Latchkey Kids

Latchkey Kids

Unlocking Doors for Children and Their Families

Bryan E. Robinson
University of North Carolina, Charlotte

Bobbie H. Rowland
University of North Carolina, Charlotte

Mick Coleman
Virginia State University

Lexington Books
D.C. Heath and Company/Lexington, Massachusetts/Toronto

Library of Congress Cataloging-in-Publication Data

Robinson, Bryan E.
   Latchkey kids.

   Bibliography: p
   Includes index.
   1. Latchkey children—United States. 2. Family—United States. 3. Latchkey children—
United States—Case studies. I. Rowland, Bobbie H. II. Coleman, Mick. III. Title.
HQ777.65.R63   1986   306.8'74   85-45521
ISBN 0-669-11929-6 (alk. paper)

Published simultaneously in Canada
Printed in the United States of America
Casebound International Standard Book Number: 0-669-11929-6
Library of Congress Catalog Card Number: 85-45521

The paper used in this publication meets the minimum requirements of American National
Standard for Information Sciences—Permanence of Paper for Printed Library Materials,
ANSI Z39.48-1984.

86 87 88 89 90 8 7 6 5 4 3 2 1

To yesterday, when being a latchkey child was not so complicated and frightening.

To today, when children and their families need the help and support of the community and its resources to ensure optimal growth and development.

To tomorrow, when the questions have been answered and provisions made for all latchkey kids.

And to latchkey kids everywhere. This book is also dedicated to:

Jamey McCullers, whose courage is an inspiration for others. *B.E.R.*

My mother, Ethel Ritch Haynes, who at age 80 continues to watch over me and nurture me in ways that open doors and reveal new meaning. *B.H.R.*

Tommy and Ruth Coleman for their steadfast support. *M.C.*

Contents

Figures   xi

Tables   xi

Preface   xiii

Acknowledgments   xv

1. **Introduction to the Latchkey Phenomenon   1**
    Emergence of Latchkey Kids   2
    Myths about Latchkey Kids   2
    Determining the Latchkey Population   4
    The Magic Age   6
    Results of Early Responsibility   8
    Looking Ahead   13

2. **Review of Research on Latchkey Kids and Their Families   17**
    Maternal Employment Studies   18
    Children in Latchkey Arrangements   19
    Parents of Latchkey Kids   26
    Alternatives to Latchkey Arrangements   28
    Conclusion   33

3. **Growth and Development of School-Age Children   37**
    Physical Development   38
    Cognitive Development   41
    Social-Emotional Development   45
    School-Age Children and Adults outside the Family   48
    Themes and Issues in Middle Childhood   49
    Programmatic and Curriculum Implications for School-Age Child Care
       Programs   51
    Matching Supervision with Development   52
    Conclusion   53

4. **Children's Adjustment to Self-Care** 57
   Planning for Self-Care 58
   Factors in Self-Care Adjustment 59
   Fears 63
   Levels of Self-Care Adjustment 65
   Conclusion 75

5. **Suggestions for Parents** 77
   Assessing the Safety Buffer 78
   In-Home Safety Strategies 82
   Selecting School-Age Child Care Programs 86
   Community Strategies 87
   Family Climate 90
   Building Family Life 91
   Making the Best of Latchkey Situations 92

6. **Suggestions for Educators** 95
   Determining Risk Factors 96
   Classroom Strategies 98
   School and Community Strategies 105
   Conclusion 109

7. **Suggestions for Researchers** 111
   Shortage of Latchkey Research 112
   Sampling and Methodology 112
   Suggestions for Future Research Studies 121
   Theoretical Guides for Latchkey Research 125
   Appendix 7A 133

8. **Public Policy, Advocacy, and Latchkey Kids** 139
   Children and Their Treatment through Time 139
   Emphasis on Prevention 142
   Cultural Context of Children 142
   Advocacy Movement 145
   Case and Class Advocacy 146
   Tools of Advocacy 148
   Initiating Community Change for Latchkey Kids:
      An Eight-Step Plan 150
   Putting the Steps into Action 153
   Conclusion 155

9. **Program Development for School-Age Children** 157
   Review of SACC Programs 159
   Developing an SACC Program 169
   Summary 174

Appendix 9A: Logistical Issues in Developing a Partnership SACC
          Program   176
Appendix 9B: SACC Project Philosophy   178
Appendix 9C: Policy and Procedure Guidelines   179
Appendix 9D: SACC Programming: A Checklist for Program
          Developers and Parents   181

Appendix: Resources on Latchkey Children and Their Families   183

Index   209

About the Authors   219

Figures and Tables

Figures

1–1. Frequency of Children in Self-Care versus Parent-Care Arrangements, by Grade 7

5–1. Neighborhood Safety Checklist 79

5–2. Home Safety Checklist 80

5–3. Determining the Safety Buffer 82

5–4. John's Schedule 84

5–5. John's House Rules 85

5–6. In-Home Safety Strategies 86

5–7. Checklist for Identifying and Monitoring SACC Programs 88

6–1. Computing the Latchkey Risk Quotient 97

7–1. An Ecological Approach to the Study of Latchkey Kids 129

9–1. SACC Project Development, 1984–1985 170

Tables

2–1. Relationship between Child Care Ecology and Child Outcomes 32

3–1. Physical Characteristics of School-Age Children 40

3–2. Thinking and Learning Characteristics of School-Age Children 44

3–3. Social-Emotional Characteristics of School-Age Children 47

4–1. Questions to Ask before Planning
Self-Care Arrangements   59

4–2. Levels of Self-Care Adjustment   66

7–1. Attributes of Studies of Latchkey Kids   134

7–2. Attributes of Studies of Latchkey Families   136

8–1. Eight Steps for Initiating Community Change for
Latchkey Kids   151

Preface

As we worked with latchkey children and their families over the past three years, we became aware of the need for a book that helps parents, teachers, administrators, counselors, clergy, nurses, social workers, psychologists, researchers, policymakers, and other practitioners understand the scope of the latchkey phenomenon and that addresses their concerns and questions.

In this book we have drawn from our own survey of 1,806 families, extensive travel to national school-age child care programs, conversations with leaders in the field of school-age child care who are attempting to address the latchkey issue, and correspondence with people from all over the United States and parts of Canada, from all walks of life, who are struggling with latchkey challenges in their regions. Parents shared their ambivalence and guilt over latchkey situations in which they often felt trapped. Teachers and school administrators told of their worry and frustration over young children leaving their charge and spending afternoons alone at home.

Researchers have reported tale after tale of unworkable (sometimes distressingly so) latchkey situations. Popular magazines and sometimes the educational arena have sensationalized the potential dangers to latchkey kids for reader appeal. Policymakers and child advocates have exhausted themselves in endless meetings pouring over solutions to latchkey dilemmas in their respective communities.

From our research and that of others, as well as our extensive correspondence and our own experiences (all the authors were latchkey kids themselves), we have come to the conclusion that most latchkey situations are not as hopeless as they have been portrayed. We have taken an ecological approach to the study of latchkey kids and suggest that latchkey arrangements can be workable.

In this book we have combined the latest scientific knowledge about latchkey kids with actual case studies of a variety of latchkey experiences. After surveying the scope of the problem, we examine the effects of latchkey arrangements on children, parents, and the family system. We discuss how many communities have met this problem. Next we detail policies and programs that have been established in many states and what families, schools, business, industry, and government still need to do to come to grips with this mounting social trend. Suggestions are also included for parents, teachers, school administrators, children in self-care, and researchers in the field of child development.

This book is an outgrowth of a desire to put the latchkey phenomenon in proper perspective, to eradicate the many myths about latchkey kids, and ultimately to unlock doors for latchkey kids and their families.

Acknowledgments

Without the cooperation and assistance of many colleagues, friends, and family members, this book would not have been possible. The authors appreciate the steadfast personal and administrative support of Mary Thomas Burke and Harold Heller. We give special thanks to the following people for contributing case study material for the book: Joy Morrison, Maureen O'Bryan, Hassie Short, Phyllis Gryder, Millie Gutherie, Mary Witherington, June Kirby, Nickey Chaney, Barbara Jordon, Swaim Strong, Nancy Ratliff, Barbara Williams, Sara Kelly Hanes, and all the anonymous latchkey kids who shared their lives with us. We also benefited from the help of Sandra Sparks and the use of her program, "The Key to Being on My Own."

We want to thank Patricia Lloyd and the Council for Children in Charlotte, North Carolina, for the commendable work they have done for latchkey kids in the state of North Carolina and for their moral support in the preparation of this book. The technical assistance of Patsy Skeen is much appreciated.

Finally, we thank the staff and our editors at Lexington Books, whose excitement, creativity, and belief in this project helped us get draft after draft of manuscripts into print.

1
Introduction to the Latchkey Phenomenon

A kindergarten teacher in Lincolnton, North Carolina, noticed children in her elementary school wearing house keys on chains around their necks. "For a long time I thought it was a new fad," she said. "I figured it was part of the punk fashion that had filtered down to the younger kids." Much to her chagrin, this teacher learned that many children wear keys around their necks to gain entry into their homes after school when parents are still working. A third-grade teacher in Statesville, North Carolina, said, "Most children won't tell me their situation, and I suspect they never tell their classmates. I only knew when I saw the strong, usually dirty, strings around their necks. The keys are always worn inside or under their clothing. When I'd ask them what's on the string, they'd tell me, 'the key to my house.'"

A principal at an elementary school in Charlotte, North Carolina, is constantly finding house keys in the hallways, gym, cafeteria, and classrooms that slip out of the pockets of elementary-school youngsters. "I'm amazed at how many young children are given the adult responsibility of taking care of themselves in mornings and afternoons while parents work," she said. "But most of the parents are single parents who must work and have no other choice but to leave children on their own."

In a suburb of a large metropolitan city, 5-year-old Mark gets off his school bus and patiently waits on his doorstep for two hours until his mother gets home from work. "The child just started kindergarten this year," protested his teacher. "Beginning school is a big step in itself. But having to wait without adult supervision for such a long time puts even more stress and responsibility on this child that youngsters his age are not developmentally prepared to handle."

Ten-year-old Heather comes home from school, unlocks her front door, and secures it behind her. She calls her mother at work to inform her that she is home safe and sound and spends the next two hours completing homework until her mother gets home. "We have strict rules that Heather must follow when she's home alone," her mother says with ambivalence. "She knows that she is not to allow strangers or friends inside when I'm not home. She has a routine that she follows every afternoon so I feel pretty secure about that. I think being alone for a few hours a day makes her more self-reliant and responsible. But I must admit that I worry about her constantly."

These cases are only a few examples we have come across in our work with parents, teachers, and school administrators of latchkey kids, unsupervised youngsters who regularly care for themselves before and after school, on weekends, and during summer vacations and holidays while their parents work. The term has been used to denote children who are regularly left during some period of the day to supervise themselves. During that time they inconsistently attend recreational programs, hang out at local convenience stores, stay home alone, cruise around the public library, play at a friend's house, are supervised by an underage brother or sister, or roam the neighborhood, idly looking for something to do.

Emergence of Latchkey Kids

The term *latchkey* emerged during the eighteenth century and referred to the method of lifting the door latch to gain access into homes. At the turn of the century in the United States, latchkey kids were referred to as "dorks" because they had their own doorkeys to get inside their homes (Wolff 1985). The terms *latchkey* and *doorkey* were revived in the 1940s to describe children who took care of themselves while their fathers were away at war and their mothers entered the labor market in massive numbers (Zucker, 1944). Historically, the word *latchkey* has carried negative associations: "The house key tied around the neck is the symbol of cold meals, of a child neglected and shorn of the security of a mother's love and affection." (Zucker 1944, p. 43).

During the 1970s and 1980s, dramatic increases in the numbers of latchkey children reemerged as a result of changes in the American family. Economic trends have led to increases in the number of families in which both parents work. The number of women entering the labor force skyrocketed in the 1970s, causing a dramatic jump in the numbers of children with working mothers (Grossman 1981; Johnson & Waldman 1981). High incidences of separation and divorce produced single-parent households and left record numbers of women as sole wage earners for their families.

The mobility of today's society and the demise of the extended family leave few adult care givers to meet children's needs. Age-segregated housing, smaller families, and the decreasing importance placed on small towns and urban neighborhoods also have led to larger numbers of latchkey kids (Galambos & Garbarino 1983).

Myths about Latchkey Kids

Although these social and economic trends have led to nationwide concern over latchkey kids, scientific study of the latchkey phenomenon has lagged far behind. Faced with insufficient data and influenced by historical stigma, parents, clinicians, educators, and other professionals have relied on a handful of anecdotal cases, articles in popular magazines, and one or two unreliable studies for information. As a result, numerous myths about latchkey kids have been perpetuated:

They are hurried children.

They face serious social and emotional damage.

They are more sexually active than adult-supervised children.

They get low marks in school and score low on achievement tests.

They have poor self-concepts and social relationships.

They develop more poorly than children in school-age child care programs.

They are more self-reliant than children cared for by adults.

They are more fearful, apprehensive, and insecure than adult-supervised children.

They have very little inner control, compared to their age-mates under adult supervision.

Ultimately research may show that many of these myths are true, but as we will demonstrate throughout this book, no current evidence exists for any of these stereotypes. Because of the negative connotations that terms like *latchkey* and *unsupervised* carry, experts are grappling with appropriate referents. Those who argue that these descriptors conjure up images of predelinquent children or of neglected youngsters prefer the use of the term *self-care* (Coolsen, Seligson & Garbarino 1985; Rodman 1986).

The term *latchkey* is not applicable to all children because many care for themselves before school but have a parent at home after school. Others stay alone only during evenings. In these situations, children do not need keys to gain entry into their homes. Additionally, other children cannot be considered unsupervised since parents supervise them in absentia by telephone or by supervisory rules during their absences (Rodman 1986).

Despite past problems with usage of *latchkey*, we have used it interchangeably with *self-care* throughout this book since the majority of children care for themselves during afternoon hours (Rodman & Pratto 1980) and since these children have received the most concern and research attention. Avoiding the word *latchkey* will not make it go away, so we might as well take pride in its usage. It has become part of the vernacular and is routinely used as a descriptor in research studies, education and social work, textbooks, and magazines, newspapers, and television.

The meaning of *latchkey* should no longer carry the negative stigma of yesteryear (Wolff 1985). It has become a common social phenomenon for which many children are properly prepared. They are not as a rule eating cold meals, neglected, or deprived of the security of their parent's love and affection. Therefore instead of throwing the term out, we have chosen to update its usage in a more balanced context and in a more contemporary and favorable light.

Determining the Latchkey Population

It is difficult to determine the extent of the latchkey phenomenon. The U.S. Department of Commerce (1976) has estimated that 1.6 million or 13 percent of the nation's children between the ages of 7 and 13 are without adult supervision before or after school hours. A more recent estimate issued by the U.S. Department of Labor (1982) puts the number of children 10 years of age and under who care for themselves when not in school at 7 million.

Other reports on the incidences of latchkey children vary by the samples studied. Estimates of children in self-care emerge from analysis by family socioeconomic status. McMurray and Kazanjian (1982), for example, found that 19 percent of the 211 poor working-class families they questioned reported that their children were left unsupervised during all or part of the day, with over one-fifth of the parents having used this arrangement when their children were 7 years of age or younger. In contrast, studies of Washington, D.C.'s wealthiest suburbs revealed that latchkey children comprised between 11 and 12 percent of the school population and in Washington, D.C., proper, 33 percent of elementary school children are reported to be in latchkey situations (Long & Long 1983a, 1983b). From our own study of a random sample of 1,806 mostly white (the sample was representative of the racial makeup of the urban area and included 56 percent white and 35 percent black), middle-income families in Charlotte, North Carolina, we found that 35 percent of the parents had latchkey children between the ages of 5 and 14 in self-care or under the charge of an older sibling (Rowland, Robinson & Coleman 1986). In a survey among readers of *Working Mother Magazine*, Rodman (1980) reported that 76 percent of the 756 mothers who responded said that their children cared for themselves daily between noon and 6:00 P.M.. Despite these statistics, it is difficult to determine the numbers of latchkey children in the United States for several reasons.

Demographic Differences

Reported figures reflect different demographic characteristics unique to the samples studied in different regions of the country. Charlotte, North Carolina, is demographically different from Washington, D.C., for example, which in turn is different from rural Pennsylvania and even suburban Washington, D.C. Currently research on latchkey kids is underway in Boston (Belle, in progress), St. Paul, Minnesota (Hedin, in progress), and Charlotte, North Carolina (Robinson, in progress). Yet no national study of this nature is planned for the foreseeable future.

Grade-Level Differences

There is no consensus among researchers on the grade levels that should be used in the study of latchkey children. A variety of school grades and age ranges have been researched. Although 10-year-olds (or fifth graders) are most commonly studied, many researchers lump together different grades, which have ranged from kindergarten to ninth grade. Some of these studies examined children in grades 1 through 6 (Long & Long 1983a), and others studied latchkey kids only above third grade because of the difficulty of locating children in self-care below that grade (Galambos & Garbarino 1983, 1985). Other researchers sampled fourth grades and seventh grades (Rodman, Pratto & Nelson 1985), and still others studied fifth through ninth grades (Steinberg 1985). Many studies group preschoolers with school-age children for study. But 14-year-olds are very different from kindergarten children, and thus the relevance of these findings to all latchkey youngsters is questionable.

Varying Types of Latchkey Ecologies

Studies comparing children of employed mothers and nonemployed mothers frequently do not specify the types of child care arrangements that children are placed in other than supervised and unsupervised. As we will discuss in chapter 2, evidence clearly shows that simply being a latchkey child does not necessarily lead to serious negative consequences. Instead the setting and type of latchkey arrangement, which we term latchkey ecology, can make a difference in positive or negative outcomes. The places where latchkey children live, for example, can make a difference in whether they are vulnerable to physical or psychological harm. Garbarino and Sherman (1980) distinguished between high-risk and low-risk neighborhoods. One attribute of neighborhood life is the prevalence of child abuse and neglect. In high-risk neighborhoods, social impoverishment is high. A school principal in one high-risk neighborhood asserted, "There are probably a significant number of 5–8-year-olds at school who got themselves up this morning. They may or may not have been at their own homes, but they got themselves to school and took care of their needs" (Garbarino & Sherman 1980, p. 197). Other data have suggested that city latchkey children living in high-crime areas may be at greater risk than those who live in relatively safe, crime-free settings in rural areas (Galambos & Garbarino 1985).

In addition to locale, the type of latchkey situation also can make a difference in children's psychological and physical risk. Some latchkey youngsters are alone at home, and some are supervised by an older brother or sister. Some children are supervised in absentia by parents through telephone calls, while others have no communication with adults. Many latchkey kids are on their own but stop off by a friend's house where no adults are present or hang out in the local shopping mall (Steinberg 1985). Recently the Los Angeles County library system has had difficulty in their forty-two sites with 300 to 400 latchkey children who hang out in the public library while their parents are working. The children have burdened library staff with discipline problems that they have neither the time nor the training to handle (*Library Hotline* 1985). Since the ecological context of latchkey children is not specified or varies among existing studies, it is difficult to generalize the findings to all children.

Methodological Problems

Control groups are absent from many of the latchkey situations, making appropriate comparisons impossible. Furthermore, an overreliance on maternal reports and questionnaires and lack of longitudinal data have limited conclusive statements. We will discuss in more detail these problems and some ways researchers can deal with them in chapter 7.

Sibling Care

Some parents report that their children are cared for by an older brother or sister, yet technically these children fall into the latchkey category since in many cases the older brother or sister is only a year or two older than the cared-for sibling (McMurray & Kazanjian 1982). A study in Oakland, California, for instance, found that 66 percent of 11- to 14-year-olds had sole responsibility for younger brothers or sisters: 10 percent on a daily basis and 25 percent between two and five days a week (Medrich 1982). Confusion over whether sibling arrangements constitute latchkey status for both sets of children often results in inconsistent reporting of statistics. Sometimes latchkey status is separated from sibling care status, and at other times, underage siblings are lumped together as latchkey kids in reporting procedures (Fosarelli 1984).

Parental Underreporting of Self-Care

The negative stigma associated with latchkey children results in parents' underreporting of child self-care. Often parents are embarrassed or feel guilty because they must leave their children alone. In some instances parents were asked at what age they would feel comfortable leaving children at home alone, and they gave an age older than when they actually began this practice (Long 1984). Others feared their children would be in danger if their latchkey status were disclosed. Others held firm to the American ethic that family problems should be kept within the family (Long & Long 1983b).

The Magic Age

Is there a magic age at which children can begin staying home alone? No. There is a wide range of social and emotional maturation rates that differ for each child.

Some children are capable of taking care of themselves at 10 or 11 years of age, and others still have not matured by age 14 or 15. Behan (1985) warns against identifying an exact age at which children can begin self-care. Instead he suggests that parents evaluate their children's maturity levels by asking the following questions:

> Is the child socially mature? That is, does he or she express a desire to do something well, show respect for another person's property, or demonstrate the ability to judge right from wrong?
>
> Can the child entertain himself or herself when parents go out?
>
> Does the child have self-discipline?
>
> Does the child accept and carry out responsibilities for home chores?
>
> Can the child accept the answer "no" with some grace?

Despite this sound advice, in practice, parents still use age as a benchmark for latchkey status. Most parents, and some experts, believe children are capable of fending for themselves when they are 11 or 12 (Long 1984). In our subsample of 886 cases, children between the ages of 9 and 11 (53 percent) were left alone more often than children between the ages of 5 and 8 (13 percent) or between the ages of 12 and 14 (34 percent). Figure 1–1 shows that, consistent with other studies, reporting self-care was dependent upon the grade level of the child.

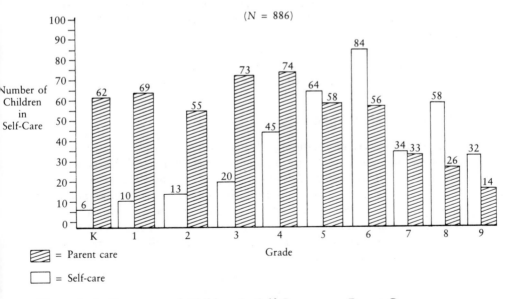

Figure 1–1. Frequency of Children in Self-Care versus Parent-Care Arrangements, by Grade

We have found that parent care was most common between kindergarten and fourth grades, and self-care was the most frequent child care arrangement between grades 5 and 9, with sixth graders having that arrangement most often. The frequency of parental care arrangements was most common in the lower grades while self-care was less frequent. Self-care increased with grade level until fifth grade, where it became more common than parent care. Self-care reached a peak during sixth grade (at approximately age 11 or 12) when parent care began to drop drastically and continued to decline through the ninth grade. These findings are consistent with other studies. One, for example, reports, "Twelve to fourteen-year-olds were found to be five times more likely to care for themselves than six to eight-year-olds and twice as likely as nine to eleven-year-olds" (Seligson et al. 1983, p. 8).

Coincidentally, the 11- to 12-year age range is a transition time that Jean Piaget cites as a cognitive shift from concrete operational thought to formal operational thought. This new cognitive status equips children to make sounder decisions regarding their welfare and safety in regard to whom to talk to and whom not to talk to, how to answer the telephone and door appropriately when a stranger calls, how to handle emergencies, and how to prepare nutritional foods. In short, formal operational children are better than younger children at handling more responsibility and unexpected situations. This age period is also a time when children begin struggling with emerging adulthood and what Erik Erikson calls the identity versus role confusion crisis. We will discuss in detail the developmental implications of latchkey status in chapter 3. In the following section we will raise the question of whether children are developmentally ready for latchkey status at this age or are being pushed to grow up too soon, as David Elkind (1981, 1984) suggests, and to handle adult responsibilities before they have had a chance to enjoy childhood. Meanwhile, although data indicate self-care is most common among older children, we must not overlook the fact that thousands, perhaps millions, of younger children like 5-year-old Mark are also latchkey kids who must fend for themselves.

Results of Early Responsibility

Despite the negative implications of being a latchkey child, research suggests that a positive parent-child relationship can offset detrimental effects and contribute to the latchkey child's development (Long & Long 1982; Woods 1972). Garbarino (1981), for example, viewed the social climate of the family as a significant factor in determining children's abilities to cope with self-care responsibilities. In addition, Harris (1981) found the quality of parent-child relationships to be viewed as more important in dual-career families than the amount of time parents spend with their children.

Other benefits have also been suggested. In their literature review, Stroman and Duff (1982) speculate that latchkey children, because of their early responsibilities, become more independent, self-reliant, and resourceful than peers who are constantly supervised. Others speculate that latchkey children learn earlier than they otherwise might to master self-help skills, assume responsibility, and solve problems (Kieffer 1981). Thomas Long (1983) admits that there are positive benefits from being a latchkey child, among them the promotion of independence and maturity. But he warns that parents must decide if the advantages outweigh the disadvantages. A survey conducted by Harris (1981) showed that the majority of family members, family traditionalists, human resource officers, and labor and feminist leaders agree that children should be expected to take on more responsibility for themselves as a result of economic demands.

Survival Training for Latchkey Kids

Numerous training programs have been developed to help unsupervised children handle more responsiblity while parents work. The Girl Scouts of America has published a survival skills booklet, *Safe and Sound at Home Alone;* the Boy Scouts of America disseminates a manual *Prepared for Today;* Camp Fire Inc. produced a program titled, "I Can Do It" for children between second and fourth grades; and the Kansas Committee for Prevention of Child Abuse developed the "I'm in Charge" program for parents and latchkey children. (The content of these programs will be discussed in more detail in chapter 9.) Researchers have studied the effectiveness of latchkey kids' training while they are in self-care. Children have learned to recognize emergencies such as fires and personal injuries and how to report these emergencies (Jones & Kazdin 1980; Rosenbaum, Creedon & Drabman 1981), how to deal with the threat of child molesters (Poche, Brouwer & Swearingen 1981), and how to escape the house in case of fire (Jones, Kazdin & Haney 1981). Food preparation, household chores, and safety during hazardous weather have been successfully taught in other survival programs (Mount & Smith 1984).

The comparative value of these programs has become the subject of some debate. Peterson (1984), for instance, studied 8- through 10-year-old latchkey kids who attended an eight-week training course on home safety and survival skills. One group of three children was trained through discussion in the "Prepared for Today" program, developed by the Boy Scouts of America. The second group of three children received behavioral instruction from the "Safe at Home" program, developed by Lizette Peterson (in press). Both programs covered such crucial issues as self-care activities (that is, selecting safe after-school activities), dealing with strangers, preparing for emergencies, and supervising younger children. Children receiving behavioral training through the "Safe at Home" program demonstrated better self-care skills than those who had participated in the discussion-oriented "Prepared for Today" program. Both training programs, however, helped reduce children's general fears of being alone and anxiety concerning home safety.

Latchkey curricula have been developed for classroom teachers to help children who are vulnerable to crisis acquire self-reliance skills and to ensure that they can cope more safely on their own (Long 1985). Lynette Long suggests that schools are the best place to teach third- and fourth-grade children what has been popularly called "survival skills." Long's nine-point curriculum comprises the following topics that prepare children for unexpected emergencies: (1) taking care of the key, (2) traveling safely to and from school, (3) maintaining safety from strangers while at home, (4) developing telephone skills to use when home alone, (5) knowing what to do in case of a fire, (6) handling household emergencies ranging from power failure to personal injuries, (7) preparing children for first aid in case of home accidents, (8) eating safe and healthy snacks when alone, and (9) reducing such fears as noises in the house or fear of break-ins. We will discuss in more detail the educator's challenge in preparing unsupervised children for self-care in chapter 6. Survival training for latchkey kids has been the subject of numerous popular magazine articles for parents as well (Chaback & Fortunato 1983; *Newsweek*, 1980).

The Controversy

Although these programs have been successful, there is considerable controversy among child development experts over whether latchkey kids (especially preschool children) should be taught survival skills. John Merrow (1985) criticizes programs aimed at teaching latchkey kids survival skills. He is against the practice of self-care (lack of adult supervision) altogether, especially for those under age 15. He believes that such terms as *self-care* and *survival skills* are "linguistic cop-outs that obscure a serious and widespread evasion of social responsibility that threatens many of our children" (Merrow 1985, p. 8). Although we agree with Merrow's argument in theory, on a more practical level his sentiments are disturbing. The term *survival skills* is not particularly appealing. It sounds as if young children are preparing for war against a world that they have barely come to know. This too is disturbing. Yet whether we like it, millions of underage children are left to care for themselves for hours every day, and many are ill prepared for this independence.

We do not advocate leaving young children in self-care and in fact believe that nothing less than good adult supervision for children when parents must work is essential. Yet despite the fact that self-care may not always be the best option for children, millions of underage youngsters are left to fend for themselves and need supportive measures for safety and security. The refusal of educators and policymakers to prepare children for potentially harmful situations is equally an evasion of social responsibility. Margaret Wolff (1985, p. 4) agrees: "If a child can be shown how to turn the obstacles of self-care into opportunities for personal accomplishment, they develop skills, personal satisfaction, *pos.*

and an attitude about meeting challenges that can be of lifelong benefit. In such a context, 'self-care' and 'survival skills' can become stimulants, not substitutes, for social responsibility." As responsible adults, we cannot abandon 5-year-old Mark who waits listlessly on his doorstep each afternoon for his parents to come home or the hundreds of other children who need proper self-care preparation.

What Price Latchkey?

What price are latchkey kids paying for the early independence thrust upon them? Staying home alone is a grown-up responsibility that some believe has an array of cognitive, social, and emotional side effects. Garbarino (1984) summarized four types of risks he considered to be associated with latchkey kids: they feel badly (for example, rejected and alienated), they act badly (delinquency and vandalism may result), they develop badly (academic failure may result), and they are treated badly (accidents and sexual victimization are more likely to occur). He implies that families with latchkey children are in a state of stress or crisis. More specifically, latchkey children can be viewed as a means by which families attempt to cope with economic, sex role, and other social changes. In fact, the early responsibility placed upon latchkey children has been viewed as symbolic of society's conflict over the family's need to maintain its standard of living and the child's need to experience childhood (Garbarino 1984). Long (1984) says that parents see high achievement as their children's ticket to success. Maturity and achievement, he insists, are associated as one in the parent's mind:

> While physical development and associated motor and mental activity progress at different rates for different children for purely biological reasons not under parental control, parents often seem to lack the patience to allow for normal development or the trust to accept that their child will develop. Also, parents often want their children to mature more rapidly in order to relieve parental stress caused by child rearing. The more capable at taking care of themselves children appear to be, the less stress arising from child-care responsibilities parents seem to experience. (Long 1984, p. 62)

This type of pressure to have children grow up quickly and assume responsibility early may produce unnecessary childhood stress (Elkind 1981, 1984). Elkind notes that hurried children were once products of low-income environments where independence was a necessary commodity in single-parent families or homes where both parents worked. But today growing up too fast too soon has no social class boundaries and can be symptomatic of children from all economic levels.

The case of Heather illustrates this growing problem. Dressed to kill in makeup, heels, and blouse and skirt, 5-year-old Heather walked into MacDonald's with her grandmother and ordered a hamburger. An onlooker remarked, "Look at that midget!" When Heather was 6, her teacher expressed concern to Heather's father that the child was not paying attention in class because she constantly pulled out her makeup and primped during lessons.

Heather is 10 now. She is on a diet so that her parachute pants will fit a more shapely figure. She has been in therapy for a year since her grades began falling in school. A tall, large child, Heather looks more mature than she is. Her designer clothes, carefully manicured and painted nails, coiffed hairdo, jewelry, perfume, and penchant for MTV and Prince deceptively mask her true age and act as a veneer of sophistication that hides her childlike confusion. She keeps a lot inside according to her grandmother, and she appears very pensive, as if she is harboring secrets that she will not share yet cannot handle either.

Exposed to things that many kids her age never experience, Heather has had to grow up fast. At 18 days, she started her whirlwind growth when she was flown everywhere she needed to be—living with her grandmother in North Carolina for a year and then her grandmother in Virginia until she was 3. Heather's parents never set up housekeeping until the child was 3, when they moved into a condominium in Washington, D.C. After a year, the parents divorced, discussing the impending split in front of their 4-year-old, who appeared to accept the divorce in stride. In the absence of her parents, however, Heather cried uncontrollably on her grandmother's shoulder. At 4 she was routinely placed on an airplane and flew alone to various relatives on the East Coast. Academically Heather is pushed to read at home. Her parents buy books to encourage reading rather than for enjoyment. The 10-year-old has difficulty playing with others her age and in fact when she does, takes the adult role of director, telling her friends what to do rather than playing like most other school-age children. From the time she was 2, Heather was in nursery school and since school age has spent after-school hours caring for herself at home alone.

Long and Long (1983b) report that adults who were former latchkey children harbor negative reactions to unresolved stress associated with too much responsibility at too young an age. These adults secretly resented their parents because of self-care responsibilities, and most of them never expressed this resentment to their parents until later life, if at all. James Garbarino (1981) appropriately summarizes the problem:

> It is the *premature* granting of responsibility, particularly when it occurs in a negative emotional climate, that seems to be damaging. No social event affects all children or youth equally. Nearly all experiences are mediated by the quality and character of the family. Thus, we know that some kids will thrive on the opportunity of being a latchkey child. Others will just manage to cope. Still others will be at risk, and still others will be harmed. It is often difficult to separate the specific effects of the latchkey situation from the more general condition of the family. (Garbarino 1981, pp. 14–15)

We can conclude that although some latchkey youngsters may be hurried children, all of them are not. Many concerned parents, like Barbara Jordon, are careful not to overburden their latchkey kids with additional responsibilities: "My oldest son seems to have developed a lot of responsibility from the experience. But I don't want to put too much on him. I still want him to do the things kids do—the extracurricular things."

Looking Ahead

Finding and affording after-school care is one of the biggest problems parents face, especially working mothers from low-income families (McGurdy 1984; Whitbread 1979). The problem of latchkey children will not go away but will continue to escalate during the 1990s, presenting one of the biggest challenges of the future for all concerned about children and youth. The numbers of latchkey kids can be expected to rise as current social and economic trends continue steady growth. It has been projected that by 1990 as many as 6 million latchkey children will exist nationwide (if they do not already) due to the influx of more mothers into the labor force (Turkington 1983). Emphasis on child care for preschoolers has resulted in the development of few programs for school-age children. Nieting (1983) suggests that this gap in services has led to a lack of direct supervision of school-agers, which leaves them vulnerable to numerous social, emotional, and health problems. Chapters 8 and 9 explore appropriate programmatic and supervisory activities and how community advocacy can direct school-agers' energies into positive channels, helping them to deal effectively with potential problems.

The nationwide concern over latchkey children has roused educators, politicians, and people from all walks of life interested in the welfare of the nation's youth. A network of parents, schools, and communities working together can alleviate many of the potential problems that latchkey kids and their families face. Researchers also have begun to study long-neglected questions about latchkey kids to determine whether some of the tentative answers are myth or reality. We will address these findings in the next chapter.

References

Behan, R.A. 1985. Should Johnny or Janet "sit" themselves? *PTA Today* 10:27–28.

Belle, D. In Progress. *Social support processes among latchkey and adult supervised children.* Boston: Boston University.

Chaback, E., & Fortunato, P. 1983 (February). A kid's survival checklist: When you're home alone. *Parents Magazine*, pp. 134–136.

Coolsen, P.; Seligson, M.; & Garbarino, J. 1985. *When school's out and nobody's home.* Chicago: National Committee for Prevention of Child Abuse.

Elkind, D. 1981. *The hurried child.* Reading, Mass.: Addison-Wesley.

Elkind, D. 1984. *All grown up and no place to go.* Reading, Mass.: Addison-Wesley.

Fosarelli, P.D. 1984. Latchkey children. *Journal of Developmental and Behavioral Pediatrics* 5:173–177.

Galambos, N., & Garbarino, J. 1983. Identifying the missing links in the study of latchkey children. *Children Today* 12:2–4.

Galambos, N., & Garbarino, J. 1985. Adjustment of unsupervised children in a rural ecology. *Journal of Genetic Psychology* 146:227–231.

Garbarino, J. 1981. Latchkey children: How much a problem? *Education Digest* 46:14–16.

Garbarino, J. 1984. Can American families afford the luxury of childhood? Unpublished manuscript. University Park: Pennsylvania State University.

Garbarino, J., & Sherman, D. 1980. High-risk neighborhoods and high-risk families: The human ecology of child maltreatment. *Child Development* 51:188–198.

Grossman, A.S. 1981. Working mothers and their children. *Monthly Labor Review* 104:49–54.

Harris, L. 1981. *Families strengths and stresses at work.* Minneapolis: General Mills American Family Report.

Hedin, D. In progress. *The family's view of after-school time.* St. Paul, Minn.: Center for Youth Development.

Johnson, B.L., & Waldman, E. 1981. Marital and family patterns of the labor force. *Monthly Labor Review* 104:36–41.

Jones, R.T., & Kazdin, A.E. 1980. Teaching children how and when to make emergency telephone calls. *Behavior Therapy* 11:509–521.

Jones, R.T.; Kazdin, A.E.; & Haney, J.I. 1981. Social validation and training of emergency fire safety skills for potential injury prevention and life saving. *Journal of Applied Behavior Analysis* 14:249–260.

Kieffer, E. 1981 (February 24). The latchkey kids—how are they doing? *Family circle,* pp. 28–35.

Library Hotline. 1985 (October 14). Latchkey children in Los Angeles, *Library Hotline* 44:5.

Long, T. 1983 (November 7). *Latchkey children: Scope of the problem.* Speech delivered at the Seventh Annual Conference of the North Carolina chapter of the National Committee for the Prevention of Child Abuse, Charlotte, N.C.

Long, T. 1984. So who cares if I'm home? *Educational Horizons* 62:60–64.

Long, L. 1985 (February). Safe at home. *Instructor Magazine,* pp. 64–70.

Long, T.J., & Long, L. 1983a. *Latchkey Children.* ERIC ED 226 836.

Long, T.J., & Long, L. 1983b. *The handbook for latchkey children and their parents.* New York: Arbor House.

McGurdy, J. 1984 (March). Schools respond to latchkey children. *School Administrator,* pp. 16–18.

McMurray, G.L., & Kazanjian, D.P. 1982. *Day care and the working poor: The Struggle for self-sufficiency.* New York: Community Service Society of New York.

Medrich, E. 1982. *Children's time study.* Berkeley: University of California Press.

Merrow, J. 1985. Viewpoint: Self-care. *Young Children* 40:8.

Mount, R., & Smith, K. 1984. Kids on their own for the first time. *Educational Horizons* 62:63.

Newsweek. 1980 (October 6). Survival training for latchkey kids. *Newsweek,* p. 100.

Nieting, P.L. 1983. School-age child care: In support of development and learning. *Childhood Education* 60:6–11.

Peterson, L. 1984. Teaching home safety and survival skills to latchkey children: A comparison of two manuals and methods. *Journal of Applied Behavior Analysis* 17:279–293.

Peterson, L. In press. The "Safe-at-Home" game: Training comprehensive safety skills in latchkey children. *Behavior Modification.*

Poche, C.; Brouwer, R.; & Swearingen, M. 1981. Teaching self-protection to young children. *Journal of Applied Behavior Analysis* 14:169–176.

Robinson, B.E. In Progress. *The after-school ecologies of school-age children: A longitudinal study.* Charlotte: University of North Carolina.

Rodman, H. 1980 (July). How children take care of themselves. *Working Mother,* pp. 61–63.

Rodman, H. 1986. *From Latchkey stereotypes to self-care realities.* Unpublished manuscript. Greensboro: University of North Carolina.

Rodman, H., & Pratto, D. 1980. *How children take care of themselves: Preliminary statement on magazine survey.* Report submitted to the Ford Foundation.

Rodman, H.; Pratto, D.J.; & Nelson, R.S. 1985. Child care arrangements and children's functioning: A comparison of self-care and adult-care children. *Developmental Psychology* 21:413–418.

Rosenbaum, M.S.; Creedon, D.L.; & Drabman, R.S. 1981. Training preschool children to identify emergency situations and make emergency phone calls. *Behavior Therapy* 12:425–435.

Rowland, B.H.; Robinson, B.E.; & Coleman, M. 1986. Parents' perceptions of needs for their latchkey children: A survey. *Pediatric Nursing* 12.

Seligson, M.; Genser, A.; Gannett, E.; & Gray, W. 1983. *School-age child care: A policy report.* Wellesley, Mass.: Center for Research on Women.

Steinberg, L. 1985. *Latchkey children and susceptibility to peer pressure: An ecological analysis.* Madison: University of Wisconsin.

Stroman, S.H., & Duff, E. 1982. The latchkey child: Whose responsibility? *Childhood Education* 59:76–79.

Turkington, C. 1983. Lifetime of fear may be legacy of latchkey children. *APA Monitor* 14:19.

U.S. Department of Commerce. Bureau of the Census. 1976. *Daytime care of children: October 1974 and February 1975.* Current Population Reports Series P-20, No. 298. Washington, D.C.: U.S. Government Printing Office.

U.S. Department of Labor. Women's Bureau. 1982. *Employers and child care: Establishing services through the workplace.* Pamphlet No. 23. Washington, D.C.: U.S. Government Printing Office.

Whitbread, J. 1979. Who's taking care of the children? *Family Circle* 20:88, 92, 102, 103.

Wolff, M. 1985 (September). A reply to John Merrow. *SACC Newsletter* 3:4.

Woods, M. 1972. The unsupervised child of the working mother. *Developmental Psychology* 6:14–25.

Zucker, H.L. 1944. Working parents and latchkey children. *Annals of the American Academy* 236:43–50.

2
Review of Research on Latchkey Kids and Their Families

"My name is Scott, I'm 11 years old, and I live outside a small town. My dad gets me up in the mornings, and then he and my mom leave for work at 6:00. I watch TV until 7:00; then I get ready for school and leave at 7:30. I get home from school at 4:00 and my parents at about 5:00. It's quiet where I live, and my neighbors are very close. Some are at home in the afternoons, and some are not. I've never lost my key because I keep it in my pocket. I've done this for two or three years. I've never been scared either. I like getting home first. It makes me feel bigger—like I can do something by myself. Oh yeah, sometimes I hear things and get a little scared. But anybody would do that—even a grown-up. Anyway, I've never had a real problem, except when the school bus was late, and I called my mom. I've learned that Mom and Dad can trust me."

"My name is Lauren, I'm 10 years old, and I live in the city. I get home at 3:30, and my mom doesn't get home until 5:30. Once I went home, and my dad was there, but I didn't know it because the door was locked. I unlocked it, and the TV was on. I checked the bedrooms, but I didn't see anybody. I heard noises too. I was scared so I went outside and waited fifteen minutes. Then I looked in the window and saw my dad.

Sometimes I'm afraid people are watching me and know when I'm alone. Once a green Volkswagen sat at the end of my driveway for a long time. When my mom came down the street, it left.

I get my key from the same place every day, and I'm afraid somebody is watching me, but it doesn't bother me now as much as it used to. If my mom was home when I get there, we might go places or do projects, but I wouldn't do other things different. It's boring by myself. I just do my homework. I don't watch TV. I asked Mom if I could go to a day care because I'm tired of being alone. There is nobody to talk to. I can use the microwave but not the stove. I've learned not to use the stove to cook because I might start a grease fire. I don't really know how to put out a grease fire—I just know to put salt on it. I know not to mess with the guns or knives. I don't search every room each day. My mom said if I heard something, just run outside and to the neighbors. They keep an eye on me. I just fix a sandwich, a cookie, and a Pepsi. I saw the movie *Adam*. He had to come home alone. I've learned not to talk to strangers and to get out of the house if there is trouble. I used to worry about losing my house key, and I'd leave it at school a lot. But now we put it in a certain place, and I have to worry about someone hiding in a closet. I get scared easily. But it doesn't bother me as much anymore."

Surveys of the research literature show that few studies have been conducted in the past two decades on children in latchkey situations (Coleman, Robinson

& Rowland 1984; Fosarelli 1984; Robinson, Coleman & Rowland 1986a, 1986b; Stroman & Duff 1982). Although the information pertaining to this topic is limited, that which does exist has contributed to our understanding of the latchkey phenomenon.

We have organized this chapter around several major areas that reflect historical evolution of latchkey research, as well as those areas with which social scientists have been most concerned. The first wave of studies appeared in the 1970s and primarily addressed the issue of maternal employment. The second wave of publications reported the effects of latchkey arrangements on children and were conducted primarily during the 1980s. We have divided these publications into the popular press literature and scientific investigations employing either urban samples or rural and suburban samples. A third wave of studies appeared during the 1980s and dealt with parents of latchkey children and their reactions to such arrangements. The fourth series of research studies examined alternatives to latchkey arrangements by assessing parental preferences and the impact of school-age child care programs. We conclude this chapter by weighing the reported advantages and disadvantages of being a latchkey child versus being cared for by adults.

Maternal Employment Studies

Latchkey research began during the 1970s under the guise of maternal employment studies. These investigations were not focused on latchkey issues and in fact often did not specify which children were in self-care compared to some other child care arrangement. Nevertheless, the literature on the effects of maternal employment on children stands as an important means of introducing such child outcomes as social and personality adjustment, academic achievement, and sex role concept formulation that are related to latchkey children.

Findings of maternal employment research and child outcomes have produced consistent evidence that children of employed mothers do not differ from children of nonworking mothers on measures of personality, social adjustment, or academic performance (Hoffman 1979; Moore 1978; Taveggia & Thomas 1974); however, children of working mothers have been found to assume more responsibility for household chores, display higher academic and career aspirations, and perceive smaller differences between masculine and feminine sex roles (Moore 1978; Zambrana, Hurst & Hite 1979). Not surprisingly, the mother's attitude toward her homemaker and work roles (Moore 1978) and the quality and consistency of substitute child care (Zambrana, Hurst & Hite 1979) have been found to mediate these child outcomes.

Comparisons of children with employed and nonemployed mothers also have been based on the age of children. Two studies were conducted by Gold and Andres (1978a, 1978b) for purposes of comparing sex role attitudes, personality and social adjustment, and academic achievement of Caucasian children whose mothers were employed or unemployed. One study focused on 10-year-old children and the other on 14- to 16-year-old adolescents. Both groups of children lived in a suburb of a Canadian city and were from low- and middle-income families. The 10-year-old children with employed mothers had more egalitarian sex role attitudes than their peers whose mothers did not work. In contrast, middle-class boys with employed mothers were found to have lower scores on language and math tests than the children with unemployed mothers.

The 14- to 16-year-olds whose mothers worked had more egalitarian sex role attitudes than their peers whose mothers did not work. Adolescents of employed mothers also had higher adjustment scores (for example, they showed a greater sense of personal worth and family cohesion) than adolescents of non-working mothers. There was no difference between the two groups on academic achievement.

Findings on employed and nonemployed parents are difficult to generalize to latchkey kids because types of child care arrangements were not specified in these studies. Not until the 1980s did studies focus specifically on children in self-care.

Children in Latchkey Arrangements

Controversy exists in popular and scientific literature over whether latchkey arrangements are detrimental to school-age children. Much of this conflict has been fostered by the popular press.

The Popular Press

A handful of popular magazine articles have offered practical tips on safety, health, and emergency rules for children at home alone (Chaback & Fortunato 1983; Leishman 1980; *Newsweek* 1980). Several new books written especially for latchkey kids also provide safety tips and constructive ways of occupying time while in self-care. (See the Appendix at the end of this book.)

Popular publications such as *Newsweek* (Langway 1981), *People* (Huff 1982), *USA Today* (Castelli 1983), *Family Circle* (Kieffer 1981), and *U.S. News & World Report* (Wellborn 1981) have generated interest and concern over the latchkey issue. But many of these reports have fostered confusion and misrepresentation of the scientific literature through a phenomenon that might be called *latchkeyphobia*. The popular literature has manufactured conclusions based on irrational, subjective, and emotional information. This tendency commonly occurs in circumstances that involve the unknown where little or no information is available about a subject.

Some mass media publications have sensationalized the latchkey child's self-care. We interviewed parents who tearfully shared their concerns that their children face serious social and emotional damage as a result of their latchkey dilemma. These worries are fueled by grim stories constantly appearing in popular magazines, newspapers, on television, and in some consumer books. Such titles as "Yes We're Afraid and We Are Lonely" (Castelli 1983), "The Unspoken Fears of Latchkey Kids" (Long & Long 1982b), "The Lonely Life of Latchkey Children" (Long & Long 1982a), and "Latchkey Blues: When Kids Come Home" (Lapinski 1982) typify the hysteria that has been generated. These publications capitalize on the potential dangers in latchkey situations for reader appeal; in fact no body of research supports these claims. (The Appendix contains a list of some of these articles.) Dangers can exist, but researchers have not detected many of the harmful consequences that have been alleged.

During the 1950s and 1960s before research was available, many professionals made the mistaken charge that day care and working mothers caused damage to children's development. Later studies refuted those beliefs. Rodman (1986) has accused the media and some professionals of repeating this mistake by perpetuating negative stereotypes of latchkey kids where no supporting data exist:

> The media love a problem. They also love a picture: children with keys around their necks or children cowering in closets. These are dramatic and personal. They make for good human interest stories. They sell newspapers and books. . . . The negative picture *may* turn out to be the more accurate one. But the media are not reserving judgment. Despite insufficient evidence, newspaper reports and popular articles often paint latchkey children with stereotype and stigma. (p. 7)

Of course, some popular articles report benefits for children in self-care, among them increased self-reliance, independence, and responsibility (Kieffer 1981). Yet no substantial body of research shows that such benefits are derived from latchkey experiences. Galambos and Dixon (1984) warn those in the child care field to examine current knowledge about latchkey kids and to abandon any popular notions that are not undergirded by solid empirical research before making decisions and policies about after-school care. These researchers also list three major reasons for conflicting reports in the popular press:

> First, little directly related empirical research actually exists, thereby restricting the pool of explicit common information. Second, many of the popular press conclusions are based largely on anecdotal data. Several authors have interviewed a handful of parents, children, teachers, or other professionals and have then generalized findings from those interviews to the entire population of latchkey children. Third, those parents, children, and experts who have been interviewed are from substantially different types of communities. (p. 118)

Long and Long Studies

Thomas Long and Lynette Long are two of the best-known writers on the subject of latchkey kids. Their interest in this topic has produced numerous popular magazine articles and television appearances, but they are best known for one of the first books on the subject, *The Handbook for Latchkey Children and Their Parents.*

Long and Long's major findings have not been published in professional journals, which means their methods of study have never been subjected to expert peer evaluation. Instead, their research findings have appeared in ERIC Reports, popular magazines, or books. The studies are vague in design and in some cases the tone of their findings is reminiscent of sensationalized stories found in the popular press.

Long and Long's findings are grim; they suggest that children at home alone are bored, lonely, isolated, terrified, and sexually active. Parents or concerned professionals reading these conclusions in a magazine or watching the authors on television talk shows never hear the details of how they were derived. Long and Long's most commonly cited study, for instance, was based on a handful of loosely conducted interviews with children of one race (all black), who attended one school, and lived in one large urban, high-crime area of the United States. On the basis of this small and unrepresentative sample, Long and Long generalized their findings to all 6 million latchkey youngsters: "Fear development should constitute a major area of concern for the parents and guardians of latchkey children, especially of those children who find themselves at home without continuous companionship" (Long & Long 1982c, p. 28).

Results of their national survey of 400 children between the ages of 12 and 15 were reported in the *Denver Post* and *Jet Magazine* (and soon will be published in book form). Long and Long (1985) concluded, "Teenagers these days don't get pregnant in motels and cars at 10 at night. Sex happens at home at three in the afternoon while Mom is away at work" (p. 32). It is unclear how children were selected for this study, what scientific procedures and controls were used, and what kinds of comparisons were made.

The Long and Long studies appear to contain serious methodological flaws. The authors do not specify the procedures for selecting subjects and conducting interviews. Vandell and Corasaniti (1985) note that in one study, "No comparable interviews were reported for children who returned home to mother or were in some other form of after-school care" (p. 2). Moreover, Long and Long apparently made no attempt to control other variables that might influence their findings. As Rodman (1986) pointed out, the Long and Long studies have emphasized the negative consequences of self-care arrangements and have referred to the extreme risks that may occur over the long term. But Rodman asserts it is difficult to know how much confidence to place in their research since the Longs "candidly acknowledged the possibility of bias due to the subjective methods they have employed" (Rodman 1986, p. 4).

Still, the Long and Long studies are important historically because they generated scientific interest and concern over the latchkey issue. Therefore we will discuss them within the context of scientific investigations. But beyond their historical importance, these studies should be interpreted with extreme caution.

Scientific Investigations

Ecological factors are important in determining the positive or negative nature of latchkey arrangements. An ecological approach further underscores a major parting of the ways from the popular literature. Studies of white middle-class children in rural areas and affluent children in suburban settings characterized as relatively crime free have not reported the same disadvantages as those of city children in potentially high-crime areas.

Urban Latchkey Children. One of the first studies to look at unsupervised children of working mothers was conducted with 108 fifth-grade black children from intact families in a ghetto area of Philadelphia (Woods 1972). Although this researcher did not specifically study latchkey children and therefore the results have limited relevance because the type of self-care ecology was not clarified, the research was a stepping-stone in the right direction. Supervised and unsupervised children were compared, some or all of whom must have been in some type of self-care situation.

Half of the children studied were unsupervised while their mothers worked, and the other half received constant adult supervision. More girls than boys reported a lack of adult supervision at home during breakfast, lunch, after school, and during summer vacations. Unsupervised girls had lower school achievement, performed more poorly on intellectual tests, and had more problems with self-concept and social relationships than their supervised peers. Children who were supervised tended to be more self-reliant than those who were not. This finding contrasts to the popular notion that unsupervised latchkey kids are more self-reliant than those under adult care. Some differences also were found between supervised and unsupervised boys, but these differences were too few to warrant serious consideration.

In a study conducted in Charlotte, North Carolina (Rowland, Robinson & Coleman 1986), parents of 1,806 children between the ages of 5 and 14 were randomly selected for inclusion. Of those children who routinely cared for themselves, a minority of 23 percent was reported by parents to be somewhat fearful and apprehensive when alone at home. The children were described as "afraid," "insecure," or not liking such an arrangement. Of the responses denoting apprehension when left alone, 51 percent were attributed to children in kindergarten through third grade, 42 percent to children in fourth through sixth, and 7 percent to children in seventh through ninth grades.

An investigation of 2,258 children between the ages of 7 and 11 and 1,748 parents revealed that 32 percent of boys and 41 percent of girls worried about staying home alone (Zill, Gruvaeus & Woyshner 1977). Thirteen percent of the children said they were frequently scared. The most common fears were of intruders—someone "bad" might get into the house—and going outside to play. Fear levels were highest among children from low-income areas and those of Hispanic origin who lived in high-crime areas.

Perhaps the most-often cited study of urban children was conducted by Long and Long (1982c), who interviewed 53 latchkey children and 32 adult-supervised children in grades 1 through 6. All the children attended the same all-black parochial school in Washington, D.C. More than 30 percent of these children who were left at home alone and 20 percent left at home with a sibling reported recurring nightmares and high fear levels; they were afraid of noises, the dark, and intruders. To cope with their fears, the children hid, played the television set loudly, or telephoned their parents, friends, or neighbors. Although latchkey children were better informed regarding self-care and emergencies than supervised children, none of the supervised children scored in the high-fear category.

Several studies suggest that urban latchkey kids experience confinement and isolation when caring for themselves. Long and Long (1983a) found that 45 percent of the latchkey children and 33 percent who were in sibling care were not allowed to play outside when parents were absent. Younger children in second grade and girls were more housebound than older sixth-grade children and boys, who had the most freedom. Eighty percent of all latchkey kids were socially constrained in that they were not permitted to have friends visit while parents worked. In contrast, 90 percent of adult-supervised children enjoyed unstructured play and friendships.

As a result of such confinement, it is not surprising that urban children complain of boredom and loneliness (Long & Long 1982c, 1983b; Zill, Gruvaeus & Woyshner 1977) when compared with latchkey children in the suburbs (Long & Long 1983a) and those in rural settings (Garbarino 1981) who are given freer reign during parental absences.

A survey of 51 elementary-school children in a large Canadian city asked youngsters about their views of having working mothers (Trimberger & MacLean 1982). The fifth, sixth, and seventh graders were from intact working- or middle-class families in which all mothers were employed outside the home in full-time positions. Of significance here were the latchkey children (52 percent) who arrived home two hours before their mothers every day. Half of the children were unsupervised when they got home from school.

Children who stayed alone after school while their mothers worked did not feel any more harmed by their mothers' employment than children who were supervised. The authors concluded, "To be alone after school and to be responsible for themselves would be perceived by the child as a positive effect of maternal employment (Trimberger & MacLean 1982, 473). On the other hand, latchkey kids who were alone after school tended to have more negative attitudes about their mothers' employment than children who were with someone. The authors suggested that the mother's absence might have contributed to the children's negative attitude toward maternal employment.

To determine the long-term effects of latchkey children's fears and confinement, Long and Long (1983b) studied 1,000 current and former latchkey kids. Approximately 50 percent of adults who were former latchkey children was found to suffer from what the authors called "latchkey syndrome." These adults, mostly minorities, had a residue from their latchkey experiences characterized by loneliness, boredom, resentment toward parents for their insensitivity, increased fears (especially of being alone), social isolation, and a tendency to enter occupations oriented around things instead of people. Thomas Long surmised that a lifetime of fear may be the legacy for latchkey kids, having sublimated unexplained fears that they suffered as children—fears that, never confronted, have never gone away (Turkington 1983).

Suburban and Rural Latchkey Kids

Research on suburban latchkey kids was first conducted in two studies during the late 1970s (Gold & Andres 1978a, 1978b). The researchers in the first study analyzed a subsample of unsupervised children from a larger investigation on maternal employment. The subsample consisted of 97 10-year-old children from intact families in Montreal, Canada, suburbs. A small percentage of boys (16 percent) was unsupervised for at least two periods during the day. No differences were found between supervised and unsupervised boys on social adjustment or academic achievement. The second study indicated no differences in social adjustment and academic achievement of supervised and unsupervised 14- to 16-year-old suburban adolescents.

A later study of latchkey kids from a relatively affluent, well-educated Dallas suburb suggests that these youngsters may not necessarily be at risk (Vandell & Corasaniti 1985). The researchers studied 32 third-grade children from intact white, middle-class families who were in self-care after school. This latchkey group was compared with three other groups: 32 children in their mother's care at home each afternoon, 13 who went to day care centers, and 13 who had sitters. Classmates were asked to list the names of children they "liked" and those they "did not play with." Questionnaires also were administered to discover what parents and teachers thought of the children and what youngsters thought of themselves. Findings revealed that latchkey kids were just as well adjusted as children who spent after-school time with mothers or sitters. Children enrolled in day care centers after school were rated the lowest on social and work study skills. Other studies of children living in relatively safe areas such as those in selected schools in Washington, D.C.'s, wealthiest suburbs showed no significant differences in academic achievement and emotional adjustment between latchkey kids and adult-supervised youngsters (Long & Long 1983b).

Rural latchkey children were first studied through a survey of 77 fifth and sixth graders in a predominantly white, low-income school district in Pennsylvania (Galambos & Garbarino, 1983, 1985). The children were divided into three groups: 21 children whose mothers were employed outside the home and were regularly unsupervised before and after school; 29 children whose mothers were employed but provided continual adult supervision; and 27 children who were continually supervised by nonemployed mothers. The study found no significant differences between latchkey kids and supervised children on school adjustment or locus of control. Findings also showed no differences between latchkey children and adult-supervised children on academic achievement and fear of being alone.

Environmental Context

Research to date indicates that being a latchkey child does not necessarily lead to serious negative consequences. Instead the places where latchkey kids live and the types of latchkey arrangements made for them determine their vulnerability to physical or psychological harm. Galambos and Garbarino (1983, 1985) suggest that the environmental context may be the most important factor in how youngsters adjust to self-care situations. City latchkey kids living in high-crime areas appear to be at greater risk than those living in relatively safe, crime-free settings in rural or suburban areas. City children are more confined and isolated and face greater threats of personal intrusion and accidents. In contrast, children in nonurban areas face fewer restrictions on outdoor play and fewer threats of personal harm. Despite these environmental differences, the grim conclusions reported in the urban studies and popular literature have been generalized to typify all latchkey children.

This stereotype did not endure even when a team of researchers maximized urban-rural diversity in their sample by selecting elementary schools from different parts of one county in North Carolina (Rodman, Pratto & Nelson 1985). They compared 48 children in self-care with 48 children in adult care to study the negative consequences of latchkey arrangements on children. They found no differences between the two groups of children on self-esteem, locus of control, or social adjustment.

This study was criticized, however, on the ground that the type of latchkey arrangement—not simply whether the child is in a latchkey situation or under adult supervision—is the most critical factor in the latchkey child's adjustment (Steinberg 1985). Some latchkey children are alone at home, and some are supervised by an older sibling. Others are on their own but stop off at a friend's house where no adults are present, or they hang out in the local shopping mall. Some children are supervised *in absentia* by parents through telephone calls and rules, while others have no communication with adults.

Steinberg (1985) found that different latchkey arrangements made a difference in children's adjustment. His study of 865 fifth through ninth graders in a suburban area of Madison, Wisconsin, showed that with respect to self-reliance, identity, and susceptibility to peer pressure, latchkey kids who reported home after school (where they were supervised *in absentia*) were no different from those who were supervised by parents at home during after-school hours. But when the after-school ecologies of elementary-age children were studied, Steinberg found significant differences within the self-care population with respect to susceptibility to peer pressure. In effect, he concluded that when the sample of self-care youngsters was expanded to include those who are on their own but not at home, youngsters who were removed from adult supervision (for example, they hung out at a friend's house or in the neighborhood) were more susceptible to peer pressure to engage in antisocial behaviors. Moreover, children who had authoritative parents (parental responsiveness that develops responsible behaviors) developed an internal psychological foundation to resist peer pressure, even among children who spent afternoons where susceptibility to peer pressure was high.

Another explanation for similarities in adjustment of suburban latchkey kids and suburban adult-supervised children may be self-selection. According to Vandell and Corasaniti (1985), "It may be that parents are only using latchkey arrangements for those children they feel have sufficient maturity and responsibility to stay without an adult present. They may place those children with less maturity with a sitter or a day care center" (p. 9). Another factor could be that a latchkey arrangement produces well-liked, responsible children, at least in suburban settings.

Parents of Latchkey Kids

A series of studies has addressed parents' feelings toward child self-care and has pinpointed a range of emotions from pride in their latchkey children's responsibility and independence to concern and ambivalence over their children's self-care arrangement.

Parental Satisfaction

Research suggests that families using different child care arrangements report different satisfaction levels, depending on the arrangement (Coleman et al., 1984). From a random sample of 492 parents of school-age children in three different child care arrangements after school, Coleman and his associates found that latchkey parents and parents who provided out-of-home care expressed lower levels of satisfaction with child care arrangements than parents providing in-home care. Among low-income working mothers, the majority expressed most satisfaction with knowing their school-age children were in group child care (Harris 1977).

Parental interviews of 91 third- and fifth-grade latchkey students in an elementary school in Summerville, South Carolina, revealed that parental satisfaction with latchkey arrangements was linked to several factors: whether the use of self-care was voluntary or involuntary, whether the child was a boy or girl, and the amount of time the child spent weekly in self-care. When self-care was voluntary, involved boys more than girls, and occurred for a shorter period of time, parents were more satisfied with the arrangement (Stewart 1981). A national survey of readers of *Working Mother* magazine reported that 82 percent were either very or somewhat satisfied with their latchkey arrangements (Rodman 1980). Others contend, however, that although parents report positive benefits from latchkey experiences, these reports often reflect inaccurate judgments or are made to ease parental guilt or embarrassment (Long & Long, 1983b).

Parental Ambivalence

One of the most common parental reactions to latchkey arrangements that consistently appears in research findings is that of parental ambivalence. From their analysis of 492 parent surveys, Coleman and his associates (1984) found that latchkey parents were the most ambivalent group about their child's self-care status compared to parents who provided out-of-home care and those who provided in-home care.

Long and Long (1983b) interviewed 100 parents who reported they were reluctant to leave their children alone or to admit to having made such arrangements. Some parents said that although they routinely left their children unattended, they would never admit this to their own parents and tried to keep their child's self-care unknown. Although some parents perceived child self-care as a positive experience for their children and others found such an arrangement convenient for themselves, most were concerned, guilty, and ambivalent about leaving their youngsters alone. Although 95 percent of the parents Long (1983) interviewed reported advantages to latchkey arrangements, most wanted their children to be adequately supervised and 50 percent worried about problems that might arise, such as accidents or break-ins.

A survey of 213 parents of children in kindergarten through sixth grade also indicated ambivalence and uneasiness on the part of adults (Sparks 1983). In that study, 87 percent said their children were not in after-school programs and that they felt their children were old enough to stay home alone.

Nevertheless, 51 percent also expressed concern about leaving their offspring at home alone after school.

Parental ambivalence was evidenced in the study by Rowland, Robinson, and Coleman (1986). Although the majority of the parents who had latchkey arrangements for their children were satisfied with the situation, 63 percent expressed concern over their youngsters' staying home alone. This concern was illustrated through the practice of checking on children in a variety of ways. During parental absences, telephone calls were the most commonly used method of keeping check on children (45 percent), followed by brother or sister (18 percent), relatives (9 percent), neighbors (9 percent), and a combination of the methods (20 percent). When children were alone, 91 percent of the parents said they had rules for their youngsters to follow. Rule setting occurred most often among children in grades 4 through 6 (47 percent), where the largest numbers of latchkey children were found.

McMurray and Kazanjian (1982) studied 211 low-income families in New York City, a substantial number of whom had latchkey children. That study showed that although parents insisted their youngsters were old enough and responsible enough to stay alone, the parents nevertheless revealed extreme ambivalence, concern, and dissatisfaction but felt they had no options. Nearly one-fifth of these parents left children unsupervised between four and eight hours a day. Many of these children had been in self-care since the age of 7, and by age 12, 95 percent routinely cared for themselves.

Statistics from industry also suggest that concerns of parents whose children are home alone manifest themselves on the job through the "3 o'clock syndrome": productivity slumps, increases in assembly-line accidents, and absenteeism (Pecoraro, Theriot & Lafont 1984).

Alternatives to Latchkey Arrangements

The inability to find and afford high-quality before- and after-school care results in many working parents' leaving their school-age children to care for themselves. Although alternatives to latchkey arrangements are not always available to parents, when they are, cost is the major obstacle that prevents parents from taking advantage of them. A study of 188 service providers and 25 child care directors of after-school programs in Charlotte, North Carolina, reported that the expense of child care is a major factor in perpetuating the latchkey phenomenon (Council for Children 1984). Forty-seven percent of parents who left their children in self-care gave expense of child care as the major reason, and 22 percent of the day care directors reported cost as a major factor in children's being removed from after-school programs. Cost aside, studies have queried parents regarding preferred types of care, and findings indicate that these parents have definite preferences.

Parental Preferences

A survey of *Family Circle* magazine readers, reporting 10,000 responses, asked parents about the child care arrangements they preferred (Whitbread 1979). The most common response (27 percent) was that parents wanted school-age child care somewhere other than at a day care center or in someone else's home. The practice of mothers staying home after school with their children tends to be more common among middle- and upper-middle-class parents (Davis & Solomon 1980; Vandell & Corasaniti 1985). Low-income mothers prefer group child care for school-age children more than any other arrangement, presumably because it is less expensive than in-home care (Harris 1977).

Asked what kind of care they would prefer for their school-age children, 26 percent of parents in another study most often said they preferred a day care center for their children ages 6 to 9 (Rodes & Moore 1975). Nearly three-fourths of the parents agreed that there were not enough places for children to go after school and that every community should have supervised recreational programs for after school. Asked about the role of public schools, nearly 60 percent agreed that the schools should provide such activities.

A survey of 1,806 parents indicated that summer programs (27 percent) and after-school programs (22 percent) were the most common parental preferences for children compared to current arrangements (Rowland, Robinson & Coleman 1986). Care during school holidays followed close behind (14 percent). Emergency care, sick care, weekend care, before-school care, night care, care for children with special needs, and educational and recreational programs comprised the remaining stated preferences, in descending order of importance (37 percent combined).

Local surveys in various parts of the country consistently indicate that most parents want more child care options, most of these being after-school programs, and that they would take advantage of available programs (Seligson et al. 1983).

School-Age Child Care Programs

The focus for child care in the past has been on preschoolers; as a result, few school-age programs exist. (We will discuss some of the different types of programs in chapter 9.) It has been suggested that because of this shortage, school-age children quickly become bored and unhappy with having to stay at a place where emphasis is on preschool care (Campbell & Flake 1985; Vandell & Corasaniti 1985).

The scarcity of school-age programs, which comprised only 3 percent of child care services in 1971 (Chapman & Lazar 1971), has led to a national movement for the establishment of extended day programs in elementary schools to assuage the problems of latchkey kids. Despite this movement, no research is available to document developmental differences between children in self-care and those in after-school programs. Many studies have shown the long-term intellectual and social-emotional benefits of preschool programs (Flake-Hobson, Robinson & Skeen 1983), so one would assume that organized after-school programs have distinct advantages that would circumvent the negative outcomes that might occur in latchkey situations. These assumptions continue to appear in the impressionistic literature despite the absence of solid research documentation. These articles laud the advantages of school-age programs as a panacea for the ills that plague latchkey kids (Mills & Cooke 1983; Nieting 1983; Rosalind 1977; Seligson et al. 1983; Stroman & Duff 1982; Zigler & Hunsinger 1977). Policymakers recommend the use of public schools for after-school programs as the best and most logical solution to the problem of children at home alone (Caldwell 1981; McGurdy 1984; Zigler & Hunsinger 1977).

Some authors claim that extended day programs offer improved mental health and increased productivity benefits to parents and children (Baden et al. 1982; Mills & Cooke 1983). Mills and Cooke (1983) speculate that such programs offer families an anchor of security:

> Parents become more productive at work, as they realize that their children are assured high quality care without leaving the school grounds. These parents no longer have to leave their jobs for child care obligations to interrupt their work schedules to telephone home to make sure children are safe. Children who attend the programs no longer feel isolated from the rest of society. (p. 149)

Other writers have made bold claims regarding the advantages of their after-school programs based on unscientific observations of one or two children:

> For four years, morning and afternoon during the year, and all day in summer, Donner-Belmont has had a chance to make a difference. We look at Angie (9-years-old) and boldly claim our share in her glowing health, her zest for life, her competence, her positive self-concept, and her regard for others. Without us, it might not have been so. (Core 1978, p. 6)

Nieting (1983) suggests that appropriate programmatic and supervisory after-school activities can direct children's energies into positive channels and help school-agers around or effectively deal with drug use, alcoholism, delinquency, obesity, pregnancy, and television addiction. A program in Portland, Oregon, reports that the cost of vandalism at three schools fell from $12,000 in damages in one year to $200 the next year—a drop that program leaders attribute to the establishment of an after-school program in the three schools (Wellborn 1981).

Based on the promising outcomes from these personal accounts and from preschool day care research, one would predict that school-age children enrolled in after-school programs would excel in some ways over their peers who do not have the advantages of such programs. The only hint that this is indeed the case comes from two inconclusive reports.

An unpublished study by Entwisle (1976) described a six-month, loosely controlled pilot project in which 40 low-income black children enrolled in an after-school care program were compared to 15 children not enrolled in the program. Located in Baltimore, Maryland, the center-based after-school program served children between the ages of 5 and 12. Program children had significantly higher grades in math and reading than children not receiving program services. The program was not a tutorial or remedial program but emphasized recreational and cultural activities, and so the academic gains made by program children were surprising. Although attitudes and self-concept improved slightly among some children in the program, the gains were not statistically significant. Entwisle warns that these findings should be interpreted with caution because of the small sample size and an inadequate comparison group for the older children.

The only other study of this nature was conducted by Mayesky (1980a, 1980b, 1980c), who followed the academic achievement of children attending an extended-day program for a three-year period compared with a comparable group of children who were not enrolled. During 1977–1978, 108 program children and 68 nonprogram children were studied; 115 program children and 65 nonprogram children were compared during the 1978–1979 school year. Group 1 consisted of youngsters enrolled in first grade between 1977 and 1978 (when the extended-day program began). Test scores were available for group 1 for three years through the third grade (1979–1980). Group 2 consisted of children who were in second grade between 1977 and 1978; however, test scores were available for this group for only two years, through third grade in 1978–1979 (fourth-grade children were not tested annually).

Mayesky found that standardized math and reading scores for extended-day children were significantly higher than those for nonparticipants. The differences in group scores also widened over the three-year period for group 1 and over the two-year period for group 2. Mayesky attributed these gains to the goals and design of the program—which included high-interest activity areas for intellectual, affective, and psychomotor learning—and to qualified staff. She concluded that the program's nonthreatening environment and small adult-child ratio also contributed to the children's achievement.

Although these two studies suggest clear advantages to after-school programs, no attempts have been made to examine long-term outcomes of after-school programs compared to latchkey situations. Vandell and Corasaniti (1985) compared children in day care centers with those in self-care and found that day care school-age children were rated more poorly by teachers on work and study skills. Day care children also were viewed more negatively by their peers. Because day care programs generally serve preschool children and do not provide organized, after-school activities especially designed for school-age children, Vandell and Corasaniti (1985) suggest that the third graders in their study disliked the day care centers and that such programs may not be appropriate for third graders: "Parents and teachers have told us that many third graders complain about going to the after-school programs because they are 'for babies'. If the activities are inappropriate, they may be fostering less than adequate development" (p. 10).

Based on the Entwisle and Mayesky findings, however, one might suspect that children in adult after-school ecologies (that is, children enrolled in age-appropriate after-school programs or under adult at-home supervision) would fare better than children left in self-care after-school ecologies. This hypothesis, however, must await the test by future researchers since both Entwisle and Mayesky compared only participating and nonparticipating children and did not distinguish the types of after-school arrangements of the nonparticipants.

Table 2–1 summarizes the research to date by type of child care arrangement and child outcomes. Data indicate that in terms of the variables studied so far, rural and suburban latchkey kids and children in adult care after school (excluding day care centers that provide baby-sitting services for school-agers) benefit more than urban latchkey kids in every arena. They are superior in academic achievement, self-reliance, and self-concept. They have fewer fears,

Table 2–1
Relationship between Child Care Ecology and Child Outcomes

Child Outcomes	Urban Latchkey Kids	Rural-Suburban Latchkey Kids	Children in Adult Care
Academic achievement	Low (1)	Not affected (2,3,4)	High (1,5,6)
Self-reliance	Low (1)	Not affected (12)	High (1)
Self-concept	Low (1)	Not measured	High (6)
Fear levels	High (4,7,8,9)	Low (2,3)	Low (4,7)
Bored/lonely	High (4,7,9)	Low (2,10,11)	Low (4,7)
Accidents	High (10)	Not measured	Low (10)
Restricted play	High (10)	Low (2,10)	Low (10)
Social-emotional problems	High (1)	Low (2,3,4,14)	Low (1,6,12,14)
Negative attitudes toward working mothers	High (13)	Not measured	Not measured

Sources: 1, Woods 1972; 2, Galambos & Garbarino 1985; 3, Gold & Andres 1978b; 4, Long & Long 1983b; 5, Mayesky 1980; 6, Entwisle 1976; 7, Long & Long 1982c; 8, Rowland et al. 1986; 9, Zill et al. 1977; 10, Long & Long 1983a; 11, Garbarino 1981; 12, Steinberg 1985; 13, Trimberger & MacLean 1982; 14, Vandell & Corasaniti 1985.

experience less boredom and loneliness, and are less vulnerable to accidents. Their play is less restricted, and they have fewer social-emotional problems.

Conclusion

More questions than answers exist on the risks of self-care. Until research can catch up with the mounting numbers of latchkey youngsters, we can make only limited speculations from a few pioneer studies that pave the way for future study.

It is not our aim to minimize the potential harm inherent in latchkey situations. Many of our own anecdotal cases, including the opening case to this chapter, contain accounts of latchkey children's fears and apprehensions. Furthermore, no study has found that latchkey children are better off than adult-supervised children, with the exception of Vandell & Corasaniti (1985). This finding may have emerged because parents are properly preparing children for self-care, or, as Vandell and Corasaniti (1985) suggest, they may be self-selecting only the most mature children for this responsiblity. Scientists' research tools may not be sophisticated enough to measure potential problems in a brief time. Future longitudinal research may unearth undetected problems after in-depth study over longer time periods.

Whatever the reason, research to date suggests that many latchkey kids are doing well and appear to be growing and developing similarly to their nonlatchkey contemporaries. In the following chapter we will discuss typical growth and development patterns of school-agers and the implications they hold for latchkey children and those in school-age child care programs.

References

Baden, R.; Genser, A.; Levine, J.; & Seligson, M. 1982. *School-age child care: An action manual.* Boston: Auburn House.

Caldwell, B. 1981. Day care and the schools. *Theory into Practice* 20:121–129.

Campbell, L.P., & Flake, A.E. 1985. Latchkey children—What is the answer? *Clearing House* 58:381–383.

Castelli, J. 1983 (August 10). Yes, we're afraid and we are lonely. *USA Today,* p. 9A.

Chaback, E., & Fortunato, P. 1983 (February). A kid's survival checklist: When you're home alone. *Parents Magazine,* pp. 134–136.

Chapman, J.E., & Lazar, J.B. 1977. *A review of the present status and future need in day care research.* Working paper. Washington, D.C.: Interagency Panel on Early Childhood Research and Development, Office of Child Development.

Coleman, M.; Robinson, B.E.; & Rowland, B.H. 1984. Latchkey children and their families. *Dimensions* 13:23–24.

Coleman, M.; Robinson, B.E.; Rowland, B.H.; & Price, S. 1984 (October 19). Families with latchkey children: A study with implications for service delivery. Paper presented at the National Council on Family Relations, San Francisco.

Core, M. 1978 (December). When school's out and nobody's home. *Record*, pp. 2–6.

Council for Children. 1984. *Taking action for latchkey children.* Charlotte, N.C.: Council for Children.

Davis, J., & Solomon, P. 1980. Day care needs among the upper middle classes. *Child Welfare* 59:497–499.

Entwisle, B. 1976. The impact of school age day care upon achievement. Paper presented at the Annual Meeting of the American Sociological Association, New York.

Flake-Hobson, C.; Robinson, B.E.; & Skeen, P. 1983. *Child development and relationships.* Reading, Mass.: Addison-Wesley.

Fosarelli, P.D. 1984. Latchkey children. *Journal of Developmental and Behavioral Pediatrics* 5:173–177.

Galambos, N.L., & Dixon, R.A. 1984. Toward understanding and caring for latchkey children. *Child Care Quarterly* 13:116–125.

Galambos, N.L., & Garbarino, J. 1983. Identifying the missing links in the study of latchkey children. *Children Today* 12:2–4, 10.

Galambos, N.L., & Garbarino, J. 1985. Adjustment of unsupervised children in a rural ecology. *Journal of Genetic Psychology* 146:227–231.

Garbarino, J. 1981. Latchkey children: How much a problem? *Educational Digest* 46: 14–16.

Gold, D., & Andres, D. 1978a. Developmental comparisons between ten-year-old children with employed and nonemployed mothers. *Child Development* 49:75–84.

Gold, D., & Andres, D. 1978b. Comparisons of adolescent children with employed and nonemployed mothers. *Merrill-Palmer Quarterly* 24:243–254.

Harris, O.C. 1977. Day care: Have we forgotten the school-age child? *Child Welfare* 56:440–448.

Hoffman, L.W. 1979. Maternal employment: 1979. *American Psychologist* 34:859–865.

Huff, K. 1982 (September 20). In their own words. *People Magazine* pp. 83–84, 87–88.

Kieffer, E. 1981 (February 24). The latchkey kids: How are they doing? *Family Circle,* pp. 28–35.

Langway, L. 1981 (February). The latchkey children. *Newsweek,* pp. 96–97.

Lapinski, S. 1982 (September 2). Latchkey blues: When kids come home. *Family Weekly,* pp. 22–23.

Leishman, K. 1980 (November). When kids are home alone: How mothers make sure they're safe. *Working Mother,* pp. 21–22, 25.

Long, L., & Long, T. 1982a (September 20). The lonely life of latchkey children. *People Magazine.*

Long, L. & Long, T. 1982b (May). The unspoken fears of latchkey kids. *Working Mother,* pp. 88–90.

Long, T., & Long, L. 1982c. *Latchkey children: The child's view of self-care.* ERIC ED 211 229.

Long, T., & Long, L. 1983a. *Latchkey children.* ERIC ED 226 836.

Long, T., & Long, L. 1983b. *The handbook for latchkey children and their parents.* New York: Arbor House.

Long, L., & Long T. 1985 (December 23). Study: Latchkey kids learning more about sex when no one's home. *Jet Magazine* 69:32.

Long, T. 1983 (November 7). Latchkey children: Scope of the problem. Speech presented at the Seventh Annual Conference of the North Carolina Chapter of the National Committee for the Prevention of Child Abuse, Charlotte, N.C.

Mayesky, M.E. 1980a. A study of academic effectiveness in a public school day care program. *Phi Delta Kappan* 62:284–285.

Mayesky, M.E. 1980b. *Differences in academic growth as measured in an extended day program in a public elementary school.* ERIC ED 184 675.

Mayesky, M.E. 1980c. Phillips extended day magnet: A successful blend of day care and academics. *Education Digest* 58:12–15.

McGurdy, J. 1984 (March). Schools respond to latchkey children. *School Administrator,* pp. 16–18.

McMurray, G.L., & Kazanjian, D.P. 1982. *Day care and the working poor: The struggle for self-sufficiency.* New York: Community Service Society of New York.

Mills, B.C., & Cooke, E. 1983. Extended day programs: A place for the latchkey child. *Early Child Development and Care* 12:143–151.

Moore, S.G. 1978. Working mothers and their children. *Young Children* 34:77–82.

Newsweek. 1980 (October 6). Survival training for latchkey kids. *Newsweek,* p. 100.

Nieting, P.L. 1983. School-age child care: In support of development and learning. *Childhood Education* 60:6–11.

Pecoraro, A.; Theriot, J.; & Lafont, P. 1984. What home economists should know about latchkey children. *Journal of Home Economics* 76:20–22.

Robinson, B.E.; Coleman, M.; & Rowland, B.H. 1986a. Taking action for latchkey children and their families. *Family Relations* 35.

Robinson, B.E.; Coleman, M.; & Rowland, B.H. 1986b. The after-school ecologies of latchkey children. *Children's Environments Quarterly.*

Rodes, T.W., & Moore, L.C. 1975. *National child care consumer study: 1975.* Washington, D.C.: Office of Child Development, U.S. Department of Health, Education, and Welfare.

Rodman, H. 1980 (July). How children take care of themselves. *Working Mother,* pp. 61–63.

Rodman, H. 1986. From latchkey stereotypes to self-care realities. Unpublished manuscript. Greensboro: University of North Carolina.

Rodman, H.; Pratto, D.J.; & Nelson, R.S. 1985. Child care arrangements and children's functioning: A comparison of self-care and adult-care children. *Developmental Psychology* 21:413–418.

Rosalind, S. 1977. Extended day. *Journal of Home Economics* 69:7–10.

Rowland, B.H.; Robinson, B.E.; & Coleman, M. 1986. Parents' perceptions of needs for their latchkey children: A survey. *Pediatric Nursing* 12.

Seligson, M.; Genser, A.; Gannett, E.; & Gray, W. 1983. *School-age child care: A policy report.* Wellesley, Mass.: Center for Research on Women.

Sparks, S. 1983. Latchkey children. Thesis, University of North Carolina at Charlotte.

Steinberg, L. 1985. Latchkey children and susceptibility to peer pressure: An ecological analysis. Unpublished manuscript. Madison: University of Wisconsin.

Stewart, M. 1981. *Children in self-care: An exploratory study.* ERIC ED 224 604.

Stroman, S.H. & Duff, E. 1982. The latchkey child: Whose responsiblity? *Childhood Education* 59:76–79.

Taveggia, T.C., & Thomas, E.M. 1974. Latchkey children. *Pacific Sociological Review* 17:27–34.

Trimberger, R., & MacLean, M.J. 1982. Maternal employment: The child's perspective. *Journal of Marriage and the Family* 44:469–475.

Turkington, C. 1983. Lifetime of fear may be legacy of latchkey children. *APA Monitor* 14:19.

Vandell, D., & Corasaniti, M.A. 1985. (May 27). After-school care: Choices and outcomes for third graders. Paper presented at the Annual Meeting of the American Association for the Advancement of Science, Los Angeles.

Wellborn, S.N. 1981. (September 14). When school kids come home to an empty house. *U.S. News and World Report,* pp. 42–47.

Whitbread, J. 1979. Who's taking care of the children? *Family Circle* 20:88, 92, 102, 103.

Woods, M.B. 1972. The unsupervised child of the working mother. *Developmental Psychology* 6:14–25.

Zambrana, R.E.; Hurst, M.; & Hite, R.L. 1979. The working mother in contemporary perspective: A review of the literature. *Pediatrics* 64:862–870.

Zigler, E., & Hunsinger, S. 1977. Day care policy: Some modest proposals. *Day Care and Early Education* 4:9–11.

Zill, N.; Gruvaeus, G.; & Woyshner, K. 1977. *Kids, parents, and interviewers: Three points of view on a national sample of children.* New York: Foundation of Child Development.

3
Growth and Development of School-Age Children

Walter is 13 years old and in his first year of junior high school. He has a younger brother, Robert, age 11 and in fifth grade. For several years they attended the same elementary school and were very close. Today they are still close but have developmentally different interests. Walter has new interests and feels that he is more serious about school now that he is in junior high.

At times Walter becomes annoyed with his younger brother. "Robert likes to have things his own way and only wants to watch comedy shows on TV," Walter reports. Instead of arguing over which programs to watch, Walter usually goes to his room to watch sports on a smaller television set.

Walter remembers elementary school clearly. He liked all his teachers and had fun most of the time. He recalls having some difficulty with math and remaining quiet in the lunchroom. Both boys complained of a red light that signaled "no talking" in the school cafeteria.

Walter, a model student, described himself as shy and modest. Perhaps he was a little defensive when he said, "I talked a lot at home and around my friends, but there was no reason to talk a lot at school."

"The thing I like to do best," says Walter, "is play basketball. The backboard that Dad put up in the driveway has been a lot of fun. All the neighborhood kids come over, and we play one-on-one."

Walter and Robert, both Tar Heel basketball fans, wear Tar Heel sweatshirts and Air-Jordan sports shoes—the rage of children their ages. They have demonstrated their allegiance to the Tar Heels since they were given their first T-shirts as infants.

During the elementary school years, Walter was active in church programs. He sang in the children's choir and attended church school each week. He has not joined the youth choir, and one of his major reasons "is that the other kids don't go."

Walter remembers being afraid of sirens and the sounds they make when he was 8. He still does not like to stay home alone in the evenings without all the lights on in the house. At times Walter and Robert are left in a semilatchkey arrangement for several hours when their mother attends a meeting and their father is out of town.

Walter and Robert help around the house. They cut grass, take out trash, and pick up things in their rooms. By their own admission, Walter is messy, while Robert is neat and orderly. Walter is not as industrious as Robert, who has started a handyman's business with one of the neighborhood youths. Robert and his friend do odd jobs for neighbors and have a business card and brochure.

Walter talked about what it was like growing up—the good times and the bad times—and about the future: "In the fourth grade, I became interested in playing football and basketball. I played on Little League teams and with the YMCA. I really like sports. But I also like to be with my friends and do things with family. The best part of elementary school was the sixth grade. We were given special privileges and choices but also a lot of work to do. I needed an extra period each day to do my homework. I've always been afraid that I wouldn't get my work done. Once in the second grade, I had to stay after school to finish my work. That was a bad time. If I have a complaint about teachers in elementary school, it is when they punish the whole class for something one kid had done. That's not fair.

"One thing I don't want to be is a 'nerd.' A nerd is someone who is too different. I'm not a troublemaker. I'm quiet, but I feel like I'm normal. I have some good friends, and I like girls who are nice and look good. What other people think about you depends on how you look. When I was in kindergarten, I liked the same girl that my friend liked. We didn't fight over her; it was a crush. When I was in the third grade, we had to folk dance with girls. Everybody had to do it, so I didn't feel different. When I was in the fourth grade, I snooped around and found the presents from the Easter Bunny. That's the same year I found out that there's no such thing as Santa Claus. It was okay.

"I know there are drugs and alcohol at my school, but I haven't seen them. You learn the kids who don't care about anything, and you stay away from them. I've seen kids walking away from school smoking. I'm in the seventh grade now, and no adult has told me about sex or sex education. What I know, I heard from other kids. When I think about the future, I'm not as worried about an atomic war now as I was in elementary school. I believe Russia and the United States are trying to work together. I wouldn't want to go to the army, and I certainly wouldn't want to fight. I think something needs to be done about terrorism. I don't know what. I want to go to college, maybe to be a veterinarian because I really like animals."

Many changes have taken place for Walter and Robert during their elementary-school years. Walter is leaving childhood behind and entering adolescence. Robert is in the swing of middle childhood and enjoys his new sense of independence and competence. In this chapter, we will examine the developmental stage of middle childhood. We will highlight physical, cognitive, social, and emotional growth. We will emphasize, as others have (Melizzi & Yawkey 1984), that after-school programs or at-home activities for latchkey kids should consider the child's maturity level as well as complement physical, intellectual, and social-emotional needs at this stage. Special emphasis will be placed on the importance of high-quality, successful school-age child care programs and how to develop them. We will look at significant adults in the lives of children outside home and the influences on children.

Physical Development

During middle childhood (ages 6–12), physical growth decelerates and from outward appearances could easily be described as a lengthening-out period. Legs become longer and trunks slimmer. Average growth ranges from two to three inches per year, and weight increases from three to five pounds (Lowrey 1978).

Children become better coordinated as motor development results in greater strength and activity. By developmental design, elementary-age children experience a strong drive to be active. Because their muscle tissues are immature, they cannot sit still for longer periods of time (Flake-Hobson, Robinson & Skeen 1983).

Body Build

W.H. Sheldon (1940) classified body build into three types and described associated personality traits. Children with chubby body builds (endomorphs) have been classified as calm and happy individuals. Athletic, muscular children (mesomorphs) are thought to be bold and outgoing. Children with thin body builds (ectomorphs) have been described as shy and withdrawn. Many children fit these descriptions, but just as many do not. Unfortunately, these stereotypes have affected the child's view of self and relationships with others, even in the preschool years.

Society generally favors the mesomorph, and children give more desirable ratings to youngsters with this type of physique (Lerner & Lerner 1977). Adult responses to children are affected by physical attractiveness even in the preschool years. Dion (1977) found that adults were more tolerant of negative behavior displayed by attractive children than by unattractive children.

Physical Skill Development

In the elementary-school years, children become competent in running, climbing, and jumping. Walter, a mesomorph, looked forward to field day at his afterschool program. He was assured of several blue ribbons. Robert, an endomorph, reported that he was not "crazy" about running. Robert was ambivalent when Walter won the softball throw and several races. He was proud but indicated that ribbons are not hard to win and therefore were not worth the effort.

Most school-age children say they are pleased with their new physical accomplishments—the ability to play games that provide practice and refinement. In high-quality daytime and after-school programs, the school yard echoes with jumping rope chants, catchball, chase, and tag games.

Principles of Physical Growth

Several principles of physical growth have direct bearing on the behavior of school-age youngsters:

1. Each child grows at a different rate and pace.
2. The physical uniqueness of each child is based on a combination of body build, physical abilities, and level of physical maturity (Maxim 1985)

3. A gradual increase in muscle mass and strength occurs, with boys having more muscle tissue than girls (Maccoby 1980).

4. Girls generally outperform boys in fine motor abilities.

5. Boys generally outperform girls in gross motor skills.

6. Sensory mechanisms continue to mature, with binocular vision becoming well developed and hearing acuity increasing (Lundsteen & Bernstein-Tarrow 1981).

7. Distinguishing between left and right laterality improves rapidly in middle childhood (Flake-Hobson, Robinson & Skeen 1983).

8. The nervous system continues refinement, and greater communication between the two sides of the brain appears (Tanner 1970).

9. Girls begin their physical growth spurt before boys and are slightly taller than boys at age 10 (Hamill et al. 1977).

10. Boys and girls tend to experience early physical maturation due to improved nutrition and health care.

Implications for After-School Activities

School-age children are physical in their approach to the world. The developmental characteristics listed in table 3–1 signify the need for latchkey kids or children in school-age child care programs to be physically involved in activities on a daily basis. School-age children typically have sat in a regimented classroom all day. Once school is out, children of this age, whether at home alone or enrolled in an after-school program, need to be physically active.

Table 3–1
Physical Characteristics of School-Age Children

Physical growth is slow and consistent.

Motor development is smoother and more coordinated than in early childhood.

Competence improves in running, climbing, jumping rope, catching ball, bicycle riding, skating, and general movement.

Good body control is evident; children can stretch, twist, and curl.

Handedness develops.

They can reproduce letters and numbers.

They can draw designs.

They demand activity.

Eye-hand coordination is accomplished.

They can perform complex motor skills.

They can suffer bone and muscle damage when activity is begun too early or carried to the extreme.

It is no wonder that some latchkey kids, daily confined to their homes after school, say they are bored; physical confinement goes against the grain of their natural urge to be active. Where city children must stay inside due to outside dangers, parents can capitalize on the needs for physical activity by helping children develop a rigorous physical exercise program that they can accomplish at home. Nightly or weekend family outings and long walks and talks also can meet growing children's physical as well as emotional needs.

Enrolling children in a weekend or after-school Y or local park and recreation department program is another way of meeting needs in a developmentally appropriate way. But regularly attending a program does not always solve children's needs for movement. Parents who have children enrolled in after-school care should make sure the program offers opportunities for physical expression: group games, sports, aerobics classes, or other recreational activities. Parents should be cautious of school-age child care that offers only sedentary activities and demands quiet or programs that are carbon-copy extensions of the school day. Quiet and inactive school-age children are unhappy children, whether they are at home alone or in after-school group care.

Cognitive Development

Middle childhood opens the door of thinking. Thinking up to this point has been mainly trial and error and a series of hunches and guesses. How things seemed to be was how they were. Time and experiences have moved on, and according to Jean Piaget (1954), children continue to add new information to old data and form new concepts.

Jean Piaget

Jean Piaget (1896–1980) was a pioneer in the study of the nature of knowledge. Born in Switzerland, he was influenced heavily by philosophers and scientists of his time. He studied the core of intelligence and sought answers to why children gave wrong answers on intelligence tests constructed by Alfred Binet in the early 1900s.

Piaget developed a theory of how children think based on studies and observations. He described a four-stage invariant sequential process. Infancy and *sensorimotor* knowing is the first stage during which the child organizes and coordinates sensations with actions. The second stage, *preoperational thought*, lasts from 2 to 7 years of age. Children see things from their own perspective and cannot reverse their thinking. The third stage, *concrete operations*, lasts from approximately 7 to 11 years and is the major mode of thinking of school-age children. Children can classify and organize their thoughts in a logical way, and for the first time can perform actions mentally. The last and most advanced stage, *formal operations*, begins around 11 or 12 years of age. Children now think in abstract ways and can conceptualize about things they have never seen.

Children's thinking, according to Piaget, results from the interaction of heredity and environment. Stages cannot be skipped or accelerated. The value of a responsive setting, where children can be involved, is stressed. Four ingredients are fundamental to Piaget's theory:

1. *The child's maturation.* A genetic unfolding sets the sequence for thinking. Piaget believed that human beings innately possess certain basic drives or needs plus the capacity to seek fulfillment.

2. *People, values, and the cultural transmitters.* Children learn by example and imitation. Society, parents, siblings, peers, and other adults portray for children their interpretation of concepts or ideas being explored. Children add this dimension to their own learning.

3. *The new or extended experience itself.* Children act on objects and events and give them personal meaning and definition. Any concept must be connected to an already-formed idea or thought.

4. *A process of equilibration.* A newly evolving concept is preceded by a sense of contradiction in meaning. Things do not fit as well as they once did, and the child manipulates the thought or idea until it becomes more focused.

School-Age Children and Concrete Operations

Children are always trying to make sense of their world. They are driven to fit things together and make them into cohesive wholes. Cognitive processes develop within two major areas: physical knowledge and logico-mathematical knowledge (Maxim 1985). Physical knowledge concerns observable properties of objects. Children manipulate objects to find out what they are useful for and what they can do. They punch, squeeze, look, drop, fold, listen, taste, and do anything else feasible to stimulate their mental activity. Logico-mathematical knowledge "involves five skill areas: (a) classification, (b) seriation, (c) spatial relations, (d) temporal relations, and (e) conservation" (Maxim 1985, p. 218).

For the most part school-age children are concrete operational thinkers. They experience shifts in the way they think. One of the major changes is from egocentrism to relativism. In this shift, children decenter and deal with two variables or aspects of a problem simultaneously. Being able to take the viewpoint of another opens new doors of communication with family, teachers, and peers. Decreased egocentrism also leads to cooperation and competition. Play activities take on new meaning as children develop systems and rules to guide their behaviors.

Other important characteristics of concrete thinkers include the newly acquired abilities of reversibility, conservation, classification, and seriation. Children can reverse their thought processes and return them to their original states. In other words, they can mentally backtrack their line of reasoning; they can find their way around an unfamiliar place like a department store and are less likely to get lost as they were a few years before. They can conserve (hold constant in their minds) the notion that basic properties of objects (such as weight, volume, number, and area) remain unchanged although the appearance of objects is modified. Robert had yet to conserve when he demanded the tall, slim glass of lemonade while Walter enjoyed his lemonade in a short, wide glass that held the same amount. Concrete operational thinkers group things together (classification) and put them in sequences and order (seriation). They understand far and near, below and above, and have abilities to understand direction and distance. They also perceive time sequences and cause and effect relationships.

Information Processing

Children's learning is tied to memory too. Processes for storing information improve during this period of development. Middle childhood youngsters develop systems for retrieving information and are able to use recall extensively (Flavell 1979). Problem solving and creativity become thinking vehicles and reach their peak at the beginning of this period. Symbols (words and numbers) become useful, and logical reasoning brings order to the child's world. A sense of competence develops, and expanding interests and resources outside the home (such as school, peers, and community) lead to a higher level of intelligence and understanding.

Implications for After-School Activities

School-age child care staff and latchkey parents can capitalize on shifts in cognitive development by providing activities for children that match their new cognitive skills described in table 3–2. Adults can find a wealth of resources for such activities in their everyday environments. One sample activity is "Measuring around objects." Instruct the child to find a number of objects throughout the house (or school or classroom), and measure around them with strings. Have them ponder which they think is the thinnest, fattest, and so forth. They then examine the lengths of the pieces of string and place the objects in order from thinnest to fattest. Finally they use the pieces of string to make a graph.

Many science and math activities of this nature will stimulate the new cognitive skills that children have acquired. These activities can be included

Table 3–2
Thinking and Learning Characteristics of School-Age Children

Their thinking skills and their ability to construct knowledge progress from simple knowing to more complex, logical thought patterns.

They learn best by doing because direct action on ideas and objects is important in forming concepts.

They understand relationships between the whole and its parts.

They consider and share the viewpoints of others.

They begin to develop the abilities to conserve number, length, liquid, area, weight, and volume.

They develop reversibility of thought.

They develop the ability to classify and categorize people and things.

Their sense of order develops as they learn to put objects in sequence.

---

in a school-age child care curriculum or sent home by daytime classroom teachers with latchkey kids to keep them constructively occupied in afternoons when they are alone. Parents of latchkey children will find activities of this sort useful as they strive to entertain the family and provide cognitive stimulation. It is important that the activities adults create involve the use of manipulative materials. Teachers will then have to prepare the concrete objects so that they can be taken home easily, perhaps in a shoebox. Besides including manipulatives, the shoebox could contain a task card with clear and legible directions; a tradebook (a children's reference book that is readable and accurate and has a pleasing format) that can expand the learning opportunities provided by the activity; and a letter to parent(s) introducing the activity.[2] The following example provides a science shoebox activity task:

Topic: Discovering Shapes That Float Best

Materials: Paper clips; ball of clay; water; cottage cheese container in which to store the paper clips and clay and to hold water for the activity.

Activities: 1. Change the ball of clay so that it floats.
2. Describe two shapes that float best.
3. Load the floating shapes with cargo (paper clips).
4. Record the amount of cargo each shape will hold before it sinks. The craft that carries the most cargo wins.

All activities should share certain characteristics. They should be educational as well as fun, often involving a game that can be repeated and enjoyed. They should appeal to a wide range of school ages and use common materials. In joint adult-child activities, adults should not tell children what they should learn because this limits and stifles personal knowing and understanding.

Instead the adult and child should talk through the learning process. The adult can ask: "How can we solve this problem?" "Do you see the solution to the problem?" "Can you predict the outcome?"

One activity, "Building a Structure," contains all these characteristics and gives children the added experience of sharpening spatial ability skills. It is designed to stimulate exploration of properties of various geometric shapes and learning directional words such as *right, left, up,* and *down.* Working with a partner, the child chooses four different blocks (this could be similar lightweight items found around the home or school). With a set of the four selected blocks, both participants sit back to back with their partners and build a structure with the blocks. Then each tells their partner how to build the same structure without looking at the model. Comparing structures, partners talk through the learning process: "Are they the same? If not, where was the misunderstanding? What could you have said?" Next, this same format is repeated for the second partner to build a structure for duplication.[1]

Social-Emotional Development

From their first interactions with others, children go through a special process of social-emotional development. They learn to behave in acceptable ways while reciprocal relationships form between themselves and others in their environment. The nature of these relationships and the expression of the child's feelings are inseparable, one influencing the other.

The social and emotional needs of school-age children are related to the social settings or contexts in which development takes place. The family and primary care givers continue to have the most important socializing influence on the child at this stage. Parents help their offspring develop social competencies needed in school and peer relationships. For the first time children realize that the rules of society are logical and reasonable. But although independence is a primary mode of behaving, children still need attention and guidance.

The importance of parents' role during this age cannot be overstated. A fine line exists between letting children go or holding them too tightly to grow. Children are entering settings where they can take care of themselves for a large part of the day. They feel a new sense of pride in their work and achievements. For the most part children need little encouragement to develop a sense of industry and accomplishment.

Industry versus Inferiority

Erik Erikson developed a theory of self-identity as a product of cultural or social factors. Erikson's (1963) psychosocial theory is based on a life span frame of reference that all individuals progress through. During each stage, a conflict or crisis occurs where personal needs and social expectations seek harmony. Erikson perceived these crises as being resolved in positive, healthy ways or in pessimistic, unhealthy ways. To develop a positive sense of self, the person must resolve each stage satisfactorily. Erikson believed that the significant persons and ensuing relationships in the life of the child are the primary shapers of the child's destiny.

For school-age children, the fourth stage in Erikson's life span frame, industry versus inferiority, is strongly influenced by support and feedback that come from important adults and peers (Flake-Hobson, Robinson & Skeen 1983). Children begin to compare themselves with others. They want to demonstrate their new physical and mental abilities. It is important for them to view themselves as productive and competent. "I can do it myself" is the prevailing attitude.

Robert worked for almost an hour putting his new train track together. The small railroad cars would soon go over the bridge and around the curves. But Walter wanted to help Robert; he thought he could speed things up. "Let me help," Walter said. "Go away," Robert answered, "I can put the track together." Robert continued to connect one piece of the track to another.

Although children need challenge, they need it within their reach. When they are pushed beyond their capabilities and experience failure, they feel inadequate or inferior. Adults must encourage independence and productivity and avoid situations where children feel shame or doubt.

The Self and Self-Esteem

Because of increasing cognitive abilities, school-age children are better able to take the perspective of others while simultaneously understanding how others view them. They have learned that their behaviors affect different people in different ways. They can act one way with adults and another with children their own age. They begin to see themselves in relationship to others. They place a value or judgment on this new self-awareness, which some researchers label self-esteem or self-concept.

Important studies focusing on self-esteem have revealed that affectionate and involved parents rear youngsters with high self-esteem (Coopersmith 1967). Parents whose attitudes are linked to high self-esteem are warm and accepting, are consistent in discipline, maintain a harmonious home, state limits clearly, participate with children in recreational activities, are available and accessible to children, and have firm but flexible rules.

Age-mates or peers are important in the social-emotional development of school-age children. The child who gives the most reinforcement in a peer group is the one most likely to receive reinforcement in return (Charlesworth & Hartup 1967). Peer interaction is reciprocal in nature. At the same time, an urge or drive to be popular exists. Being well liked is related to a positive self-concept. Studies show that being happy and showing concern for others can lead to popularity (Hartup 1970).

Overall school-age children are forming new ideas about themselves that are influenced greatly by their families, peers, and others in the community. They have become aware of the importance of their physical attributes, their behaviors, and their personality traits. They place a value or judgment on themselves that can be positive or negative and can influence their individuality.

Implications for After-School Activities

Social-emotional needs of elementary-school children such as those listed in table 3–3 can be matched through a variety of activities in child care programs: sharing time through group involvement, free choice experiences, outdoor and indoor physical exercise, quiet time for individual expression, and opportunities for productivity alone and in groups.

Adults, whether parents or care givers, can present children choices of activities that correspond to developmental abilities. Kindergarten children, for instance, can be given choices that are narrower and limited to perhaps two or three. Building a terrarium or painting a picture are examples of two choices. Adolescents can handle a wider range and variety of such choices as house repair and housekeeping, sports, club meetings, and field trips (Melizzi & Yawkey 1984). Volunteers who manage help-lines and receive children's calls report that advice varies according to the caller's developmental abilities: "For example, a young child may be asked to cover a broken glass, while an older child is instructed in ways to pick it up safely. Children then report back to the volunteer" (Soto & Guerney 1984, p. 105).

School-age children need activities that permit them to be industrious. During this stage, children want to fix things, demonstrate new physical skills,

Table 3–3
Social-Emotional Characteristics of School-Age Children

Conformity and the peer group become significant factors influencing their social development.

They depend on the emotional security and support of their peer group to begin weakening ties from parents.

As they detach themselves from their parents, they continue to depend on parental affection, attention, and guidance.

Their growing contact with the outside world provides important influences from adults, such as teachers and civic leaders.

The need to be industrious and to have the products of this industry valued are essential to their developing self-concept.

Being well-liked by others, especially peers, has a bearing on their developing self-concept.

Their fears, thoughts, interests, and humor reflect their expanding knowledge of the world at large.

create, and learn. Creative skills such as woodworking, clay modeling, painting, and arts and crafts yield concrete products. More process-oriented activities such as memberships in clubs and civic organizations, like Girl and Boy Scouts, teach children to be competent, productive members of society. Dance or music lessons nurture creative skills. Organized sports such as soccer, board games such as Monopoly and checkers, and computerized games appeal to the school-age child's emerging competitive spirit. Group games such as blindman's bluff, chasing games, hide-and-seek, and red rover are popular at this age. They give children opportunities to let off pent-up energy, develop physical-motor capacities, and build social skills. Children this age love to collect and categorize objects as evidence of their productivity.

Whether latchkey kids develop industry or inferiority is strongly influenced by the support and feedback from parents and teachers. Latchkey youngsters, for instance, should be adequately prepared by adults so that they can feel successful in assuming responsibility for their own welfare. (We discuss the parent's role in chapter 5 and the teacher's role in chapter 6.) Constructive after-school activities, structured by school-age child care (SACC) teachers or by latchkey parents, and the adult's recognition and approval of a job well done can foster feelings of worth, confidence, and industry.

School-Age Children and Adults outside the Family

Parents are no longer the only significant adults in the lives of children. As youngsters move into the community for longer periods of time each day, they are exposed to a variety of disciplinary and leadership styles (Flake-Hobson, Robinson & Skeen 1983).

Teachers

Teachers, who exert the strongest influence on middle-age children, can provide an environment that tests the child's newly developed capabilities. Their training has prepared them to match curriculum activities and programming with the ways children learn and think best. When teachers know children developmentally, they can offer a creative curriculum that questions and encourages. They can provide needed choice and some freedom and make available opportunities for decision making. A developmentally aware teacher strikes a balance between guidance and instruction.

Community Leaders

Coaches, scout leaders, church workers, and other community leaders and their institutions begin to play a major role during middle childhood. Team games and sports serve as vehicles for trying out new rules and regulations. Organizations that offer children a chance to build their talents are viewed as attractive and important. The community is full of resources and models. Albert Bandura (1977) believes that children's learning occurs largely through observing parents, peers, and other significant people in the community. He reports that children are more likely to copy the behavior of those they most admire. The importance of warm, trusting adults in these significant roles cannot be overemphasized.

Robert thought Mrs. Kersh, the children's choir leader, was the greatest. She always had a quick smile and kind words. Robert was sometimes mischievous, but Mrs. Kersh did not seem to mind. She would say, "Now, Robert settle in!" Robert liked to sing, but what he liked best were the skating parties and trips to the pizza parlor. Once each month, the children and Mrs. Kersh chose a special event or treat. Many times the group would take Robert's suggestion, and that always made him feel good.

Advocates

With the changing family and the changing views of childhood, new problems and concerns for school-age children have emerged. Certain individuals and groups, such as the Children's Defense Fund in Washington, D.C., have responded quickly to child care needs. Other advocates, like the Council for Children in Charlotte, N.C., have sought solutions to recognized community problems. Efforts have been made to improve children's status and to provide them with quality programming opportunities. Advocacy is examined in detail in chapter 8.

Themes and Issues in Middle Childhood

Themes

School-age children have new interests and powers. They form new relationships with peers and begin to select additional adult role models. Their need to achieve enables them to turn out work. To make something work is satisfying and helps to build self-esteem. Schools and churches give children other points of view and transmit new perspectives into their cultures and values. The developmental and cognitive shifts that children experience in middle childhood make these developments possible. In our achievement-oriented society, boys and girls need an environmental climate that creates a balance between accomplishments and dreams.

Issues

In the complex process of growing and developing, children need skills for dealing with the new and unexpected. Because each child is different, what works for one child may not work for another. Sometimes children are unduly penalized for differing opinions when it comes to deciding what is best for them. Research examining influences on children, parenting strategies, and teacher effectiveness has been limited. The outcome has been one of debate and disagreement. Varying opinions have been proposed in regard to the best means for helping children learn to help themselves. Some conflicting opinions center around the following issues:

Discipline. Ways to control the behavior of youngsters are debated constantly. Some believe in punitive measures; others advocate positive approaches. Reliable evidence negates the use of punishment as an effective means of changing behavior (Hyman 1979). Logical consequences—with the child participating in the decision of how to handle the problem—has met with favor by many elementary school counselors and parents.

Violence on television. Television affects the thinking and feelings of school-age children. Some experts say that television hurries children (Elkind 1981) and forces them to deal with information for which they have no foundations of understanding. Bandura (1978) reported that children repeat what they see and hear on television. Other studies indicate that when children view television violence, they are prone to act aggressively (Liebert, Sprafkin & Davidson 1985). Little argument can be found for positive effects of aggression on television. Some advocacy organizations such as Action for Children's Television (ACT) claim that television is a major educator of young children and that its lessons are poorly planned. ACT was instrumental in reducing commercial time on children's programs and in prohibiting advertisements for fireworks, vitamins, and junk food aimed directly at children.

Nutrition and diet. Parents and teachers are concerned with promoting good health. Junk food eating has contributed to this problem more than any other source. Underweight children suffer too. They may lack stamina and the energy needed for an active life. Good nutrition is critical throughout childhood. Links between childhood nutrition and later development of health problems such as high blood pressure and calcium deficiencies cannot be ignored.

Anxieties and fears. Fears and anxieties during middle childhood are related to the child's expanding world (Williams & Stith 1980). Realistic concerns of everyday life cause anxiety and worry. Often children cannot pinpoint the source of their worries. They tend to generalize bad feelings and experience unhappiness and sometimes perform poorly in school. Children in some self-care situations experience stress for which they may be unprepared (Long 1983). Debate continues on the effect of the child's emotions when self-care is the primary out-of-school arrangement.

Educators and child development specialists are recognizing a new problem: child abuse. Data indicating child abuse as an increasing problem led to new laws and procedures. Programs aimed at prevention of abuse are adding new pressures to childhood. Children are being taught to stay away from strangers, to talk about the "funny tummy feelings" they might experience, and in many other ways not to trust all adults. Television commercials target children's safety. School programs are being developed to give children necessary skills for protecting themselves in unexpected situations (see chapter 9). There is no doubt that children are vulnerable, but the debate comes when emphasis is placed on survival skills and not on the responsibilities of parents or community-based support systems. What price is paid in the context of developing relationships when children are taught to fear unknown persons or events and what fears and anxieties are cultivated when children have to stay alone for extended periods of time are unknown. Some experts suggest that society, in trying to protect children through such procedures as fingerprinting, is actually instilling irrational fears in young people (Spock 1986).

Play. Play is unstructured activity—a basis for children to get to know their bodies and natural flow of movement. It promotes growth not only in the physical but also in the cognitive and social-emotional domains. Middle childhood is a prime time for games and sports when learning rules and cooperation results in feelings of pride and accomplishment. Children need opportunities to contribute to other's enjoyment, and play opens many such doors.

Constance Kamii (1972) helped to clarify how play activities help youngsters gain knowledge of the physical world. Furth and Wachs (1975) devised a curriculum based on thinking games and play for elementary-age children. Math and reading were the major content areas. There is much support for allowing children time to explore new ideas through play. Children are naturally curious and will seek out creative choices and decisions in a play-oriented environment.

Programmatic and Curriculum Implications for School-Age Child Care Programs

The influence of developmental principles should be reflected in all school-age child care programs. Little is gained from knowledge about growth and development if it is not applied to curriculum decisions and program offerings. All activities should be selected on the basis of what best serves the growing and changing child. Schedules also should reflect the child's physical and learning needs. We have already discussed several examples of appropriate developmental activities. Other resources for curriculum ideas are listed in the Appendix at the end of this book.

Aside from specific activities, there are general needs that all school-age children have: opportunities to be cooperative and responsible and to be treated with dignity and respect and recognized for their individual styles of learning. Current debate exists over the best type of education for children. Some educators stress self-awareness and interpersonal relationships; others believe the major task is to provide a traditional education and transmit basic academic skills.

No way has been devised to decide the best educational plan or the one most likely to increase the optimal growth of school-age children. What is clear is that good education can occur anywhere and at any time (Samples, Charles & Barnhart 1977). People who plan out-of-school experiences need to emphasize alternatives and choices. No one plan is suitable to meet all needs. Children are complex. They need to be challenged and protected. In curriculum and programming, special attention should be given to:

1. Providing activities of high interest.
2. Recognizing that there are many ways to learn.
3. Letting children make choices about what they want to learn.
4. Nurturing ways of knowing through guidance and encouragement.
5. Creating an atmosphere of trust and honesty.
6. Accepting children as they are—bold or timid, serious or "silly".
7. Providing opportunities for children's successes.
8. Reinforcing children's achievements.
9. Allowing time for spontaneous and natural play.
10. Encouraging creative thinking and behavior.
11. Taking into account what activities the children have been involved in throughout the day.
12. Recognizing and planning for individual differences.

Matching Supervision with Development

Often it is difficult for adults to decide the best plan for latchkey kids. We have categorized the various types of out-of-school programs to assist in this decision-making process. As we have stressed, latchkey kids are not all alike, and neither are the neighborhoods in which they live. Different needs from child to child and community to community have resulted in the establishment of multiple types of programs to match the developmental needs of youngsters and their families. (Programs are discussed in more detail in chapter 9.)

Some children, especially younger school-age children living in urban settings, need close before- and after-school supervision. Older upper elementary and junior high school children still need supervision but less of it, and the same holds true for many latchkey kids in more rural-like settings. Generally programs that we have classified as proximate supervision fit best for younger children because they provide direct and close supervision, usually through organized program curricula. Proximate supervisory programs include extended-day programs where enrichment activities are offered in afternoons by public schools; agency-run programs sponsored by such organizations as parks and recreation centers or Ys; and home-based care that provides supervision by neighbors who are responsible for keeping children in their homes before and after school.

Programs classified as distal supervision fit best for older children because these programs offer indirect, more removed supervision in which adults are available but children are given more responsibility for being on their own. Distal supervisory programs include help-lines that are locally based and offer advice for children at home alone; check-in programs where designated mothers in neighborhoods serve as check points for older elementary-school and junior high children who wish to pursue activities in their communities; emergency care in which certain homes, with identifiable logos in the windows, are designated as places where children can retreat in emergencies such as when a stranger follows them home from school or an accident requires medical attention; and survival skills programs that offer safety tips for latchkey kids who have no alternative but to stay home alone or because they are older insist on the responsibility and independence of being on their own.

Conclusion

School-age children take themselves seriously. Walter and Robert are fortunate to have experienced a varied, enriching environment at home and school. Their parents, neighbors, teachers, and community leaders have opened doors for them to practice their newly developed abilities. They have been allowed to ask questions and to seek new information. Because they were well prepared for elementary school, they experienced new independence and satisfying relationships. Cognitively they have formed systems of reasoning with chances to make choices from supportive adults.

As with all others in middle childhood, peers are influential in the ways Robert and Walter see themselves. They internalize new ideas and values from their expanding social system. Having had their share of crises, they have made mistakes and bad judgments. But on the whole they have done what was expected of them. Physically they are better at running, climbing, and jumping and can contribute to team efforts. Emotionally they are relatively stable, with only occasional ups and downs that characterize all school-age children when overly stressed or pressured.

Programs and plans for middle-school children should take into account these characteristics by nourishing and supporting growth and development. Matching leisure and enrichment activities to developmental changes will result in better school-age child care and home experiences. In the next chapter we will use this growth and development information as a backdrop for discussing how different children adjust to their self-care arrangements.

Notes

1. This section was written by Catherine R. Conwell. It is used with permission. For additional activities of this nature, write EQUALS Program, Lawrence Hall of Science, University of California, Berkeley, California 94720.

2. Each year *Science and Children* publishes a review of tradebooks in the March issue. Write to the National Science Teachers Association, 1742 Connecticut Avenue, N.W., Washington, D.C. 20009.

References

Bandura, A. 1977, *Social learning theory*. Englewood Cliffs, N.J.: Prentice-Hall.

Bandura, A. 1978. The self system in reciprocal determinism. *American Psychologist* 33:344–358.

Charlesworth, R., & Hartup, W. 1967. Positive social reinforcement in the nursery school peer group. *Child Development* 38:993–1002.

Coopersmith, S. 1967. *The antecedents of self-esteem*. San Francisco: W.H. Freeman.

Dion, K. 1977. Physical attractiveness and evaluations of children's transgressions. *Journal of Personality and Social Psychology* 24:207–213.

Elkind, D. 1981. *The hurried child*. Reading, Mass.: Addison-Wesley.

Erikson, E.H. 1963. *Childhood and Society*. New York: Norton.

Flake-Hobson, C.; Robinson, B.E.; & Skeen, P. 1983. *Child development and relationships*. Reading, Mass.: Addison-Wesley.

Flavell, J.H. 1979. Metacognition and cognitive monitoring: A new area of psychological inquiry. *American Psychologist* 34:906–911.

Furth, H., & Wachs, H. 1975. *Thinking goes to school: Piaget's theory in practice*. New York: Oxford University Press.

Hamill, P.; Drizid, T.; Johnson, C.; Ried, R.; & Roche, A. 1977. *NCHS growth curves for children birth to 18 years*. U.S. Department of Health, Education and Welfare Publication No. 78-1650. Washington, D.C.: U.S. Government Printing Office.

Hartup, W. 1970. Peer interaction and social organizations. In P.H. Mussen, ed. *Carmichael's manual of child psychology*, vol. 2. 3d ed. New York: Wiley.

Hyman, I. 1979. Psychology, education, and schooling. *American Psychologist* 34:1024–1029.

Kamii, C. 1972. A sketch of the Piaget-derived preschool curriculum developed by the Ypsilanti Early Education Program. In S.J. Braun & E.P. Edwards, *History and theory of early childhood education*. Belmont, Calif.: Wadsworth.

Lerner, R., & Lerner, J. 1977. Effects of age, sex and physical attractiveness on peer relations, academic performance, and elementary school adjustment. *Developmental Psychology* 13:585–590.

Liebert, R.M.; Sprafkin, J.N.; & Davidson, E.S. 1985. *The early window: Effects of television on children and youth*. 2d ed. New York: Pergamon Press.

Long, T. 1983 (November 7). *Latchkey children: Scope of the problem.* Speech delivered at the Seventh Annual Conference of the North Carolina Chapter of the National Committee for the Prevention of Child Abuse, Charlotte, N.C.

Lowrey, G.H. 1978. *Growth and development of children.* 7th ed. Chicago: Chicago Medical Yearbook.

Lundsteen, S.W., & Bernstein-Tarrow, N.B. 1981. *Guiding young children's learning.* New York: McGraw-Hill.

Maccoby, E.E. 1980. *Social development: Psychological growth and the parent-child relationship.* New York: Harcourt Brace Jovanovich.

Maxim, G.W. 1985. *The very young child: Guiding children from infancy through the early years.* 2d ed. Belmont, Calif.: Wadsworth.

Melizzi, M.A., & Yawkey, T.D. 1984. School-age child care: Considerations for preservice educators. *Educational Horizons* 62:104–105.

Murray, J.P. 1980. *Television and youth: 25 years of research and controversy.* Boys Town, Neb.: Boys Town Center for the Study of Youth Development.

Piaget, J. 1954. *The construction of reality in the child.* New York: Basic Books.

Samples, B.; Charles, C.; & Barnhart, D. 1977 *The wholeschool book.* Reading, Mass.: Addison-Wesley.

Sheldon, H.H. 1940. *The varieties of human physique.* New York: Harper & Row.

Soto, L.D., & Guerney, L. 1984. Latchkey children count on phonefriend. *Educational Horizons* 62:105.

Spock, B. 1986 (April 9). *Influences on children and families in the nuclear age.* Speech given at the Seventh Child and Family Development Conference. University of North Carolina at Charlotte, Charlotte.

Tanner, J.M. 1970. Physical growth. In P.H. Mussen, ed. *Carmichael's manual of child psychology.* 3d ed. Vol 1. New York: Wiley.

Williams, J.W., & Stith, M. 1980. *Middle childhood: Behavior and development.* 2d ed. New York: Macmillan.

4
Children's Adjustment to Self-Care

Charles, who is 7 years old, has a 14-year-old brother, a 12-year-old sister, and a 3-year-old sister. His father works out of town during the week, and his mother is a department store clerk and works most afternoons and Saturdays. Big brother lets Charles tag along when he plays in the nearby park, goes double-bike riding, or plays touch football with his friends.

Charles and his brother have rules they must follow, such as checking in with their mother by telephone. They are at times at odds with the older sister, who keeps her eye on their 3-year-old sister after the sitter goes home at five o'clock. Their mother comes home a little after six and hurries to put supper on the table. There are good days and bad ones. As long as there are no emergencies, the children fare well. The time the older brother hurt his leg, the time Charles slipped and broke his collar bone, and the day the baby sister ran a high fever and threw up all over the bed are examples of the stressful times.

Charles has had to adjust to multiple authorities. He has to please his big brother, his older sister, and his parents—a large order. At the same time, he is supervised and has a somewhat loosely tied safety net.

Vicky, a third grader, comes home from school on the bus. Although tall for her age, she complains that the boys pick on her while on the bus and that the driver is not much help. Her mother is a church secretary; her father died when she was 5 years old. Vicky stays home alone and lets herself into the house with her key. She is careful to lock the door behind her and to check through the house before she begins her homework. Usually she makes herself a snack and watches television. Vicky says she is afraid sometimes at home alone because the house makes noises and her imagination runs wild. She never plays outside when she is in self-care.

David, a fourth grader, goes directly to a neighbor's house to check in before he goes home. If he needs anything, he contacts the neighbor, who keeps a watchful eye on him. He can play outdoors, visit with his friends, and have a snack that was left for him that morning.

Carla, a fifth grader who has been taking care of herself for years, does not go directly home. She stops at the park, goes by the shopping mall, and sometimes visits a friend. She does not like attending the day care center after-school program. She said it was for babies and besides cost too much money. Carla lives with her grandmother, who works at the neighborhood library. On cold or wet days, Carla spends her afternoons among the stacks of books. Although she enjoys reading, she would rather read in her own room, not in the library. When not in school, she spends most of her time alone.

Will, a second grader, lives close to his school, where his mother meets him each afternoon for the walk home. Will's mother has arranged a flexible work schedule with her employer because she believes her only child should be at home after school. She is concerned that he have time alone that is supervised by an adult: "Being in school all day is about as confining as Will can handle. It was not easy to negotiate my work schedule so that I could be home with my son, but it was so important, and we worked it out."

So far this book has focused on latchkey trends, research, and growth and development issues. This chapter draws information from the main source: the children. Through anecdotal case material from interviews, we trace how sixty latchkey kids (ages 6–14) adjust to their individual arrangements. Our goal is to illustrate points presented throughout this book, not to conduct a scientific analysis of latchkey arrangements. Although each situation was different, planning for self-care seemed to make a difference in adjustment patterns.

Planning for Self-Care

Planning for self-care is a gradual, developmental process that begins long before the school-age years. The journey starts when toddlers begin to exercise their autonomy within the boundaries of a parental safety net. The toddler takes that first step and reaches for curious objects to explore. There are gentle "no-no's," and breakable objects are put out of reach on high shelves. Under close adult guidance, children learn such self-care responsibilities as putting on sweaters, buckling shoes, and staying out of the street. Errors and mistakes occur within a parental safety buffer where no threats to body or mind exist.

In those earliest days, the care giver is solely responsible for the child's safety. Consider 2-year-old Kevin who refuses to let his father hold his hand as they walk through the shopping mall. And Alisha, a 3-year-old who comes bounding into the room, stomping with her new cowboy boots, refusing to take them off even for a nap. Gradually the care giver or parent relinquishes control to the child and acts as a guide to wise decision making. Limited choices are given: whether to have a second helping of peas, to play with blocks or to paint, or to stay with Daddy or go with Mommy (Flake-Hobson, Robinson & Skeen 1983). These simple decisions keep the shield of protection in place yet promote autonomy—the bedrock for later latchkey responsibilities.

When children reach middle childhood, they have many opportunities to practice self-reliance. They are away from their primary support system and can venture into unknown waters. The teacher, scout leader, or other community leader provides guideposts by calling a halt to unacceptable behaviors that become out of bounds. The community leader's place and role are not open to challenge, and the child accepts the support and safety net provided. With experience, school-age children learn their limits and can follow rules and regulations. The children we interviewed were quick to tell us what they could and could not do and generally were resistant to take on more than they could handle.

Factors in Self-Care Adjustment

By nature, self-care has inherent characteristics, such as age and maturity, that require children to adjust to premature responsibilities and decision making. Responsible adults must play matchmaker between an age of protection and an age of preparation in order to nurture children with coping skills. Table 4–1 presents eight questions to ask about children before they are left alone on a regular basis. A "no" to any one of these questions would indicate that adjustment is not likely to occur and that latchkey arrangements should be reconsidered.

Latchkey kids adjust differently depending upon combinations of certain personal and ecological characteristics: the child's age, maturity level, preparation, type of neighborhood, community resources, length of time alone, parental attitude, and type of self-care arrangement.

Age

Generally children below age 12 are too young to assume the responsibilities of self-care. A 9-year-old boy who stays by himself every day said, "I'm scared when the wall cracks. I lock the doors and hide when I'm scared." Developmentally, younger children lack the necessary cognitive and emotional skills

Table 4–1
Questions to Ask before Planning Self-Care Arrangements

Is the child old enough to be left alone?

Is the child emotionally mature enough, regardless of age, to assume the responsibility of self-care?

Has the child been adequately prepared for the basics of self-care?

Does the child reside in a safe neighborhood where crime is low and community cohesion high?

Can neighbors and community facilities be depended upon as support systems?

Does the child stay home for short time periods?

Do the parents have a positive attitude toward the child's latchkey experience?

Does the child's self-care arrangement provide for some type of distal or proximate adult supervision?

essential for sensible decision making. They are not equipped to foresee all possibilities and problems that can arise from deviating from the agreed-upon rules and regulations. Too many tragedies have been reported when very young children were left alone for only a brief time. Even when they have committed rules to memory, the impact of the moment takes over their actions and clouds their judgment. The child-like side dominates, and all the rehearsed safety plans are forgotten or pushed aside. One 9-year-old boy entrusted all responsibilities to his 14-year-old sister: "I don't answer the telephone. My sister is supposed to do that. If it rings before she gets there, I just let it ring. If the doorbell rings, we just turn off the TV and stay still." Older children, like this 14-year-old sister, take on latchkey obligations with greater ease but still need adult direction and guidance.

Maturity

It is a mistake to assume that all 12-year-olds are candidates for self-care. There is no magic age. The child's maturity level is an overriding factor that outweighs age as an important consideration. Certain clues indicate which children are mature enough to be on their own: how well the child follows rules and exercises self-control in the parent's presence; how the child handles brief periods alone when a parent runs out to do an errand; the degree to which the child gets bored easily or can occupy himself or herself during free time. Parents can usually pick up hints from casual observation to determine when or if their children have reached a satisfactory maturity level. Some children give direct messages that eliminate any second guessing about self-care readiness. A 6-year-old boy said, "I don't like going home by myself. I wish somebody was there. I don't like for my mother to work. She calls me at home from work to check on me. But I'm still afraid when somebody knocks at the door. I just don't answer it, and I don't answer the telephone either. I just let it ring." Chronologically and emotionally unprepared, this child limps through his days alone after school.

Preparation

Aside from the early developmental start that parents give their children, other more immediate preparations are in order. Adults are responsible for setting limits and pointing out dangerous pitfalls of carelessness and poor judgment. Attention to the physical environment by providing securely locked doors and windows is paramount. The importance of home security to the child's psychological well-being was reflected in an 11-year-old boy's comment: "I'm afraid that somebody may be in the house on the days the side door doesn't catch good." Mutually agreed upon safety precautions and rules also must be in place. The following ten rules for self-care were written especially for school-age children:

1. Go straight home from school. If you will be later than usual getting home from school, call your parents and let them know.
2. As soon as you get home, lock the door and call Mom or Dad at work to let them know you are home. *Always* keep doors locked.
3. Know where a telephone is available if there is not one at your house.
4. If a window is broken, the door is open, or things don't look just right, do not go into your house. Go to a neighbor's house.
5. *Never* let a stranger at the door or on the telephone know that you are alone.
6. Don't stay on the telephone for long periods of time.
7. Do not let friends inside to play or go outside to play with them unless you have permission from your parents.
8. Never use the oven, stove, or other appliances unless an adult is with you.
9. Clean up after snacks and activities.
10. Know when and how to get help if there is an emergency.[1]

Almost all children we interviewed reported some sort of daily routine after they got home: usually changing clothes, getting something to eat, completing household chores, finishing homework, and almost always watching televison. A 12-year-old boy shared his routines: "I do my homework and then I do housework (trash, dishes, ashtrays, get wood, bathroom, fold clothes, sometimes wash then sweep) and watch TV."

The majority of children had sets of rules to follow, such as locking the front door, refraining from using electrical appliances, staying inside, and not answering the door or telephone unless a certain number of rings had been predetermined as a code for answering a parent's call. An 11-year-old boy expressed comfort in these preparations: "I've never been afraid by myself. I have a code to answer the phone only after two rings, and they call back. If it doesn't [ring twice], I don't answer it."

Emotional preparation must also be made. A climate of mutual trust and open communication is prerequisite to successful adjustment to self-care. Yet emotional preparation was frequently lacking in the lives of many of the children we interviewed.

Neighborhood

Latchkey children who live in fairly safe neighborhoods (often these tend to be suburban or rural areas) tend to function better. A 13-year-old girl who lives in a rural neighborhood said, "I enjoy being alone because I have time to think, and it gives me a sense of responsibility. There are four houses within walking distance of mine, and I can always contact my grandparents who live down the road."

Those in high-crime areas where neighborhood solidarity is low have more problems. A less fortunate 11-year-old boy reported low community cohesion: "I live in a two-story white frame house, and I live around a lot of old people, and old people can't help you if something happens. So it's kinda scary. They'd say, 'I can't right now' or 'We don't want to get involved with it.' So you just have to protect yourself on your own." Parents who judge their neigborhoods as too unsafe with few support systems may be putting their children at physical and psychological risk.

Community Resources

Many of the children we talked to reported feeling secure because of nearby neighbors whom they could contact for help. Some children routinely checked in with a neighbor after school, and others had entrusted door keys to neighbors in case they misplaced theirs. Children who know their neighbors and know that they can depend on them in times of need feel more comfortable being alone. An 11-year-old boy said, "I've never been scared alone. I have neighbors nearby, and if I had to, I could go and get them to help out."

Community facilities also play a role in latchkey arrangements. Emergency services (police, fire, and rescue departments) should be within reasonable distance and their telephone numbers readily accessible so that children feel an extra anchor of security. A 14-year-old girl felt confident with her emergency plan: "I've never had an emergency, but if I had to call the police or fire department, I have their numbers."

Length of Time Alone

Time alone can be a major factor in children's adjustment. Children who spend unusually long hours in self-care are more likely to have more adjustment problems. The longer they are alone, the greater are their chances of having an accident or expressing fears, especially after nightfall. Longer hours also are more likely to produce boredom and loneliness. Brian, an 11-year-old who is alone for eight hours until eleven-thirty every night, said, "In the afternoons it's boring and lonely, and at night it's scary." Shorter time periods, say for an hour or two, are long enough for children to complete homework and chores and to enjoy some time alone. Jennifer, an 8-year-old, is alone for one hour in the afternoons and says she likes the time: "I'm usually not scared. It makes me feel big." Jennifer's one hour in the afternoon is a dramatic contrast to Brian's eight hours at night and shows how amount of time alone can affect children's adjustment.

Parental Attitude

Parental attitudes toward self-care can be subtly transmitted to children. Fears, worries, and uncertainties harbored by insecure parents can be sensed by youngsters, thus causing them to share parental concerns. Parental guilt over leaving children alone or mistrust of their children can turn an otherwise workable arrangement into a nightmare. June Kirby, struggling with after-school arrangements for her 8-year-old daughter, told us why she refused to leave Nickey in self-care:

> She's too mature to be in a day care center. I took her out because there were no kids there her age, and she was being used to take care of the younger children. She's never stayed home alone by herself because she's too afraid. She's too young to stay by herself because she couldn't defend herself. She's so friendly she might let a stranger in the house. And if I set rules she probably wouldn't follow them.

Nickey agreed with her mother's assessment: "I'd like to go home, but I'm scared to stay there by myself because there's been a lot of kidnapping in my neighborhood." Rightly or wrongly, insecure latchkey parents beget insecure latchkey kids.

Type of Latchkey Arrangements

The degree to which a child has some kind of adult contact can influence self-care adjustment. Telephone calls to or from parents or neighbors and even *in absentia* guidelines can undergird afternoons with a sense of comfort and security for all parties. Daily telephone calls from his mother acts as a lifeline for one 7-year-old boy: "I like going home by myself. I play in my room. I like for my mom to work. I call her sometimes, and sometimes she calls me. I'm never afraid of things."

Situations where unsupervised children float freely in their neighborhoods or at the local video arcade often lead to poor adjustment and negative consequences. Sibling care arrangements, although sometimes workable, also can cause problems. The older child may resent the added responsiblity, or constant squabbling between siblings can complicate an already stressful situation, as this 8-year-old girl confessed: "My brother (14 years old) beats me up and plays tricks on me. One time he folded me up in the sofa bed, and another time he went off and left me by myself."

Fears

Of the children we interviewed, 57 percent said they liked or did not mind being alone and never had any fears. It is important to note that the majority of these children lived in small towns or in suburban or rural areas outside small towns. The following comments are representative of the children's responses.

"I'm okay." (10-year-old boy)

"It makes me feel big." (8-year-old girl)

"I've learned more responsiblity." (9-year-old boy)

"I like being alone because I can do anything I want to." (10-year-old boy)

"It gives me time to think." (14-year-old girl)

Of the children who liked being alone, some cited advantages of having parents at home in the afternoons:

"I wouldn't have to let myself in and don't have to worry about losing my key." (14-year-old boy)

"I wouldn't have to clean as much and not have as much responsibility." (12-year-old girl)

"It would be great!" (14-year-old girl)

"I could eat when I got home." (14-year-old boy)

Older latchkey children who were unafraid had difficulty seeing any advantages to adults at home:

"It would be boring." (14-year-old boy)

"I wouldn't have time alone to myself." (13-year-old girl)

"I would have to start homework right then with no TV." (14-year-old girl)

"I would have less time to myself and to talk to my friends on the phone because my parents regulate my phone use when they are home." (13-year-old girl)

"It would probably be a drag." (13-year-old boy)

"I would have a hard time adjusting to them being home, and I wouldn't get to talk on the phone as much." (13-year-old girl)

Forty-three percent said they were frightened sometimes or all the time when they were home alone. Fears usually were generated by such house noises as dishes settling against one another in the kitchen or the house creaking. Many of these children, though, admitted (without prodding) that even adults are sometimes uncomfortable hearing these noises. Following are a few other examples of what children shared with us:

"I'm afraid because there are wild dogs outside." (14-year-old girl)

"Sometimes I feel like someone is always there." (13-year-old girl)

"We have people call and play practical jokes." (14-year-old boy)

"I'm afraid of being kidnapped." (12-year-old girl)

Levels of Self-Care Adjustment

The level of self-care indicates the ways children adjust to their latchkey responsibilities. Adjustment levels also reflect how latchkey kids view and respond to their respective arrangements. We have constructed five levels of self-care adjustment that emerged from the interviews (table 4–2). These levels are descriptions only; they are not necessarily sequential and have not been scientifically tested. Each level will be accompanied by appropriate parental instruction and guidance that can foster children's adjustment at that level.

Level 1: Orientation

In the initial stages of self-care, children are preoccupied with survival. House sounds like creaking walls still take some getting used to. Questions are raised with regard to the do's and don'ts of self-care. Occasionally children at this stage forget to practice every rule, as when 8-year-old Michael, who has been caring for himself for nine months, sometimes forgets to lock the door behind him.

Case of Michael

"I used to go to Sandbox Nursery where my little sister goes, but I stopped going last year in the second grade. The first two or three weeks, it kinda got boring and stuff at the day care center. It wasn't much fun. I just didn't want to go back. In day care if it gets too cold, they won't take you outside to play. I didn't feel very good because there was not much freedom. I wanted to be home instead of in a day care center because I can play with my friends. I just didn't want to go back. I told my mom about it, and she said we'll start letting you go home and see if you do okay.

When I get home at about 3:10, I get my key and go inside. Sometimes I lock the door, and sometimes I forget. I put my stuff in my room, turn on TV, and get something to eat. If I have homework, I wait till Mom gets home to do it. She gets home at about 6:00. She usually calls me, though, at 3:30 to make sure I got in all right and that I'm okay. If I had a problem, I'd call her. She works at the bank, and I know her number by heart now.

After Mom calls me, I do my chores (clean up my room) and go outside and play with my friends. When it gets dark at home, I get kinda scared because I hear all these funny noises. Sometimes dishes will slide down and hit together, and that scares me. My imagination is really what scares me the most, because I think I see people running around in the house and stuff. But nothing bad's ever happened, and everything's going fine so far."

Table 4–2
Levels of Self-Care Adjustment

Level 1: Orientation	Children learn the ropes of their new arrangements.
Level 2: Questioning/ resentment	Children question and may even resent the responsibilities that they feel have been thrust upon them.
Level 3: Toleration	Children tolerate their latchkey status, although they may often become bored.
Level 4: Acceptance	Children have learned to accept and understand their latchkey status.
Level 5: Appreciation	Children at this level not only accept their lot, they also appreciate parental efforts.

Case Analysis. Michael has been caring for himself less than a year and is still somewhat negligent about routines. But he chose against a boring after-school program in favor of self-care though he had to put up with scary sounds and his imagination. Clearly Michael, not the parents, made the choice. Many children probably choose to care for themselves rather than attend inadequate programs. Apparently Michael decided that being with his friends after school was worth the risk of his apprehensions. His choice also points out an area that research has never considered: that there are different degrees of fear. All school-age children are fearful at times, whether they are in self-care or not, and even many adults feel uncomfortable alone when the house settles. One of the authors, at age 40, is still apprehensive when home alone at night. Fear levels reported in previous studies may have been normal fears that anyone would report but not necessarily devastating enough to cause prolonged psychological harm. If they did, children would obviously choose another arrangement in those cases where they had the option to choose.

Michael is too young to be alone, especially for such a long time period. Although he has rules and routines, he often forgets to lock the door. Perhaps his negligence results from his young age or perhaps he just needs more time to learn the routines. Anchors in Michael's arrangement that probably add to his security are his playmates and his mother's daily telephone calls to check on him. He seems self-assured that he could reach his mother in the event of a problem, and knowing her telephone number is a comfort.

Although Michael is still at the orientation level, by his own admission he seems to be adjusting extraordinarily well for an 8-year-old. As he adapts to the fears he identified, they will undoubtedly subside unless he is confronted with problems, such as obscene telephone calls, strangers at the door, or a traumatic accident. His confidence, or lack of it, in dealing with the unexpected could put him at another level.

Instruction and Guidance. At this level, instruction and guidance should center on basic precautions. Parents should be firm and insist that children follow the rules. The following suggestions should be implemented by parents and children together:

Create a set of guidelines for the child to follow when no adult is present. The guidelines should be created by parent and child and discussed thoroughly.

Establish a check-in system. The child should call the parent or a neighbor to make contact for additional instructions and guidance.

Prepare a first-aid kit and instructions of what to do in an emergency.

Make a list of important telephone numbers. Whom to call and when to call for help is important.

Discuss possible situations that might arise. Children should be well versed in how to answer the telephone, when not to open the door, and what to do when friends want to come over. They should understand what safety precautions to take.

Make a detailed description of how the parent can be reached. It is important to make very clear when the parent is expected home. It is equally important that parents be on time.

Parent and child can talk openly about their apprehensions regarding the latchkey arrangement. Parents can calm children's fears by sharing their own feelings and by instructing kids that a little fear is a good thing to have.

Level 2: Questioning/Resentment

Children now begin to compare their self-care experiences with the after-school arrangements of their peers. They question and may even resent their arrangements, sometimes becoming quite philosophical. They may seek information about other options. Eleven-year-old Sue and 12-year-old Chuck are cases.

Case of Sue

"When I get home at 3:15, I do light housework, start supper, and watch after my 9-year-old sister. We lock the door and stay inside until Mother gets home at 5:00. She doesn't allow us to go outside for any reason. To tell you the truth, I don't mind cleaning and cooking, but I hate looking after my little sister. That should be for an older person to do. The only time I get scared is walking from the bus stop to home when my sister isn't with me."

Case of Chuck

"Somebody called and wouldn't tell me who they were. I told them my dad was home, but he wasn't. When I called him to come to the phone, they hung up. I cried all afternoon. I called a neighbor to come stay with me and got out all the knives, a letter opener, a gun, and the fire extinguisher. My parents don't get home until after dark. I turn on all the lights and play Atari or something. I'm not with my parents much, except mornings and weekends. Kids whose parents are there when they get home get more done. They get to be around parents more and know about them and what they do. I'd rather not be alone. I wish my parents were home. But we get to do things together on weekends."

Case Analysis. Children at level 2 feel cheated; they feel that certain aspects of their arrangements are unfair. Sue resents supervising her younger sister and believes, perhaps rightly, that this is too much responsibility for an 11 year old. Her only fear revolves around her responsibilities for the 9 year old's welfare. Chuck feels that children whose parents are at home in the afternoons have more advantages than he has. He misses being with his parents and feels deprived of knowing them better.

Some children at this level may not be emotionally mature enough for certain aspects of self-care. Sue does not mind her duties of cooking and cleaning, but the responsibility of another child is too much for her. Helping her move out of this level to another level, of toleration or acceptance, for example, might require removing the burden of sibling care.

Girls in middle childhood tend to develop physically and emotionally faster than boys. Although a year younger than Chuck, Sue seems to be emotionally more prepared for her latchkey status. Chuck, on the other hand, does not seem to be adjusting well to any aspect of self-care. Anonymous telephone calls are traumatic for him, and he copes with them in unconstructive ways: crying all afternoon and assembling an assortment of weapons. Emotionally, too, he seems to feel deprived of a special relationship that he needs with his parents. Helping Chuck move out of this level could require better preparation on how to handle problems. He needs instruction on how to handle anonymous calls (see chapter 6). He also needs emotional reassurance from his parents, perhaps from better preparation to help him feel more secure. Chuck stated flatly that he would rather not be alone. Parents need to heed children when they utter such complaints. More time for Chuck and his parents to spend together might help, or he may need a different arrangement altogether.

Instruction and Guidance. Instruction and guidance at this level should focus on opportunities provided by schools, clubs, and groups serving young people. Arrangements may need to be modified or reassessed. Resources should be sought and ways to obtain them investigated.

For Children

Talk to other children, and find out how they use their time alone.

On your parents' day off, visit local museums, recreation centers, and other community resources for materials and supplies that will stimulate new ideas.

Use suggestions made by your teachers, scout leaders, and others to make your time alone more interesting.

Take responsibility for expanding your interests. Use your imagination and creativity.

Select a topic each week to learn more about.

Learn to play a musical instrument.

Read a book on self care. (See the list in the Appendix at the end of this book.)

For Parents

Talk to your children and ask them how they feel being on their own in afternoons. Take their fears and concerns seriously, reassure them, and seek ways to resolve scary feelings.

Reassess your children's latchkey arrangements by asking yourself if you have given them more responsibility than they can emotionally handle. If so, modify the current arrangement or explore the possibility of other options.

Instigate a program in the schools such as "I'm in Charge" to better help your child constructively cope with self-care.

Purchase how-to books and activity manuals that describe at-home activities and ways of preparing kids for latchkey situations. (See the list in the Appendix at the end of this book.)

Make special arrangements for your children so they can participate in outside activities of their choice such as scout groups, dance or music lessons, and sports.

Plan a special outing for yourself and your children on a weekend or your day off. Quality time is important. Make this a special ritual and something to look forward to.

Level 3: Toleration

The child becomes tolerant of self-care and decides that the situation is okay. But boredom may set in, and the child may tire of the routines. Eleven-year-old Ralph does not like being by himself after school but has learned to tolerate his situation after five years as a latchkey child.

Case of Ralph

"It's kinda boring, and it can get lonely at times when there's nothing to do. My parents work at night a lot—usually until about 11:30. It scares me to be alone at night by myself. Somebody called one night and said my brother was in a wreck. They said he died in a hospital in the emergency room. I thought to myself, What would my dad think about it? When my dad told me it was a prank, it gave me a little confidence.

Dad took me out in the country and showed me how to shoot a .22 semiautomatic rifle. The reason my dad taught me to use the rifle is to be protective, so I won't worry if anything was to happen. He doesn't want me to mess with the pistol he's got because I might not be able to aim it as good as the other one [the rifle]. It's the way my dad wants me to be, and that's the way his feelings are about it.

At night when I'm alone, I sit by the TV, and there's a gun rack above me so in case a robber came in or something was to happen, I'd be prepared for anything and I'd have a weapon to fight back.

I've managed it [self-care] for five years. It's not the best thing a kid would want to do. But when it comes down to it, it's the way I have to be. I can live with it and handle it. Overall, I'm pretty comfortable with the situation."

Case Analysis. Tolerant children no longer question their self-care arrangements but have learned to live with them. Although they may have been in the arrangement for a long time, certain problems may arise and lead to maladjustment causing them to dislike being alone after school.

Ralph is alone for approximately eight hours, a long time for a child his age. He is bored and fearful. He lacks constructive ways of occupying his time; he seems to be idle. At night he is afraid of anonymous callers and intruders.

To help Ralph adjust better to his situation, his parents could help him find activities that capture his attention and interest. The fears Ralph has are probably attributed to the poor attempts at preparation his dad gave him. Teaching an 11-year-old to protect himself by firing a gun can instill more fear than it eradicates. The presence of firearms and instruction in their use tells children that they have a lot to fear. Expecting such a young child to defend himself through such violent measures can be overwhelming. A child who constantly wonders when and if he or she will have to kill someone will become emotionally strained. A parent who perceives a self-care arrangement as life threatening enough to equip a child with dangerous weapons should remove the child from it.

Ralph does not question or resent his father's survival skill tactics. Instead he sees it as the way things have to be. He sees no alternatives. Although he tolerates his position, Ralph does not cite any positive aspects of the arrangement. In his case, tolerance can mask deep-seated fears and resentments toward parents. Obviously Ralph's self-care situation is destructive. His parents need to instruct him on more positive ways of answering the telephone, adjusting to boredom, and coping with fears. They need to question their child's maturity level, reassess their own negative attitudes, rethink the amount of time they are leaving him alone, and make reasonable adjustments. We were not surprised to learn that Ralph is awaiting a court appearance to hear charges that he had illegal drugs—LSD and marijuana—in his possession.

Instruction and Guidance. Level 3 instruction and guidance should include patience and understanding. Boredom can be relieved by focusing on activities children can do on their own. Emphasis should be on enrichment and high-interest activities. Suggestions include:

For Children

Find new ways to relieve boredom.

Take time to do homework and put away books and papers for school the next day.

Reexamine your interests and take time to get involved in something new. Make a plan of activities for the following week. Use ideas from library books and magazines.

Choose a project to work on from a list of activities. Plan the materials and supplies you will need with your parent.

Select television programs from a schedule that a parent has approved.

Begin a new hobby or project or start a new collection.

Use magazines and activity books to gain new ideas.

For Parents

Reevaluate your child's latchkey arrangement by candidly answering the questions in table 4–1. Make appropriate adjustments to the child's situation where questions are answered "no."

Consider alternate provisions where financially and practically possible, especially when the child's tolerance level is low.

Remind the child of the reasons for the arrangement and let the child know that you appreciate tolerance.

Take time to determine with your child his or her favorite activities and those things most likely to attract time and energy.

Make lists, develop a schedule, create a calendar, and discuss each day's plans with your child.

Communicate appreciation for tasks well done and work accomplished.

Help your child plan and carry out some of the Boredom Busters described in chapter 6.

Level 4: Acceptance

This can be described as the "make it or break it" level. Children accept, not just put up with, their situations. Reciprocal understanding on both the parent and child's part is essential. Rex, an 11-year-old, has reached this level.

Case of Rex

"I don't mind being alone. I'm not afraid unless a stranger comes to the door. If somebody knocks that I don't know, I don't answer the door. I stay in my room. But I really don't worry about anything. My next-door neighbors are home most of the time, and we keep the key hidden most of the time. So I don't worry about losing it. Staying home by myself doesn't bother me at all. I like getting there [home] first. It makes me feel bigger, like I can do something by myself. I've learned that Mom and Dad can trust me."

Case Analysis. As a rule, children at the acceptance level have few worries, and, if they do worry, they feel confident that they can resolve problems. Rex does not mind being alone. He has several anchors of security: he knows what to do if a stranger knocks at the door; he has the security of his next-door neighbors in the event of an emergency; and unnecessary worry about losing a key was removed by establishing a safe hiding place for it.

Rex has been prepared so that he does not have to worry about the unexpected. Children like Rex who have accepted their status cite positive aspects of their arrangements. Rex, for example, likes getting home before his parents because it gives him self-confidence and a sense that his parents trust him. Apparently these payoffs outweigh the fear of a stranger coming to the door.

Instruction and Guidance. Instruction and guidance at Level 4 should be personal. Trust, special attention, and honesty with one another are signs of mutual understanding. Suggestions include the following:

For Children

Tell your parents you love them in a variety of ways. Do not hesitate to say it often.

Make something special to share with the family.

Clean up your room without being told to do so.

Make a special effort to be cooperative. Think twice before doing something foolish.

Celebrate your independence. Demonstrate your self-reliance and reliability by following rules and guidelines that you have agreed upon.

For Parents

Tell your children you love them, you are proud of them for assuming their responsibilities, and they have earned your trust.

Leave notes in surprising places that remind the child of your love and care.

Make frequent telephone calls on a regular basis to check on your child.

Refrain from negative comments. Keep things pleasant and life a joy.

Emphasize that you love and accept the child just the way he or she is rather than making acceptance contingent upon the way you would like the child to be.

Level 5: Appreciation

This is the stage in which children acquire an appreciation for self-care arrangements. Self-care has worked out fairly well for everyone, and there is a good feeling and a sense of accomplishment. Improved communication and mutual sensitivity develops between parents and children when self-care is not too stressful. Eight-year-old Jennifer's views on her latchkey arrangement are classic of this level.

Case of Jennifer

"I've been going home by myself since I was in the first grade, and I'm in the third now. When I get home, I do my homework, wash dishes, and sometimes collect the garbage and dirty clothes and watch TV. If I have trouble with my homework, my mom helps me when she gets home. After I'm home an hour, my mom comes home. We watch TV together, or she goes upstairs and writes letters and I help. My favorite thing is to talk to her. I tell her how my day in school was and how I'm doing in school.

I have rules and stuff when she's not home. I lock the door behind me, can't use the phone, and can't go outside. I can't use any electrical things either—just the microwave—and can't answer the door. If somebody does come to the door, I just don't answer it. But I'm usually not scared 'cause there's somebody down the road that's home. It makes me feel big. I'm used to staying home alone. I stay inside the whole time. I do my homework at about 3:30. I'm used to doing things at a certain time, but I don't have a certain schedule. I can't call Mom, and she can't call me because she works in a factory. But I know the numbers to call the police department or neighbor if I need to. They're up by the phone. But I've never had to call anybody. I like for my mom to work. She's always worked. If she didn't work, we wouldn't get anything."

Case Analysis. Children at the appreciation level not only accept their self-care arrangement but appreciate the benefits they and their parents derive from the experience. This can be a difficult concept for some children to grasp. It involves empathy and role taking, a skill achieved only at the concrete operational level of cognitive development. It also entails open communication between adults and children, one of the ingredients missing the most in latchkey care.

Jennifer could not reach her mother in an emergency, but she has other safety nets: telephone numbers of neighbors and the police department. She also has the security anchor of rules and routines that she abides by in her mother's absence. And she has quality time with her mother every afternoon. They share an open line of communication; she likes to talk to her mother about how things are going on a daily basis. Another security factor is that Jennifer has been caring for herself for two years, and she is alone for only one hour. Jennifer's one hour in the afternoon compared to Ralph's eight hours at night can make all the difference in the world in a latchkey child's adjustment.

Jennifer seems to be thriving from her latchkey experience because she has been properly prepared. She has neighborhood and community support, and the amount of time she spends alone is not unrealistic. Jennifer gets several payoffs as a latchkey child and expresses no fear. She enjoys the responsibility because it makes her feel big. She knows what is expected, feels she can manage the expectations, and expresses confidence in her brief time alone. She also appreciates her mother's working because she knows it is necessary so that they can have all the things they have. Most important, Jennifer has quality time with her mother to which she looks forward each afternoon.

Instruction and Guidance.. Instruction and guidance at this level should include communicating appreciation for one another and at the same time remembering that children are children and should not be burdened in the same way as adults. Suggestions include:

For Children

Trust your own feelings when it comes to decisions about right and wrong.

Leave yourself several options for dealing with the unexpected.

Establish yourself with your peers as someone who sticks up for your beliefs and standards.

Make changes in your habits if you find it necessary.

Show the competence you possess.

Turn off the television and enjoy a good book or conversation.

Tell your parents how much you appreciate them.

For Parents

Continue to examine your assumptions about how children form their ideas of self-worth.

Be flexible, and be a calm and optimistic role model.

Heighten your awareness of your child's feelings as you guide and encourage your youngster into new avenues of interest.

Encourage your child to get in touch with his or her feelings and share them.

Let your child know how appreciative you are for his or her role in helping the family function on a daily basis.

Conclusion

Observers raise important questions about the social development and sense of self-esteem of latchkey kids. They ask about fears and long-term resentment for having experienced premature adulthood. They look at the child's self-reliance and self-control. Some seem quite surprised that boys and girls are affected differently by child care arrangements. Others believe that there are no differences in children's functioning when self-care and adult-care children are compared. Evidence mounts, and the number of children in self-care continues to rise.

The impact may be one of confusion. Should children be left alone? Will instruction and guidance, special programs, latchkey curricula, films, and brochures help to guarantee safety? What about Charles who has an older brother watching out for him? Is he in a better arrangement than Vicky or Ralph who stay in their houses after school? David has the run of the neighborhood. Is he gaining independence and self-confidence? What about

Will? What will be the benefits of being home alone with his mother? Carla explores the park and the mall. Is she safe and secure?

Obviously more questions than answers exist. Because scientific inquiry has only begun to examine these areas, it is important for concerned professionals to refrain from generalizing negative or positive effects to all latchkey kids. Instead the issue is to create workable latchkey arrangements that match the unique characteristics of each family and contribute to the growth of each child. We believe that a close analysis of each individual arrangement should be made to determine each child's potential adjustment. We have suggested that latchkey kids adjust differently depending on eight personal or ecological factors in their arrangements: age, maturity, preparation, neighborhood, community resources, daily length of time alone, parental attitudes, and type of self-care arrangement. Each of these factors combines in such a way as to provide children with different levels of adjustment.

Ultimately, checks and balances between protection and preparation lay in the hands of parents. We will present a more detailed discussion of suggestions for parents in the next chapter. Meanwhile, we conclude this chapter with words from a wise single mother of two latchkey kids who speaks to all other latchkey parents:

> I think, typically, we feel a lot of stress, and I think we are frustrated by lots of things. And I think it's important that we are very careful that we don't take our frustrations out on our latchkey children—that we make them feel as comfortable as we can—that they know they can call Mother or Daddy, maybe, if they feel unsafe for some reason. Or it's important that there's somebody in the neighborhood that knows that they [the children] are alone, and they can go to that particular person until Mother can get home to handle whatever the situation is. I also think it's important that you listen to your kids. It's important that you listen anyway, but somehow or another it becomes even more important to me that I actually hear what they're saying. So I try very hard to listen and sometimes it's kinda hard between the kids, the job, and the home. It's hard making all the decisions, and sometimes I wonder if I'll ever get a chance to take care of me. But there's no "ifs," "ands," or "buts" about it—I have to do it!

Notes

1. Sandra Sparks, *The key to being on my own* (Charlotte, N.C.: University of North Carolina, 1984). Reprinted with permission.

References

Flake-Hobson, C., Robinson, B.E., & Skeen, P. 1983. *Child development and relationships*. Reading, Mass.: Addison-Wesley.

Sparks, S. 1984. *The key to being on my own*. Charlotte: University of North Carolina.

5

Suggestions for Parents

Barbara Jordan, a single working mother, has two sons: one 5 and the other 11. She sums up her latchkey situation simply: "It's not my first choice, but it's all I can afford. It's stressful, very stressful. There are many things you worry about. Seeing as I'm chairman of the board, I have to make all the decisions, and it's difficult sometimes deciding what's best. As soon as I get to work in the mornings, I call my older son, who is responsible for getting himself and his younger brother off to school. In the afternoon, they must call me as soon as they get home."

What does Barbara worry about? "I worry about lots of different things," she states. "I worry that nobody is watching and really paying us any attention . . . and some crazy might try to do something."

Threats from outside the home are not the only concerns Barbara expresses. She fears for her two sons' safety within the home. She states, "They roughhouse a lot. They are told not to, but what do you expect? I'm afraid somebody might run and bump something or cut something."

What about house rules? Barbara answers quickly. "Oh yeah, there are lots of rules. First rule is that they cannot let anybody, other than one particular lady, inside. They are told not to roughhouse. They cannot cook or use any electrical appliance—not even television. They can't play with anything sharp, and of course they can't run. They are not allowed to go outside."

Characteristic of some other parents, Barbara attempts to relieve the guilt she feels over imposing so many house rules by arranging for special night and weekend activities. She still worries, however, about her eldest son, who must care for his younger brother. "I'm kinda caught between the devil and the deep blue sea," she states. "My oldest son seems to have developed a lot of responsibility from the experience. But I don't want to put too much responsibility on him. I still want him to do all the extracurricular things." This type of ambivalence is characteristic of many parents we have talked to. On the one hand, they express pride in their children's ability to assume responsibility in the home, but on the other hand they feel guilty over asking their children to assume responsibility at such a young age.

Despite the stress associated with being a latchkey parent, Barbara remains upbeat. She notes, "I want everything to be perfect, and I'm hoping to strike a happy medium. I try to be careful that I don't take my frustrations out on my sons. It's important that I actually hear what my kids say to me. Sometimes though I must admit its hard . . . between the kids, and the job, and the home and decisions. Oh well, even chairmen, or I should say, chairpersons of the board have to listen!"

Parents like Barbara are not helpless, although at times it may seem that way. With some thought and planning, parents can create reasonably safe latchkey home and community environments. In this chapter, we will discuss assessment strategies for determining what we call the latchkey safety buffer. Next, we will discuss strategies for creating safety within the home setting, followed by a guide for selecting high-quality school-age child care programs. We will discuss strategies for parents to follow in stimulating community awareness and action to deal with latchkey issues and conclude with a section on eliminating family stress and building family life.

Assessing the Safety Buffer

The diversity of family structures and roles makes pat answers to the latchkey issue difficult. Educators and human service professionals are faced with such a variety of home and family situations that sometimes it seems there are no answers. A single mother of an 8-year-old has different needs from those of a single mother of a 4-year-old, who in turn has different needs from those of the dual-career parents of a 13-year-old. But some common issues do exist that all parents of latchkey kids can address in planning and implementing a safe latchkey environment.

Neighborhood

Begin by assessing the neighborhood. Does it have a low or high crime rate? What are the most common types of crime that occur in the neighborhood? The police department can supply this information. How heavily traveled are the roads surrounding your home? During what hours is traffic heaviest? The local planning office can supply this information.

How close is your home to hospitals and police and fire stations? Identify the locations of these service agencies on a simple map that you and your child develop together. Post the map on the refrigerator door, in your child's bedroom, or in some other prominent site. A list of telephone numbers and names beside each agency will enable your child to act with haste and confidence when services are needed. Periodically check your child's ability to use the map by playing a game. Ask your child to use the map and direct a walk to each service agency within walking distance, or if too far to walk, drive to the agency while your child traces the route on the map. Upon arriving, chat with workers at the agency so that your child and the workers associate faces with names. Your child will feel more comfortable calling upon service agencies if a friendly relationship is established.

Crime rates, traffic flow, and location of service agencies are not the only neighborhood characteristics to consider. Next-door neighbors, the location of bus stops, and the characteristics of adjoining neighborhoods are some other factors to consider in sizing up the safety and danger areas. A more complete safety checklist for assessing a neighborhood is provided in figure 5–1. (This figure will be used later to determine the safety buffer.)

Home

The home environment represents a major source of potential danger to latch-key kids. Some factors to consider in assessing the home include the safety of utilities, unprotected electrical outlets, and unlabeled foods and medicines. A more complete checklist for assessing the physical safety of your home is

---

Evaluate the areas of your neighborhood that are safe using the following checklist:

Crime rate is low.
Supervision is supplied by a well-trained and responsible adult.
Traffic flow is light.
Area is protected from traffic.
At least one community agency that can respond to an emergency is located close by.
Area is free of dangerous objects and equipment.
Area is free of pollution.
Area is protected from surrounding dangerous neighborhoods.
Area allows for quiet activities.
Police or security guards regularly patrol area.
At least one adult leader is available for every ten children.
A check-in system is used to document a child's presence.
Activities are well supervised and developmentally appropriate.
[List other safety items you think are important.]

Considering all the safety items, check the areas of your neighborhood that are safe.

Area	Time of Safety	Name of Adult Supervisor	Distance from Home
___ Park	_____	_____	_____
___ Lake or pond	_____	_____	_____
___ Recreation center	_____	_____	_____
___ Shopping mall	_____	_____	_____
___ Church	_____	_____	_____
___ Library	_____	_____	_____
___ School	_____	_____	_____
___ Friend's home	_____	_____	_____
___ Other	_____	_____	_____
_____	_____	_____	_____

Figure 5–1. Neighborhood Safety Checklist

Evaluate the areas of your home that are safe using the following checklist:

____ Electrical and mechanical equipment are locked away.
____ Locks on all doors and windows are secure.
____ Smoke alarm system is operative.
____ Foods and medicines are separated and clearly labeled.
____ All appliances are in good working condition.
____ Directions for using appliances are clearly written and posted.
____ Electrical outlets are covered with a protective plate.
____ Broken electrical cords are replaced.
____ A map of local emergency service agencies is posted.
____ Emergency telephone numbers and names are posted.
____ A schedule of after-school activities is posted.
____ A list of safety do's and don'ts is posted.
____ Broken glass is replaced.
____ Areas where children may get trapped are secure.
____ Areas from or over which children may fall are secure.
____ The temperature of the home is self-regulated and comfortable.
____ Loud noises from surrounding areas are masked.
____ Broken furniture is repaired or thrown away.
____ A check-in system is established.
____ Procedures for answering the telephone and door are established.

Figure 5–2. Home Safety Checklist

provided in figure 5–2. In-home safety practices will be presented later in this chapter.

The physical characteristics of the home represent only part of the safety issue. Safety is also dependent upon the child's behavior. A broken appliance is safe if the child follows instructions not to use it. A wood-burning stove is safe if the child follows correct operating instructions and knows what to do in case of an accident. Clearly the child's competence is an important in-home safety feature.

In general, older latchkey kids are less at risk than younger latchkey kids. Latchkey kids with a history of responsible behavior are less at risk than those who are not responsible. Other age and behavioral characteristics listed below will help to determine a child's safety features:

Age	*Safety*
5 or younger	Very unsafe
6–12	Somewhat safe
13 or older	Most safe

Behavior	*Risk*
Responsible	Less at risk
Impulsive	More at risk
Introspective	Less at risk
Curious	More at risk
Honest	Less at risk
Dishonest	More at risk
Enjoys reading and school	Less at risk
Prefers sports to school	More at risk
Good-natured	Less at risk
Argumentative	More at risk
Good family relations exist	Less at risk
Poor family relations exist	More at risk

The LRQ (latchkey risk quotient), presented in chapter 6 for educators, is also useful for parents in assessing at-risk children.

Safety Buffer

The checklist provided in figure 5–1 will enable you to define the safety buffer surrounding your home. Follow the three steps in figure 5–3.

If your responses to items 1–3 were all "yes," your latchkey safety buffer allows you to specify where, when, and with whom your child's safety is entrusted. A map that depicts this information will provide a more complete picture of how to implement the safety buffer. In some cases, the location, time, and caretaker components will be present but not coordinated. For example, the identified safety areas within a neighborhood may be accessible only by car or with an adult escort. You will need to coordinate your safety time slot and caretaker person to get your child to and from these areas. If coordination is not possible, the practical use of your safety buffer will need to be reassessed. All three components must be in place for a latchkey kid to be safe outside the home setting.

If you responded "no" to items 1, 2, and/or 3, you have a limited safety buffer. A safe space, time, and adult caretaker are needed to ensure your child's well-being. But take heart. Things can change. Parents need to reassess their safety buffer on a yearly basis. Our society is highly mobile and undergoing rapid change. The characteristics of your neighborhood and home may be quite different a year from now.

1. Are there areas surrounding your home that are safe during at least some part of the day?

   ____ Yes   (List the areas and their proximity to your home.)

   _____

   _____

   _____

   (Go to step 2.)

   ____ No   (Stop. Your child's safety outside the home is not possible.)

2. Do the times of safety for each area meet your child's after-school needs?

   ____ Yes   (List the times of safety for each area.)

   _____

   _____

   _____

   (Go to step 2.)

   ____ No   (Stop. Your child's safety outside the home is not possible.)

3. Is there at least one responsible adult who can check on your child's activities in each area?

   ____ Yes   (Name the adults for each area.)

   _____

   _____

   _____

   ____ No   (Stop. Your child's safety outside the home is very questionable.)

Figure 5–3. Determining the Safety Buffer

In-Home Safety Strategies

Regardless of the extent of the safety buffer, there are certain in-home strategies that all parents must consider. At one time or another most children find themselves alone at home. A parent who runs out to the market and leaves a child at home alone briefly may not consider this a latchkey situation, but this short time period can be as stressful and dangerous for children as when parents are gone for more extended periods of time.

House Key

The symbol most associated with latchkey kids is the house key. When worn around the neck the house key advertises a child's vulnerability. The key should be kept on a key chain or in a wallet, purse, or pocket. Under no circumstance should the child show or loan the key.

Some parents and children hide an extra key in case the original is lost. Creativity is needed in finding a good hiding place. The doormat and mailbox are poor choices. A loose brick or box buried in the shrubbery is a good choice in some instances. Leaving an extra key with a trusted neighbor is also a good idea.

Getting Home

When children go to and from school on their own, certain strategies can ensure their safe arrival. It is important for the child to follow only those routes that have been agreed upon. Experimenting with short-cuts is a dangerous practice, as is accepting rides.

Many school-age children find it difficult to leave interesting after-school activities and return to an empty house, and parents feel guilty about imposing rules that isolate their children from friends. These problems can be mitigated by planning weekend outdoor activities. These activities can be as simple as roller skating in the park with a friend and as elaborate as a fishing trip with a boys' or girls' club. Regardless of the activity, the focus should be on providing the child with informal socializing experiences that he or she misses on weekdays.

Checking In

Check-ins allow both parent and child to feel more confident. Check-ins also allow for potential problems to be avoided. There are a number of check-in possibilities.

The 3 o'clock syndrome refers to the disruption of work activities when parents call home to check on their latchkey kids. In some instances children call their parents. In other instances, a neighbor or relative serves as the contact person who makes periodic telephone or personal checks on a latchkey child.

Parents who work under demanding schedules need a creative check-in procedure. A child can call a parent's office and leave a message. Another procedure is for the child to call the office three times in succession beginning at a certain time. With each call, the child allows the telephone to ring three times before hanging up. Obviously this system has bugs. You may be called away at 3:25 or receive a business call between your child's second and third call. Finally, parents who have access to a computer at work and at home check in with their latchkey kid using a telephone modem.

House Rules

The home safety items checked in figure 5–2 can provide a guide for establishing house rules. Many parents feel that a locked door is a major safety rule. A latchkey kid may feel more is needed. Young children are often fearful that someone is hiding in a closet or under the bed. A child who includes these checks in the house rules will feel more secure.

One way to structure house rules is to develop an after-school schedule. Schedules give children a sense of control over their home environments. An example of one latchkey kid's after-school schedule is given in figure 5–4.

3:30	Arrive home	• Lock door • Check rooms and closets • Pull front window shades
3:30–3:45	Mom calls (Yea!)	
3:45–5:00	Free time	• Snack • TV, radio, telephone, calls • Feed cat (please!)
5:00–5:30	Begin homework (Boo!)	
5:30–6:00	Mom arrives (Yea!)	

Mom's signature		Date	
John's signature		Date	

Figure 5–4. John's Schedule

A few points about the after-school schedule are noteworthy. First, it should be simple and short. The example in figure 5–4 provides direction without overloading John with details. Second, the schedule must be flexible. Large blocks of time are used that give John ample opportunity to complete all tasks. Third, humor makes the schedule less demanding. Some children may choose to decorate their schedule or place checks beside items they accomplish. The less imposing the schedule is, the more likely it will be followed. Finally, there is a space for Mom and John to sign and date the schedule. John's signature serves a dual purpose: it indicates that he helped develop the schedule and that he agrees to follow the described routine.

The placement of the after-school schedule is important. Most school-age children head for the refrigerator as soon as they arrive home. The refrigerator door thus is an ideal spot for the schedule and other materials relating to your child, such as a map with the telephone number and names of local agencies.

Another technique to remind latchkey children of house rules is to post a list of do's and don'ts. An example of the list placed next to John's after-school schedule and map of local agencies is presented in figure 5–5. Notice that John's list has the same characteristics as his after-school schedule; it is simple, humorous, and signed. Also, for every don't, there is an alternative do. Telling children what to do is more informative than giving the ambiguous command, "Don't." Safety practices to consider in developing a list are listed in figure 5–6.

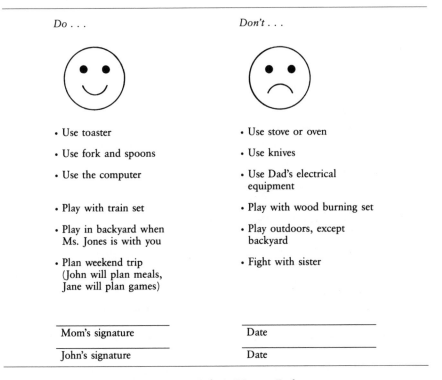

Do . . .	Don't . . .
• Use toaster	• Use stove or oven
• Use fork and spoons	• Use knives
• Use the computer	• Use Dad's electrical equipment
• Play with train set	• Play with wood burning set
• Play in backyard when Ms. Jones is with you	• Play outdoors, except backyard
• Plan weekend trip (John will plan meals, Jane will plan games)	• Fight with sister

Mom's signature	Date
John's signature	Date

Figure 5–5. John's House Rules

Emergencies

Mapping community service agencies and listing telephone numbers and names is the first step in helping a child respond to emergencies. Practice in using the map and meeting service workers gives the child practice in implementing emergency procedures. A schedule of daily events and a list of do's and don'ts provide structure for activities within the home. Finally, the National Crime Prevention Center recommendations listed in figure 5–6 address logistical issues to preventing and responding to emergencies.

Latchkey children who have completed a survival skills program will be better prepared to respond to emergencies. In chapter 9, summaries are given of two programs, one sponsored by the Boy Scouts of America and the other by the Virginia Cooperative Extension Service. Local Boy Scout clubs and county extension offices can provide information on nearby survival skills programs. In addition, the PTA, YMCA, YWCA, and Camp Fire Organization have educational programs that teach children the decision-making and life skills needed to respond to emergencies.

Teach your children:

To memorize their name and address, including city and state.

To memorize their telephone number, including area code.

To use both push-button and dial telephones to make emergency, local, and long-distance calls and to reach the operator.

To check in with you or a neighbor immediately after arriving home.

Not to go into your home if a door is ajar or a window is broken.

How to work the door and window locks of your home and lock them when they are at home alone.

How to get out of the home quickly in case of fire.

How to answer the doorbell and telephone when they're home alone.

Not to go into anyone else's home without your permission.

Never to go anywhere with another adult, even one who says you have sent him or her. Adopt a family code word to be used if you have to ask a third party to pick up your children.

To avoid walking or playing alone.

That a stranger is someone neither you nor they know well.

That if they feel they're being followed, either on foot or by a car, to run to the nearest public place, neighbor, or safe house.

To tell you if anyone asks them to keep a secret, offer them gifts, or money, or asks to take their picture.

Always to tell you if something happened while they were away from you that made them feel uncomfortable in any way.

National Crime Prevention Council, Woodward Building, 733 Fifteenth Street, N.W., Washington, D.C. 20005. Reprinted with permission.

Figure 5–6. In-Home Safety Strategies

Finally, emergencies can be avoided. Locking away dangerous equipment, separating and labeling foods and medicines, and making periodic home inspections and repairs protect against mishaps.

Selecting School-Age Child Care Programs

Many parents have given up on finding a school-age child care program. The cost of services and the difficulty in providing transportation to and from program sites are more than they can handle. Another problem is getting the school-age child to attend such programs. Children often view themselves as too old for babysitting. Still another problem parents face is distinguishing appropriate from inappropriate programs. Leita Evette (1985) has developed a checklist to assist parents in selecting and monitoring programs. This checklist is presented in figure 5–7.

Community Strategies

The latchkey problem is not a child problem, and it is not a family problem. It is a community problem. Parents have a responsibility to protect their latchkey children within the home setting, but they need additional help within the community. School-age child care program development is discussed in chapter 9. Here we will discuss how parents can stimulate community awareness and action to deal with the latchkey issue.

Publicity

The first step is to educate the community about the latchkey problem. Many people do not know what the phrase *latchkey kid* means. Writing letters to the local newspaper is one way to educate the public and stimulate community action. Writing radio public service announcements or spots is another educational strategy. Radio stations air public service spots, like the following one, free of charge:

FOR IMMEDIATE NEWS RELEASE
Topic: Latchkey Children

Does your child arrive to an empty home after school? If so, you have a latchkey child. Latchkey children care for themselves when not in school and while their parents are at work. Communities from across our country are developing programs to protect latchkey children. [*Name of community*] has *no* program for its latchkey children. If you are interested in working on this problem, please join [*name of parent group*]. Call [*telephone number*] for more information.

Networking

Networking, discussed in chapter 9, is the most efficient means to resolve the latchkey problem since individual parents can accomplish only so much. Parent groups have great visibility and resources. The first step in forming a parent group is to develop a plan of work. Some parents will be interested only in public education. Others will want to establish informal block parent groups. Still others will want to serve as advocates and work with community agencies in developing school-age child care programs. We discuss the role of advocacy in addressing the school-age child care issue in chapter 8.

It is a good idea to survey individual members to learn their interests and talents. Subcommittees can then be formed to work on different areas. Some type of administrative structure is needed to coordinate the activities of the group.

_____ Is the program safe? Every precaution must be taken to insure protection from hazards to health and physical safety.

_____ Is the program closely supervised? Adequate teacher/pupil ratios should be maintained. Ideally, the ratio should be one teacher for every ten children to allow for child-centered activities.

_____ What ages of children are served? There are many choices: Kindergarten–third grade; first–sixth grade; and even first–ninth grade! Choose a program that gives attention to the age of your child.

_____ Do the teachers express a caring attitude toward the children?

_____ Are opportunities provided for in-service training of the staff?

_____ Does the program meet during the hours you need? Some programs offer only after-school care; others provide both before and after-school care. Also ask about holidays during the school year and whether or not the program is extended in the summer.

_____ Is the program accessible to your child? What provision is made for your child to get to the program after school? Programs have various policies such as personally providing transportation for school-age children, using public school buses, or organizing car pools. The best accessibility is offered when the program is either near the child's home, the child's school, or the parent's place of employment.

_____ Does the program encourage parent involvement? Even though parents using these programs have limited time for participation, provision should be made for regular communication with and input from all parents. Whenever possible, parents should be used as resource persons in the program.

_____ How long has the program been in operation? Longevity in the community often is an indication of program stability.

_____ Does the program have clearly defined purposes?

Perhaps even more important than parental preference in choosing school-age child care are criteria that deal with the developmental needs of children. A successful program will be responsive to the unique needs of the children who attend. The following checklist will help determine whether or not the needs of children are being taken into consideration:

_____ Is time provided for physical activity? Time should also be allowed for relaxation. Children who come from school need a time to wind down. They also need plenty of space for using energy constructively.

_____ Does the program encourage children to develop competence? Are there opportunities for them to achieve? A balanced program provides children ways to sense their value and their ability to contribute to the group. School-age child care should also provide a low risk environment for the child to try new skills. These include academic as well as motor and social skills.

_____ Is there an emphasis on helping the child learn more about himself? The staff must be sensitive to the child's feelings about himself. A relaxed schedule which allows time for informal conversation with the staff and peers helps the child gain a sense of self-awareness.

_____ What encouragement is given to creative activities? Are there opportunities for involvement in art, drama, reading, and music? Children can find creative expression through sports and recreation, gardening, and games. Effective child care centers will strive continually to provide varied creative opportunities in order to keep programs interesting and attractive.

_____ Is there social interaction with peers and adults on the staff? Program activities are not as important to the child as are relationships with the staff and the peer group. Emphasis should be given to drawing out the positive relationships. Many times this will minimize negative behavior.

—— Are there clearly defined expectations for children in the program? Do they know what is expected of them? Clear boundaries within which the children can function are critical. Rules about behavior should be explicitly stated. Children function productively, are more cooperative, and become more secure in an environment which is influenced by the love and care of teachers who set limits for safety and behavior.

—— Does the program allow for meaningful participation? Activities and schedules must be conducive to the child's involvement in the program. This is true both in the daily routine and in special projects. Many school-age programs offer mission- or service-oriented activities. A balanced program will offer a variety of activities for diverse interests.

From *Living with children,* July–September 1985. © Copyright 1985 The Sunday School Board of the Southern Baptist Convention. All rights reserved. Reprinted with permission.

Figure 5–7. Checklist for Identifying and Monitoring SACC Programs

Employers

Employers can help with the latchkey problem. Those who know the policies of the company and the personality characteristics of the employer will be able to be more effective in helping companies develop ways of dealing with family-related programs.

A number of suggestions are feasible, including a 3:00–3:15 P.M. break to call home, flextime, job sharing, and after-school programs. Parents can supply figures and charts to show how their suggestions will benefit the company; increased productivity, less absenteeism, and greater loyalty among workers may result. Employees can volunteer their time to look into the feasibility of those suggestions that their employer is interested in pursuing. An employer who may not be interested now may reconsider later.

The Church

Churches can sponsor after-school programs that can be as simple as a discussion group or as elaborate as an activity center. Churches often can cut through red tape and recruit funds and staff to resolve family-related problems. The church is also a valuable partner in educating the community about the latchkey issue. Some people will listen to clergy while ignoring a human service worker or politician.

Community Agencies

Many community agencies already have programs that address the concerns of parents with latchkey kids, although the programs are not coordinated. The fire department, police department, church, PTA, county extension office, parks and recreation department, YMCA, girls' club, and mental health office have child development or child safety programs. These programs can be packaged with some coordination. A local community center or church can conduct a series of programs about the issues. Each community agency can develop a schedule detailing the times and types of activities it offers. A small fee may be required to cover utilities or materials, but most parents will be willing to pay.

Parental coordination efforts can represent the beginning of program development. Communities sometimes need a demonstration of their resources and capabilities before a commitment to programming is made. Publicizing the program will help convince community leaders that school-age child care is needed and feasible.

Family Climate

We suggested in an earlier chapter that not all latchkey kids are hurried children, but many contemporary families, latchkey and nonlatchkey, live life in the fast lane. Parents rush to work in the mornings, put in a full day, rush home to take children to lessons, rush back to pick them up, rush home to prepare dinner (or grab a bite out), rush to an evening meeting, and rush back to get the children in bed. Children rush to school in the mornings, rush home (or to music lessons, scout meetings, or after-school programs) in the afternoons, hurry to get their homework and household chores completed, grab a bite to eat, and collapse after a full-day of work.

Parents, teachers, and the principal of an affluent private school recently told us that the stress their children are under is overwhelming. Everyone was afraid to let up for fear of being criticized. Parents said the stress was a self-imposed competitive urge by children to keep up with one another. "Kids compete with each other," said one mother. "We don't pressure them." Indeed some children had weekly schedules that would make a top corporate executive's appear lax. One mother said her child had no time to play during the week: "My child has a full weekly schedule of club meetings, dance classes, music lessons, Girl Scouts, and cheerleading practice. In between she has tons of homework every evening. And she's not willing to give up anything for fear of being left behind!"

Teachers blamed parents and said they needed to let up. Parents complained that teachers were overloading children with too much homework. One teacher responded, "If we reduce the work load, then parents will criticize us for not doing our jobs." And the principal complained, "If we let kids play, when will they learn?"

This scenario is repeated every day among many families on the go. No one is willing to take responsibility for imposing stress, so the cycle continues. It is the parent's responsibility to intervene on behalf of their stressed children. The best way to do that is to create, where possible, a stress-free family climate. The following suggestions may be useful:

1. Do not hurry your children. Let them grow and develop at their own pace, according to their own developmental time-tables.

2. Encourage children to play and do things children do. Some of our fondest memories are of our childhood experiences.

3. Do not forcefeed learning. Have reasonable expectations based on what children are capable of performing at their respective ages.

4. Let children have some daily and flexible schedule at home with free time built in for choosing from activities that match their interests.

5. As much as possible, protect children from the harsh pressures of the adult world, with time to play, learn, and fantasize.

6. As much as possible, provide children a peaceful and pleasant home atmosphere, shielded from excessive marital disputes and involvements in parental conflict.

7. Try not to pass your stress on to your children. Give them opportunities to talk about their own worries and stresses.

8. Guide children toward wise decision making by introducing limited choices that match their emotional maturity.

9. Reward children for their triumphs and successes, no matter how small. Let them know you love them and are proud of them for who they are, not who you want them to be.

10. Start the day on a positive note with pleasant words and calm routines.

11. Plan special times together each week as a family (without television), and listen to what your children have to say.

12. If you do push your child, ask the question, "Am I doing this for my ego or for the child's benefit?"

Childhood is threatened with extinction as youngsters are pressured to achieve, succeed, and please (Elkind 1981). The period of childhood, compared to adulthood, is the shortest time in the life span. Some children burn out before they have lived through this brief period. Childhood lays the bedrock for adult lives, and youngsters who have a chance to be children will become healthier, more well-rounded adults.

Building Family Life

As a rule, latchkey kids stay alone a lot because one or both parents work. Children who care for themselves on a regular basis deserve a reward occasionally for a job well done. One of the best gifts of appreciation parents can give is to build family strengths. By that we mean taking special care to plan a few evenings together as a family. Preparing meals together and having pleasant conversations at mealtime (without television) give latchkey families a chance to communicate.

Children need their parents' undivided attention every so often. Parents who work find it easy to get caught up in paying bills, bringing home extra work, civic obligations, or keeping their social life active to the exclusion of their children. But they must be sensitive to the balance children need in their daily lives. Grollman and Sweder (1986) talked with over a thousand children and gathered do's and don'ts for working parents with children.

Discuss with your children the nature of your job. Let them know where you go and what you do all day long. Listen to what they have to say too. Find out what they have been up to during the week. Avoid too much television watching as a family and save newspaper reading until the children are asleep. Plan time with youngsters by helping them with homework, playing board games, scheduling weekday or weekend family outings, or conducting family projects. Start the day on a positive note with pleasant words and calm routines. Sometimes this might mean getting up fifteen minutes earlier so the family is not rushing to get out the door. Make your home a safe place where children can be alone and be happy and safe.

Do not make snap judgments and criticize children unnecessarily. Every situation has a positive and negative side. Try to focus on the positive things children do rather than always harping on the negative. This is not to say that children should not be disciplined, only that they should not be used as scapegoats when parents are tired. Do not spend all your time working. Limit the amount of work you bring home in the evenings and on weekends. Save some of that time for special moments with your most precious resources, the children. Do not come home in a foul mood. Children have bad days too. Try to unwind and set a pleasant tone for family evenings. Do not make a habit of leaving your children at home a lot in the evenings and on weekends; they already spend most of their time at home alone. Be sympathetic to their needs. Limit the number of times you go out or make provisions to take them along whenever possible.[1]

Making the Best of Latchkey Situations

The kinds of problems children incur from latchkey arrangements ultimately depend on parents' attitudes toward self-care and the degree to which they prepare children for this experience. Child's age and maturity level, neighborhood location, and type of supervision are also contributing factors. Guilt, worry, and ambivalence may be the overriding parental emotions associated with latchkey arrangements, but channeling these feelings into positive action can improve an otherwise difficult experience for both parents and children.

Parents should examine the safety of their homes and neighborhoods in terms of physical and psychological risks. Where such risks prevail, they can take appropriate safety measures to ensure children's protection. Parents can analyze the soundness of their latchkey arrangements and make supervisory provisions in absentia. Pondering questions such as the following helps clarify situations that should be rectified:

Does my child promptly report home after school and telephone me right away or check in with a reliable neighbor? Or does he or she stop off at a friend's house where there is no supervision?

Does he or she have a favorite hangout?

What rules have I established for my child to follow inside and outside the house in my absence?

Parents can find out what is available in their areas or work with other parents to establish organized after-school supervision for their youngsters. They can critically evaluate research reports on latchkey kids instead of taking them at face value. How many and what age children were studied? Where and how was the study conducted? How representative are these children? What types of latchkey arrangements were studied? How are these situations similar to my own? By asking such questions, parents can identify information that applies to them.

Close scrutiny of the existing family climate is important too. By eliminating undue stress and tension where possible, the family functions more smoothly. A searching and fearless inventory of parental attitudes about self-care and feelings of guilt and ambivalence might uncover subtle influences on adjustments to self-care.

Once parents take these actions and provide the best child care arrangement possible, they should give themselves a break, worry less, and make the best of their situation for their psychological well-being as well as the child's. Teachers and other educators share many of the same concerns as parents. In the next chapter we will explore ways that school personnel, working in concert with families, can address latchkey children's needs.

Note

1. Do's and don'ts for working parents with children were taken from "Tips for Working Parents—From Kids," *Reader's Digest* (Feb. 1986), pp. 107–110, condensed from *The Working Parent Dilemma*, copyright © 1986 by Earl A. Grollman and Gerri L. Sweder (Boston: Beacon Press).

References

Elkind, D. 1981. *The hurried child.* Reading, Mass.: Addison-Wesley.

Evette, L. 1985. School-age child care programs: Options for parents. *Living with Children* 8:22–23.

Grollman, E.A., & Sweder, G.L. (1986). *The working parent dilemma.* Boston: Beacon Press.

6

Suggestions for Educators

Several of the children I teach are latchkey kids, and I'm constantly racking my brain on what I, as a second-grade teacher, can do to help them adjust to being alone in the afternoons. Even after they leave school, I find myself worrying about them. Because of this concern, I sometimes feel that I'm working twenty-four hours a day. One child in particular caught my eye.

Eight-year-old Steve goes home to an empty house each day. He's in the second grade and walks home alone after school. Concerned about his safety, the teachers I work with and myself paired him with a little girl in his class who was going his way. That didn't work because they didn't get along. So Steve ended up walking home by himself or riding his bicycle.

When he gets home, he doesn't need a key because the door lock is broken, but he can lock the door from the inside. The first thing he does, once inside, is call his mother; then he watches television. He worries a lot about and is very protective of his dog, Brownie. He fears that other animals in the neighborhood will eat his dog's food. One child, an older girl, is allowed to visit Steve, but she doesn't come over often. When I asked him how he felt about staying at home alone, he replied, "Sometimes lonely, sometimes scared."

"What makes you scared?" I asked.

"Noises and when Brownie barks," he replied.

He says he hides in the bathroom when he gets scared. "If I think somebody is trying to get in, I get a knife."

He says a policeman lives across the street, if he ever needs someone to help him. Steve's mother and stepfather work irregular hours, and they don't always have the same hours. They may arrive home at five, six, or at nine P.M. Steve calls his mother to find out when someone will be there. Throughout the school day, he never knows how much time he will be alone when he gets home that afternoon. This uncertainty seems to cause him some anxiety during school hours.

At five o'clock, if no one is home, Steve walks across the street to the day care center to pick up his 3-year-old sister, Stacy.

"What do you and Stacy do?" I asked him.

"We watch television. She loves cartoons. But you know the hardest part?"

"What's that?" I queried.

"It's when Stacy messes her pants! I just hold my nose!"

Swaim Strong
Monroe, North Carolina

A kindergarten teacher told us of an incident involving 5-year-old Jamie, a student in her classroom. One afternoon after school, he jumped off some steps into a broken plastic milk crate, severely cutting his leg and requiring twenty-five stitches. His mother was working at the time, and his sitter, a sixth-grade neighborhood girl, did not know where the boy's mother worked; moreover, there was no telephone in the house. The mother had hired the sixth grader because she could not afford after-school care. The mother came to school to tell the teacher what had happened and said that she felt terribly guilty about the accident. She said she was trying to find an adult sitter to stay with Jamie after school. Neither the children nor the parent had properly prepared themselves for emergencies. This lack of preparation compounded the problem and left emotional after effects for parent and children.

Educators can assist parents and children in preparing for such emergencies while relieving themselves of excessive worry after children have left their supervision. We will first discuss ways classroom teachers can prepare children and parents for self-care and then examine a school-wide and community-wide approach to prevention.

Determining Risk Factors

The teacher's ability to work effectively with latchkey kids is crucial as the numbers of children in self-care spiral. With parents at work, teachers become the prominent adults in many children's lives. In effect, they become parent substitutes. As the case indicates, many teachers we talked to are concerned about children who leave their charge and feel helpless about those who go home to empty houses. They want to do something but do not know where to start. Several writers suggest the teacher's first step in prevention is to determine which children go home to empty houses by a quick survey (Long 1985; Scherer 1982). Although a survey will tell which children routinely care for themselves, it will not tell which ones are at risk. As we have pointed out, not all latchkey kids are in jeopardy. Some have workable latchkey arrangements; others have harmful ones. Once teachers determine which students are latchkey children, the next step is to determine their level of risk. Then teachers can provide the basics in self-care for all pupils (since almost all children are alone occasionally even if it is while parents are shopping) and give special attention to high-risk children.

Some of the factors that we discussed in chapter 4 can be used to screen children in possible jeopardy. Factors such as maturity level, parent's attitude toward leaving their children alone, degree of preparation, and community resources are difficult for classroom teachers to measure and for young children to verbalize. But teachers can easily gain and assess information on age of the child, where the child lives, the amount of time the child is left alone on a daily basis, and the degree of supervision after school each day. Figure 6–1 presents a scale that teachers can use to measure the degree of risk for children in their classrooms.

Read each factor and decide the degree to which it pertains to the child. Circle the number that best describes the child's latchkey situation. Calculate each child's LRQ (latchkey risk quotient) by adding the four numbers circled in each category: *LRQ = age + location + amount of time left alone + degree of supervision.* The higher the score is, the higher is the risk for the child when left alone. A score from 4 to 9 is a low-risk score. Low-risk children have few or none of the combinations that would cause them to be hurt by being alone. Twelve-year-old Marie is an example. She lives in a Lincolnton, North Carolina, suburb, where she spends her one hour alone after school doing homework, after calling her mother to let her know she is home. Her rules are to do her chores, keep the house in order, complete homework before watching television, and avoid turning on the oven. Marie says she enjoys staying home alone and is seldom afraid.

A score from 10 to 14 shows moderate risk. Moderate-risk children are those who have some combinations to place them at risk. A good example is 14-year-old Sam, who lives in Washington, D.C., is alone for five hours every afternoon, but calls his mother as soon as he gets home and has clear rules about what he can and cannot do.

1. *Age of the latchkey child*

1	2	3	4	5
14 and over	12–13	10–11	7–9	6 and under

2. *Location that best typifies where the child lives*

1	2	3	4	5
rural area	suburbia	small town	city (population under 300,000)	city (population over 300,000)

3. *Amount of time left alone after school each day*

1	2	3	4	5
1 hour	2 hours	3 hours	4 hours	5 hours or more

4. *Degree of supervision after school each day*

1	2	3	4	5
supervised by parent in absentia (daily telephone calls and clear set of rules)	checks in with a next-door neighbor	supervised at home by underage sibling	unsupervised at friend's house	unsupervised hanging out in neighborhood

Figure 6–1. Computing the Latchkey Risk Quotient

A score of 15 to 20 is a high-risk score that contains many or all of the factors that place latchkey kids at risk. Typically, high-risk children are the extreme exceptions like 6-year-old John, who lives in Philadelphia and comes home each day to an empty house. His mother works odd hours, which requires that he care for himself between the hours of three and eight o'clock. Because he does not have a telephone, his mother cannot check on him, so instead of staying home, he usually hangs out at a local video arcade. John has the highest possible risk score, 20.

This simple test has not been scientifically validated and is intended only as a screening aid for classroom teachers. As we have emphasized, four other factors also influence the child's risk of being alone. When parents accept and feel comfortable about their latchkey arrangements, for example, children are more likely to have positive attitudes toward being left alone (Pecoraro, Theriot & Lafont 1984). Nevertheless, the LRQ can provide useful information that will help reduce high-risk scores through classroom interventions, as well as prevent stereotyping of all latchkey kids. A higher score could indicate greater risks of accidents, getting into trouble, and exposure to sexual victimization. It is possible, too, that higher-risk children could face educational and social obstacles such as low academic achievement and poor self-esteem and social adjustment than lower-risk youngsters. Teachers can plan appropriate classroom interventions that can reduce high-risk scores and help all children, latchkey and nonlatchkey, prepare for self-care.

Classroom Strategies

Latchkey curricula have been developed for classroom teachers to help children who are vulnerable to crisis acquire self-reliance skills and to ensure that they can cope safely on their own. Children who have self-confidence in their abilities to care for themselves when alone are more likely to concentrate and perform better in school rather than dwell on their apprehensions.

Boredom Busters

No matter what after-school arrangement is used, children will be bored from time to time. Some latchkey kids we interviewed were bored by their after-school day care programs, others were bored being home alone, and one 14-year-old said it would be boring if a parent were home in the afternoons. Apparently boredom can affect children regardless of their after-school arrangements. Helping latchkey kids find suitable, constructive, and interesting outlets, whether in organized after-school programs or in self-care arrangements, is an ever-present challenge for teachers and parents.

Following a school-age child care survey in an elementary school in North Carolina, Sandra Sparks, a teacher, wrote a curriculum for latchkey children. The curriculum offers twenty-four Boredom Busters for elementary children who are alone. These activities offer suggestions to make the latchkey experience safe and happy and help children adjust to their respective levels of self-care. They can be selected and adapted to the interest and age of the child.[1]

Boredom Busters

1. Make a scrapbook. Staple blank paper together to make a book. Then tape or glue in anything that has special meaning to you—souvenirs, postcards, movie tickets, awards, pictures, and so forth.

2. Get a state map and trace the route to some location you think would be fun to visit. Use a yellow crayon or marker so the highway numbers will show. Plan what you would need to take on your trip and what you would like to see on your trip.

3. Be a pen pal and have fun learning about other people and other places. For possible pen pals write these places: Around the World Friends, 550 Fifth Avenue, New York, New York 10036; American Friends Service Committee, 160 North Fifteenth Street, Philadelphia, Pennsylvania; International Friendship League, 40 Mount Vernon Street, Boston, Massachusetts. Or you may write the United Nations.

4. Try chalk painting. You will need colored chalk, paper towels, and a pan of water. Dip the chalk into the water, and use it to draw anything you want on the dry paper towel. Experiment with different colors and designs. Allow the picture to dry before you hang it up. Have a special place in your house to display your art.

5. Make up a funny song, pantomime, story, or jokes to share with your family at supper.

6. What's in the future? Design clothes, cars, houses, and so on—whatever you like for the year 2001.

7. Make a bird feeder. Mix bird seed and peanut butter together. Stuff the mixture between the petals of a pine cone. Tie a string or a piece of yarn around the top of the cone to hang it up by. You may also string raisins and popcorn. When your parents get home from work, you can hang the bird feeders on a tree branch facing a window of your house so you can watch the birds each day.

8. Plan a dinner for the president. What would you serve?

9. Write a story for your favorite television show.

10. Go shopping with a catalog and pretend you have $100 to spend. What would you buy? Would you buy one or two expensive items or many less expensive items? What if you had $500 or $1,000?

11. Make a puppet. Paper bags, an old sock, a mitten, or a glove with yarn hair and button eyes or a painted face works fine. The easiest puppet to

make is simply to draw a face on the palm of your hand and wrap a fabric scrap around your hand and arm for a costume.

12. Make a puzzle. Glue a picture from a magazine on a piece of cardboard or posterboard. Let it dry. Use a black ink pen or marker to mark the picture into sections. Cut along the black lines to make the puzzle pieces.

13. Make your own greeting cards. Create messages, verses, and pictures with markers, crayons, or paints on plain or solid-colored paper. Make different sets of cards to give: birthday, get well, thinking-of-you, and so on.

14. "Green Thumb Project." Put a sponge on a dish. Wet the sponge. Sprinkle grass seed on top of the sponge. Wet the sponge a little each day when you get home from school. The seeds should sprout in about one week. For extra fun, have Mom or Dad help you cut the sponge into an animal shape the night before you are going to plant it.

15. Have you got a question for the president or something you would like to tell the president? Write him!

The President
The White House
Washington, D.C. 20500

16. Write and draw pictures for a storybook to share with a younger brother or sister or a neighborhood friend. Maybe you can make up funny endings to nursery rhymes or stories.

17. Try fingerprint art. Press your fingertips down on an ink pad; then press your fingertips on paper. Draw lines and other details to make fingerprints into bugs, monsters, animals, people, and other objects.

18. Write a note, story, secret code, or letter to a friend using typed letters and words cut out of the newspaper. Be careful cutting. Glue or tape the letters and words in the correct order to say what you want them to say. Be sure to use an old newspaper that has already been read.

19. Keep a daily journal. Staple blank sheets of paper together and decorate the cover. Each day write about what happened that day at school or while you were home.

20. Plan the house and yard you would like to have someday. Arrange and glue magazine pictures of houses, trees, flowers, shrubs, and so on on posterboard to show your dream house to friends.

21. Try washcloth painting. Ask permission first. Be sure to do this only on a cabinet or kitchen table top that has a Formica (plastic coating) top. Wet a dark-colored washcloth, and put it on the kitchen table. Run a bar of soap back and forth on the washcloth until it is sudsy. Draw pictures in the suds with your fingers. Smooth over to erase. Remember to rinse the washcloth out in the sink when finished and to dry the table!

22. Pretend you are a radio disc jockey. Make up your own commercials or some "deejay chatter" to perform for your family.

23. Draw a picture of an animal, shape, person, or any other item. Glue yarn around the outline of the picture. Then fill in the inside area of the picture with dry beans, popcorn, seeds, cereal, or macaroni, which you glue in place.

24. Pretend you have your own restaurant. Make up your own menu. What would you serve? How much would you charge for your food? What would you name your place?

Homework Assignments

Once teachers have determined which children spend their afternoons on their own, they can give personal attention to those children and assign homework in accordance with children's afternoon schedules. Many children no longer have adults at home in the evenings to help them complete homework assignments. Strother (1984) suggests that teachers could initiate a telephone hot line for homework, staffed by teachers or volunteers. Older high school students, many latchkey kids themselves, could offer their tutoring services in this manner while spending their time in a constructive way. Adults also could be drafted to assist young children by telephone while realizing a sense of purpose.

Organization of After-School Time

Many children are addicted to television and spent much of their afternoons glued to the set. Scherer (1982) suggests that teachers provide discussions of a variety of after-school activities that would be fun replacements for television watching. A unit on time management could include instruction on the basics of simple time scheduling and managing homework, chores, and leisure time efficiently. Developing time schedules integrates math and sequencing skills, and a theme on "planning my afternoons" sharpens language arts abilities. The subject of health could be taught through the cultivation of nutritional food habits, eliminating poor diets. Children would learn simple food preparation, selection of nutritious snacks, proper use of equipment, and cleanup procedures (Pecoraro, Theriot & Lafont 1984).

Key Care

Latchkey children often have difficulty holding on to their keys. Educators report that they find keys everywhere on school grounds, and many times children arrive home to discover that they have lost their key and cannot get in their home. Key care has been identified as a critical issue to address in a curriculum aimed at self-care (Long 1985; Scherer 1982). Children should be taught to keep their keys in a safe place. If they carry their keys, they should be chained around the neck or pinned or tied inside a pocket or belt where they are hidden from view. A safeguard is to leave an extra key with a neighbor. As a class activity, Long (1985) suggests that students write down their plan of action in the event of key loss and draw a map of the route they would take to procure a replacement. Such an activity integrates geography, math, writing, and many other basic academic skills.

Safety Precautions

The teacher in the opening case said that she was concerned with Steve's walking home alone in the afternoons and tried pairing him with another child, a solution that did not work. The teacher's best approach is to instruct children on appropriate safeguards to take en route to and from school since there is no assurance that one child will always be accompanied by another. Traffic safety, precautions with strangers, handling emergencies, accident prevention, and entering a safe house are topics that can be included as part of a health unit on safety.

One approach to teaching a safety unit is to create a latchkey awareness week. Community workers who visit classrooms often provide important information that teachers may not have at their fingertips. Police officers give safety tips on walking to and from school, as well as what to do when a stranger approaches. They can teach children to detect signs of an intruder and when it is safe or unsafe to enter a house alone. Firefighters talk about precautions to be taken at home against tnreat of fire. Nurses and physicians demonstrate proper procedures for administering first aid, where to go for help, or how to handle emergencies such as Jamie's cut leg.

Setting up special role plays of latchkey situations and following them with discussion can help youngsters cope with unexpected events. Long (1985) suggests the following role play, followed by discussion, as a method for teaching children rules on safe travel:

> Jeff is walking home from school in one of the first snowstorms of winter. He didn't wear boots or gloves today, and he's very cold. He still has several blocks to go when a woman pulls up beside him in a car and offers Jeff a ride home. He has never seen the woman before, but his teeth are chattering and his toes are freezing. What should Jeff do? (a) Get in the car. (b) Explain he cannot ride with strangers. (c) Keep walking and say nothing. (p. 65)

Observing Children's Emotions

By observing children over a period of time and in many different situations—in group work, alone, and on the playground—teachers get a better picture of the child's emotional makeup. Behavior cues help teachers identify and understand children's feelings, problems, and strengths. Activities such as art projects, puppet shows, and individual conversations offer insights into such emotions as fear, isolation, depression, anger, loneliness, and boredom that have been linked to latchkey kids. Teachers help children recognize and express these feelings through such curriculum activities as painting, flannel board activities, clay, drawing, writing stories about the child's day, dramatic play, woodworking, music, and movement.

School counselors can help teachers structure special lessons on latchkey families and encourage children to talk about being alone. In this way, children learn that it is not unusual to be afraid, lonely, or bored and that other children their age share many of these same feelings.

A small lending library in one corner of the classroom that includes publications for children and parents is an excellent resource for latchkey families. Children can work through their feelings from reading books that deal with children's emotions or that give special attention to adjustment to self-care. Newsletters and professional journals received through membership in national or local organizations and books on latchkey issues are also helpful to adults in preparing children outside the classroom. The resource list in the Appendix provides audiovisual information, names of national organizations and their publications, and other literature for adults as well as children.

Telephone Skills

Adults and children alike must be careful of how they answer the telephone. Children at home alone are especially easy prey for those who abuse the telephone system. The classroom is an ideal place to instruct children on how to handle calls. Anonymous or obscene calls or strangers asking personal questions can be dramatized through role play. Children should be taught to never tell an anonymous caller that a parent is not home. When someone asks for the child's mother, for example, the child should be instructed to use such phrases as "Mom can't come to the phone right now" instead of "She won't be home until six o'clock." Obscene callers should be dealt with by hanging up immediately rather than attempting to identify the caller.

Scherer (1982) suggests inviting the telephone company to bring closed-circuit telephones and demonstrate proper procedures to the class. Many areas have telephone warm lines for latchkey children to use when frightened by calls or unusual sounds in the house or faced with emergencies. Children should know important telephone numbers—for the police department, fire station, poison control, parent's work, and nearest neighbor or relative—or the numbers should be placed in a safe and accessible place for children to use in emergencies. They should practice finding and dialing these numbers swiftly, using the telephone book, and reaching the operator.

Household Rules

Most parents of latchkey children provide their youngsters with a set of rules to be followed in their absence. These rules vary from family to family. Sometimes the rules are few and other times many. Teachers can have children write a theme on rules their parents have established. Then through group discussions, the class can compile a master list from the individual themes by listing the most important ones. In cases where some children's rules are weak or vague, teachers can help children clarify them. The comprehensive class list could be duplicated and sent home to parents in a special latchkey newsletter or shared at a PTA meeting.

Classroom teacher Sandra Sparks (1984) developed a pamphlet, *Tips for Parents*, that provides ways parents can prepare children for self-care. Many of these tips can be used by teachers as classroom activities as well. The pamphlet, which included the following points, was sent to all parents in Sparks's elementary school[2]:

1. It is important to make sure your child understands why it is necessary for him or her to stay at home alone, how long it will be until you get home, how you will check on your child and safety rules that are enforced.
2. Important phone numbers (office, the 911 emergency number, an at-home neighbor's number) and your address (work and home) should be taped to the telephone. Other often used phone numbers may be put on the wall near the phone.
3. Teach your child basic first aid and select a special location for a first-aid kit.
4. Go over safety rules including such basic rules as: don't climb on furniture, don't play with matches, don't use knives or kitchen appliances without an adult present.
5. Have your child call you each day when he/she gets home so you will know everything is okay.
6. Have your child talk about how he/she feels about being alone. A pet may be a good "friend" for companionship and also give your child a sense of security.
7. If you will be late getting home from work, call your child and let him/her know when to expect you.
8. Make sure your child knows not to let strangers into the house for *any* reason.
9. Give your child a set of keys and a key chain but do not put your home address on them. Instruct your child to keep the keys out of sight. If your child wears a key on a yarn necklace, have your child wear the key inside his/her shirt. Visible keys "mark" a child who will be alone. Be sure to tell your child what to do if the key gets lost.

10. Prepare your child for various phone calls by having pretend phone conversations. Tell your child not to say that he/she is alone. Your child should say that you are busy and will call back later. If your child feels uneasy about the call, have him/her call you at work to talk about it.

11. Make sure your child knows your full home address and phone number in case it had to be given in an emergency situation.

12. Teach your child what to do in case of a fire. Hold practice fire drills showing exits and use of the 911 number. Smoke detectors should be installed in your home. Children should know to leave the house if it sounds.

13. Let a neighbor know when your child will be staying alone so the neighbor can "watch-out" for your child. If you do not have a home phone, ask a neighbor for permission for your child to use their phone in an emergency.

14. Have family meetings to decide matters such as house rules, any simple chores to be done, how much television may be watched, whether or not friends may come over and under what conditions.

15. Discuss basic things to do in adverse conditions such as bad weather, power outages, etc.

16. Break daily routine by planning some after-school activities that your child would enjoy such as Scouts, sports, Y Programs, and so forth.

17. Provide for safe snacks by putting snacks on a low shelf or table and furnish plastic cups and containers for juice. Let your child help plan healthy snacks.

18. Praise your child often for his/her grown-up behavior. Your trust and praise will promote pride and a sense of responsibility.

School and Community Strategies

The latchkey issue has become a school-wide and community concern. School administrators, counselors, and PTAs around the country have involved themselves in cooperative efforts to help latchkey children.

School Administrators

Classroom teachers need supportive school administrators behind them to implement latchkey classroom strategies. Principals and other school officials are latchkey facilitators. As driving forces behind successful programs, they set the tone of their institutions. The degree to which they encourage and support teachers in their efforts can determine whether intervention strategies succeed or fail. Long (1984), for instance, reports that principals sometimes deny latchkey programs access to schools after regular school hours out of concern over excessive use of facilities.

Administrators can facilitate the establishment of policies and procedures that ultimately benefit children and their parents. School officials can begin by examining the degree to which existing policies and procedures address the needs of latchkey kids. Reevaluating negative attitudes toward use of school space and facilities and visualizing the benefits everyone will share is a beginning step. Efforts to change the school calendar so that it more clearly matches the world of work also has been recommended. School schedules have no need to reflect the agrarian culture of yesteryear. Long (1984) suggests lengthening the school day and year to shorten the amount of time children are left unattended and provide increased time for learning. Procedures for contacting working parents in emergencies should be established. Long (1984) describes the following incident: "One eleven-year-old, who fractured her wrist during gym class, was sent home despite the school staff's failure to reach her mother, a single parent. It took the girl one and a half hours to locate her mother. Later, the school administrator explained that he had no staff person who had the time to wait with the child in a hospital emergency room" (p. 64). When appropriate, principals can help parents work out strategies for responding to such situations as a child's illness or injury at school (Strother 1984). Backup emergency contacts for sick and injured children and methods of care for these children when parents cannot be reached are essential considerations for school officials (Long 1984). Such procedures would stop the practice of sending sick children home alone where they must fend for themselves.

A latchkey task force, in conjunction with the PTA, could advise principals in making school decisions and address urgent needs of latchkey families. Parents, teachers, administrators, and the school counselor working cooperatively on a task force would provide common goals, bring multifaceted expertise to latchkey issues, and improve communication. Projects might include developing policies for emergency and sick care or determining the need for before- and after-school care for school children.

Other school-wide approaches include provisions for in-service training. Counselors and teachers often feel that they lack necessary skills to deal effectively with many problems they face. Administrators can provide flexible scheduling for teachers as well as time and funds for travel to workshops and conferences that address latchkey themes. And administrators can seek out guest speakers and launch a latchkey conference on school premises.

School officials have even greater effects when they become advocates at the community, state, and national levels. As advocates for children in their school systems, administrators must first accept school-age child care as a legitimate need. Once this step has been taken, they can acknowledge this need publicly through professional organizations and local, state, and federal branches of government (McNairy 1984). Locally, administrators can act as liaisons between school and community by tapping outside resources and forming partnerships with private and public sectors. (We will discuss networking in more detail in chapter 8.) They can build coalitions with community groups to offer programs and activities during school vacations, holidays, and after school. One model for consideration is the after-school playground program established by the Dallas Independent School District (Campbell & Flake 1985). Playground supervisors (composed of teachers, paraprofessionals, and community leaders) work in 103 elementary schools and oversee such team sports as soccer, volleyball, football, and basketball.

Enlisting the aid of high school students in organizing special recreational programs before and after school also has proved successful in some parts of the country. In one example, Future Homemakers of America (FHA) students presented a proposal to the school administration and parks and recreation department (Hall 1985). In their program, individual elementary school facilities would be used for before- and after-school programs of crafts, games, snacks, and other recreational activities. Programs would be staffed by FHA students, with a small fee paid by parents to the parks and recreation department, which would administer the program. Mutual benefits would be possible for students, who would receive part-time pay as well as constructive use of time, and the community, which would receive inexpensive yet beneficial services from their youth. Students also would learn the value of cooperative planning by working through elementary school counselors to obtain names of families needing alternatives to latchkey situations. As part of the plan, students would offer workshops for latchkey kids and their families on techniques of self-care.

Above all, school officials should involve themselves in latchkey issues at the community level and communicate to others their readiness and willingness to participate in cooperative ventures. Community groups often are reluctant to approach public schools because partnerships are hard to negotiate and administrative hierarchies are difficult to interpret (Campbell & Flake 1985). To break these barriers, educators can advocate after-school programs; participate in planning out-of-school options for children and their families; contact city and county officials; and, if necessary, spearhead a community study to document needs and gaps. The most viable programs have emerged from broad-based community support, almost always including, and often initiated by, school personnel.

Parent-Teacher Associations

Parent-teacher associations (PTAs) play a key role in dealing with latchkey issues in their respective schools. Many of the suggestions already given for teachers and school administrators pertain equally to PTAs, since membership is composed of teachers, school officials, and parents. The National PTA has been an instrumental force in advocating for latchkey kids and their families. This parent-school network is perhaps the strongest way to alleviate potential problems on a national and local scale.

Local PTAs can begin advocacy efforts by investigating choices for after-school care available in their areas. Calls to community child care referral agencies and departments of social services as well as inquiries about local child care options are beginning points. PTAs can inform other parents of their findings at regularly scheduled meetings or through special newsletters. Some PTAs publish brochures advising parents on what to look for in quality after-school programs. (See chapter 4 for a sample checklist.) In some areas informal talks with other parents and school officials about the possibility of starting an extended-day program is the next step. A more formal needs assessment, however, is often essential to determine the need for after-school care. A sample needs assessment form is available from the National PTA (Carter 1985).

Another method for determining local needs for latchkey families is to plan a special latchkey night at a PTA meeting. The film *Lord of the Locks* (see the Appendix at the end of this book for ordering information) could be shown to stimulate questions, reactions, and discussion. Brainstorming ways of addressing school and community needs in small groups can follow the film. The small groups then can share their proposed solutions in a large group meeting where a master proposal is generated from small group lists.

Depending on the results of the needs assessment, PTA groups can explore the possibility of starting some type of after-school program or organized supervision that matches school needs. Some schools have instituted extended-day programs, neighborhood block mothers, after-school check-in programs, afternoon help lines, or concerted efforts between community agencies in operating before- and after-school centers.

The John Adams PTA and the North Brunswick Township Department of Human Services established a school-age child care program in their New Jersey community (Carter 1985). The program attracts children by offering computer instruction, gynmastics, dramatics, arts and crafts, and cooking activities for forty-four children in kindergarten through six grades. Additional activities include field trips to a planetarium, an environmental education center, a water treatment plant, and a fire station. Staff include a program supervisor, four high school students, a senior citizen, and a college student. Fees are between $15 and $20 a week.

Block mother programs oversee safe travel as children walk to and from school. A reprint of an article published in *PTA Today,* "Block Parent Program That Keeps Children Safe in the Streets" can be obtained from the National PTA (Carter 1985). Check-in programs are designed to provide flexible care and supervision for older elementary school and junior high students. Designated mothers serve as check-in points for children who wish to spend time in their own homes, visit friends, play outside in their neighborhoods, or attend special community events (McKnight & Shelsby 1984). Carter (1985) also recommends that PTAs conduct a campaign to help teenagers become better babysitters. Additional ideas can be generated that match the unique needs of the school association and community.

Conclusion

The school environment is a large part of a child's life that is integrally tied to the home. Children bring to school all the joys and burdens that accompany their self-care arrangements. Public schools must confront the latchkey issue at every level—before school, during school, and after school—because all levels affect the child's learning, development, and general well-being. Teachers, school administrators, and PTAs working cooperatively is the ultimate hope of creating the most optimal ecologies for school-age children. By networking with community agencies, educators can meet the difficult challenge of opening doors for latchkey kids and their families. Educators with a sense of commitment and vision who can see the overall picture of classroom, school, and community interlocking and working harmoniously are the ones who will ultimately realize the greatest success in this endeavor.

Notes

1. Sandra R. Sparks, *The key to being on my own* (Charlotte, N.C.: University of North Carolina, 1984). Reprinted with permission.
2. Sandra R. Sparks, *The key to being on my own* (Charlotte, N.C.: University of North Carolina, 1984). Reprinted with permission.

References

Campbell, L.P., & Flake, A.E. 1985. Latchkey children: What is the answer? *Clearing House* 58:381–383.
Carter, D. 1985. The crisis in school-age child care: What you should know . . . what you can do. *PTA Today* 10:4–8.
Hall, J.M. 1985. Latchkey children: Is anybody home? Our responsibility. *Illinois Teacher of Home Economics* 28:117–119.
Long, L. 1985. Safe at home. *Instructor* 104:38–40.
Long, T. 1984. So who cares if I'm home? *Educational Horizons* 62:60–64.
McKnight, J., & Shelsby, B. 1984. Checking in: An alternative for latchkey kids. *Children Today* 13:23–25.
McNairy, M.R. 1984. School-age child care: Program and policy issues. *Educational Horizons* 62:64–67.
Pecoraro, A.; Theriot, J.; & Lafont, P. 1984. What home economists should know about latchkey children. *Journal of Home Economics* 76:20–22.
Scherer, M. 1982. The loneliness of the latchkey child. *Instructor* 101:38–41.
Sparks, S. 1984. *Latchkey children*. Thesis, University of North Carolina.
Strother, D.B. 1984. Latchkey childen: The fastest-growing special interest group in the schools. *Phi Delta Kappan* 66:290–293.

7

Suggestions for Researchers

Angie, a student in one of the author's classes, was upset about the upcoming exam. "I don't think we should be tested on latchkey kids," she bravely announced. "You said that there are no firm facts, so how can we study for the right answer?" Most of the other students in the class agreed. A freshman named Carter noted, "If I was a parent, I would not even try to figure out the latchkey thing. It's too complicated." Charlie, a more critical thinker, joined the discussion: "Yeah; I don't think there really is a problem. If people are doing research on this thing, why don't we know more? Professors just need something to study so they can give tests and get tenure."

The frustration and doubt Angie, Carter, and Charlie expressed is shared by human service and child care workers. Professionals are frequently asked to provide information about the safety of a latchkey home and the adjustment of latchkey kids. There are few answers, however, since researchers are just beginning to study the latchkey problem. In the meantime, parents remain confused. One working parent with a latchkey kid noted, "It's very frustrating. I read books and articles that are supposed to help me raise my latchkey child, but the final sentence always reads, 'We need more research.' I have a hard time believing much of what I read."

Families with latchkey kids are a popular topic for magazines and other mass media, but researchers have given little attention to the latchkey phenomenon, and it is sometimes difficult to distinguish information based on speculation from that based on scientific fact. The lack of research on latchkey children and families also can account for the differences found in school-age child care programs. Indeed most after-school care programs have not included a collaboration between researchers and child care professionals (Galambos & Dixon 1984).

In this chapter we will assume the role of consumer of research as we assess latchkey investigations. We will examine four areas: reasons behind the shortage of latchkey research, the sampling and methodological techniques that characterize latchkey research, suggestions for future latchkey studies, and theoretical guides for latchkey research.

Shortage of Latchkey Research

A number of conceptual papers (Garbarino 1981; Long & Long 1983a; Stroman & Duff 1982), books (Baden et al. 1982; Long & Long 1983b), and popular media articles (Chaback & Fortunato 1983; Iacobucci 1982) detail the experiences of latchkey children and their families. In contrast, few empirical latchkey studies exist. Although some articles have contained the phrase *latchkey children* (Taveggia & Thomas, 1974) the studies reviewed actually dealt with children of working mothers. It is unclear how many children of working mothers are actually in self-care or some other child care arrangement. A number of other problems also have prevented research on latchkey kids.

Defining the Problem

Because the latchkey issue has developed recently, it is a difficult topic to study since any new area of research brings with it the need for a clearly defined problem. It is difficult to determine exactly how the latchkey child should be defined in terms of age, hours at home alone, and type of child care arrangement.

The informal and undefined nature of the latchkey arrangement makes it difficult for researchers to ensure that a random sample of children or families is obtained. Researchers must often follow a lengthy and complex process to identify a latchkey population, making it easier for them to study children within more formalized settings, such as day care, since these populations are more readily accessible (Rodman, Pratto & Nelson 1985) and more easily defined.

Social Stigma

The family is considered a private social institution in our society, and family scholars are aware of the difficulty in convincing family members to talk honestly about their interpersonal relationships. This is especially troublesome for the latchkey issue and other topics that for some still have a negative social stigma.

The implied danger and negative stigma associated with self-care arrangements account for the low profile of latchkey kids (Jones 1980; Long & Long 1983b). Fear of community condemnation, legal arrest for child neglect, and concern over their child's safety are reasons parents may hesitate to discuss their latchkey arrangements. These types of concerns represent a logistical barrier to researchers in studying the extent and nature of the problem.

Sampling and Methodology

Latchkey children do not live in isolation. They are part of a family, school, and community. Researchers are beginning to focus on what might be called the ecological or context issue (Galambos & Dixon 1984; Galambos & Garbarino 1983). "Context issue" refers to the recognition that there is no one type of latchkey child or family and that to understand fully the latchkey phenomenon it is necessary to consider the type of social and physical environments within which subgroups of latchkey children and their families live.

The context issue represents a major advance in latchkey research, especially since policymakers now recognize that there is no one dominant family form (Levitan & Belous 1981) and that the demographic differences characterizing families are related to their unique social experiences and family relationships. For example, black and Hispanic families differ from each other in income (Terry 1983), occupation (Hayghe 1982; Terry 1983), and the age and education of spouses (Hayghe 1983). Whites are more likely to live in married-couple families where unemployment is relatively low and multiple family workers are frequent, while blacks are more likely to live in families maintained by women who are disadvantaged in the labor market (Klein 1983). These factors obviously influence the types of child care arrangements made by families with school-age children, as well as the adjustment of latchkey children and families.

Understanding the characteristics of samples and methodologies used in latchkey studies can shed light on the information we have about children and their families' experiences. In this section, we assess the samples and methodologies employed in child and family latchkey studies. We have included only studies that yield sufficient sample information. Although a study by Gold and Andres (1978b) is often classified as a latchkey investigation, these researchers identified only unsupervised children in their adolescent sample as not supervised by their employed or nonemployed mothers. No discussion was made of whether another adult, such as a father or neighbor, might have assumed child care responsibilities for these children. A study by Stewart (1981) is omitted due to the lack of sampling and methodological detail.

Appendix 7A provides an overview of this research.

Child Studies

Independent Variables. Not surprisingly, researchers have most frequently used the supervisory arrangement for school-age children as the independent variable of interest. A number of problems are associated with the definitions used for this independent variable. The major problem is that researchers have simply compared supervised children with unsupervised children without addressing different types of contexts within which these children live. Instead precise definitions are needed about the nature of the supervisory environment.

Steinberg (1985) found no difference between children who were broadly defined as supervised and unsupervised. But with a more precise definition of "unsupervised," he found that children at home alone were less susceptible to peer pressure than children who play at a friend's house after school.

The most susceptible children to peer pressure were those reporting to "hang out." Vandell and Corasaniti (1985) found that children from two-parent, highly educated, white homes were most likely to return home to mother after school. When this in-home supervisory arrangement was eliminated from analysis a similar proportion of black and white, two-parent and single-parent, and low and high parent education families used latchkey and out-of-home care arrangements. Other possible ecological comparisons to consider in relation to an unsupervised environment include the family's demographic background, the number of hours children are at home alone, the presence of older or younger siblings, and the home structure imposed by absent parents. For example, how does family income relate to the types of parental checks made in absentia? Does one hour home alone have a different impact on children than three hours? How do the parents' childhood experiences relate to their attitudes toward a latchkey arrangement?

Supervised environments also need more precise definition. Do children supervised by a sitter behave differently from those under the charge of parents, siblings, or day care professionals? Long and Long (1982) combined these arrangements into one supervised category. Other researchers have made similar errors of using *adult supervision* or *adult care* as catchall terms to describe children receiving some form of care by a mature individual. Steinberg's (1985) findings indicate that such general definitions of supervised children do not suffice.

Comparisons of different school-age child care situations will allow researchers to develop a better picture of who, when, and in what types of situations unsupervised arrangements are more harmful or beneficial than supervised arrangements. Steinberg (1985) summarizes this best:

> Perhaps the most important conclusion to be taken away from this study is that variations within the latchkey population—variations in the setting in which self-care takes place, variations in the extent to which nonpresent parents maintain distal supervision of these children, and variations in patterns of child rearing—are more important than are variations between adult-care and self-care, broadly defined. (p. 23)

Other independent variables used in latchkey studies also lack precise definition. A number of studies indicated that employed mothers were working full time, but only Woods (1972) compared the satisfaction of mothers' employment with the mother-child relationship and childhood adjustment. Other definitions of mothers' employment could include age, marital status, number of children present in the home, income, number of years employed and number and quality of support systems. Fathers' employment, as with many other family issues, has been neglected by researchers.

Perhaps the use of children's sex and school grade as independent variables comes the closest to addressing the context issue. To date, however, researchers have used different school grades, making comparison among studies difficult. And conflicting findings characterize the importance of children's sex as an independent variable in latchkey research. Woods (1972) and Steinberg (1985) found children's sex to distinguish the adjustment of unsupervised and supervised children. Galambos & Garbarino (1985) found no link between sex and children's supervisory status.

Dependent Variables. Researchers most frequently have used academic achievement, social adjustment, and personality characteristics as dependent variables. Measurement of these global constructs has varied among studies, and comparisons are difficult. Replication studies focusing on well-selected dependent variables are needed to establish the reliability of findings in relation to different dependent measures employed.

Also needed are behavioral dependent measures. Do children in unsupervised environments display poor study or time management skills as a result of fear and anxiety? If so, we would hypothesize poor performance scores on academic achievement tests. Do latchkey kids curtail their exploration and activities in the home setting until their parents arrive home? If so, we would hypothesize poor scores on self-esteem and curiosity tests. Do latchkey kids who follow highly structured routines when at home alone display poor social skills when placed in an unstructured situation with their peers? These types of behavioral measures will complement paper and pencil tests by adding a realistic dimension to the adjustment of unsupervised children.

Sampling. Steinberg (1985) has been the only researcher to employ a random sampling procedure to recruit a large sample. Thus he was able to address the susceptibility of school-age children to peer pressure under three different supervisory arrangements. It should be noted that Steinberg's study was not designed as a latchkey project but was a study on autonomy and family relations during the early adolescent years. Steinberg's sample thus consists of children who for the most part are older than the other samples in appendix 7A.

The remaining latchkey studies employed nonprobability sampling procedures to recruit relatively small samples. One sample (Gold & Andres 1978b) was actually a subsample from a larger study on children of employed and nonemployed mothers. The reason for the problem of samples is the newness of the issue and the negative stigma of the latchkey phenomenon; these factors present a barrier to recruiting large representative samples. Small numbers of nonrandomly drawn subjects reduce the power of statistical analysis and the extent to which findings can be generalized to other groups. We cannot be sure that the results of these small sample studies are truly representative of any other group except those studied. Only the random selection of large samples from well-defined populations can ensure that results are representative of the larger population.

A problem related to sample size is the return rate of questionnaires or the number of parents contacted who actually gave permission for their children's participation in the latchkey studies. Long and Long (1982), Vandell and Corasaniti (1985), and Woods (1972) did not specify how parental and child agreement to take part in their respective studies was obtained. Of the remaining studies, only Trimberger and MacLean (1982) and Steinberg (1985) collected data on more than 70 percent of the children they contacted. In Rodman, Pratto, and Nelson (1985), parental agreement for their children's participation exceeded 70 percent for only one grade level. Fewer than 70 percent of the parents contacted agreed to their child's participation in the studies conducted by Galambos and Garbarino (1983, 1985) and Gold and Andres (1978b).

Gay (1981, p. 164) gives a 70 percent return rate as the minimal level at which valid conclusions can be drawn from data. Studies with return or agreement rates lower than this are biased since the researcher does not know how individuals who did not take part in the study differed from those included. For example, the parents who returned Vandell and Corasaniti's (1985) questionnaire were relatively affluent and well educated. These researchers were not able to address the characteristics of disadvantaged families with lower levels of education. Thus, many of the studies listed in appendix 7A present a qualified picture of latchkey kids, since we do not know the response characteristics of children whose parents did not allow their participation.

We can better understand the difficulty of interpreting studies with small, nonprobability samples by looking at some of the sample characteristics of the studies examined (see appendix 7A). Only Gold and Andres (1978b), Vandell and Corasaniti (1985), and Woods (1972) focused on a small age range, and only Rodman, Pratto, and Nelson (1985) used grade level to match their sample of supervised and unsupervised children. The other researchers drew samples from across more than two grade levels and made no attempt to match or otherwise control for the range of age differences represented in their small samples. Large and well-defined age groups are needed in latchkey studies to establish the adjustment of latchkey kids across the developmental years.

Most researchers believe that family composition is an important mediating variable in the adjustment of latchkey kids, but few have given attention to this variable. Most researchers controlled for family composition. For example, Gold and Andres (1978b) and Trimberger and Maclean (1982) included only children from two-parent families in their studies, and Rodman, Pratto, and Nelson (1985) used family composition as a matching variable in their sample of supervised and unsupervised children. Of those studies employing single- and two-parent homes, only Long and Long (1982) and Vandell and Corasaniti (1985) made comparisons between the two. Woods (1972) and Galambos and Garbarino (1983) failed to specify the exact composition of their families.

Future studies will need to investigate the relationship between family composition and the adjustment of latchkey kids. Some potential research issues related to family composition might include a comparison of single families headed by mothers versus fathers, a comparison of families from different socioeconomic groups, and a comparison of two-parent homes with one versus two or more latchkey kids of different ages and/or sex. Vandell and Corasaniti (1985) found that white latchkey kids from relatively affluent, well-educated, two-parent and single-parent homes did not receive lower social, emotional, or intellectual ratings when compared to children in three other after-school arrangements.

Two of the five samples compared in appendix 7A were drawn from large eastern cities, one from a Canadian suburb, and another from a Canadian city. One sample each was drawn from a southern, midwestern, and southwestern city. Two samples represented an eastern rural area. This diversity of geographic locations has allowed for a general comparison of latchkey kids. Currently, a need exists for national samples that make direct and specific comparisons of children from different geographic locations.

Methodologies. The number and types of research instruments used in data collection are usually defined by the purpose of the study and the resources of the researchers. Generally a range of instruments is useful in serving as a set of checks and balances against such errors as subjects' misunderstanding of test items or unrecognized flaws in measurement instruments. The greater the number of instruments are used, however, the more difficult it becomes to interpret large amounts of data. Many researchers choose to conduct uncomplicated studies that rely on one or two well-selected instruments. Other researchers choose more elaborate studies that require a greater number of assessment devices. Differences in selection of research instruments are evident from the studies compared in appendix 7A, where most researchers used two or more types of measurement.

Of those researchers employing standardized tests, only Rodman, Pratto, and Nelson (1985), Gold and Andres (1978b), Trimberger and MacLean (1982), and Steinberg (1985) addressed the reliability or validity of their instruments. Rodman, Pratto, and Nelson (1985) gave a general statement that their instruments had a record of demonstrated reliability and validity. Gold and Andres (1978b) gave a test-retest reliability coefficient for one of their instruments. Trimberger and MacLean (1982) established the internal validation of each of the five measures included in their questionnaire. Steinberg (1985) addressed the internal consistency of his standardized tests. Galambos and Garbarino (1983, 1985), Vandell and Corasaniti (1985), and Woods (1972) did not give the reliability or validity of their instruments, and Long and Long (1982) to our knowledge have never made their interview schedule available for public scrutiny.

The use of self-report instruments such as rating scales, questionnaires, and interviews adds bias to latchkey studies. Self-report methods are dependent on the objectivity and memory of the individual being studied. Both conscious and unconscious alterations of fact will go unmeasured unless steps are taken to check the accuracy of information. One way to do this is to collect data using multiple measures on the same person for comparison purposes. None of the researchers in our investigation followed this procedure. When multiple measures were taken, each measure focused on a different variable (for example, social adjustment or academic achievement). It is also possible to collect data from multiple sources and thus compare the perceptions of different individuals. Only Woods (1972) collected data from more than one family member to address the same issue (in this case, mother-child relations).

Measurements on multiple family members are needed in latchkey research. Some researchers (McMurray & Kazanjian 1982; Rowland, Robinson & Coleman 1986) have found that parents are ambivalent about their use of a latchkey arrangement. Comparison measurements taken from parents, children, employers, and teachers would yield a more complete understanding of parental ambivalence, as well as the impact of latchkey arrangements on family members both within and outside the home setting. One issue that might require data collection from multiple sources is the family's stress reaction resulting from a latchkey arrangement. A potential source of stress is the employer's attitude toward the parent's work productivity between 3:00 and 5:00 when the parent calls home to check on his or her children. Another source of stress is the teacher's attitude toward a child's tardiness that results from the inability to get to school on time independent of an adult's supervision.

Behavioral dependent measures are also needed in latchkey research. Observational studies will complement the use of paper and pencil tests through depicting actual parent-child relationships, childhood behavior in the home setting, and peer relations. For example, Steinberg (1985) found that children who are raised authoritatively (democratically) are less susceptible to peer pressure when they are left unsupervised after school. Observational recordings will provide a better record than paper and pencil tests of the types of democratic home interactions that take place between these children and their parents.

Results. In general, little consistent evidence exists to suggest that latchkey kids are hurt by or benefit from their self-care experiences. The few differences found among studies must be regarded as tentative due to the limitations of most latchkey studies. Independent variables were narrowly defined, dependent variables were limited to global constructs, behavioral measures were ignored, small and nonrepresentative samples limited generalizations, methodologies were inconsistent and/or limited to self-reports, and no clear theoretical rationales were stated for conducting the studies.

One mediating factor in the adjustment of latchkey children is geographic location. Some studies (Long & Long 1982; Woods 1972) finding a harmful effect for latchkey kids based their conclusions on samples drawn from inner cities. Studies (Galambos & Garbarino 1983, 1985; Gold & Andres 1978b; Rodman, Pratto & Nelson 1985; Vandell and Corasaniti 1985) finding no harmful effect for latchkey kids based their conclusions on samples drawn from small city, suburban, affluent, or rural areas.

The studies by Trimberger and MacLean (1982), Steinberg (1985), and Vandell and Corasaniti (1985) suggest other possible mediating factors in need of study. Trimberger and MacLean's somewhat conflicting findings regarding latchkey kids' perceptions of their mother's employment suggests the need to consider the types of daily activities that mediate children's feelings about being left home alone. Steinberg's study of peer susceptibility suggests the need to consider the specific types of after-school arrangements and parenting styles that mediate school-age children's adjustment in self-care situations. Vandell and Corasaniti's study suggests the need to consider the relationship between the types of activities conducted in different after-school arrangements and the adjustment of children.

Family Studies

Few family latchkey studies exist. Of the studies we examined, two (Long & Long 1982; Woods 1972) are actually continuations of child studies. The study by Coleman and associates (1985) represents a subsample from a larger school-age child care study. The sampling and methodology limitations characterizing child studies hold true for family studies. The following review will thus be brief while pointing out some of these limitations. (Appendix 7A provides an overview of this research.)

Independent Variables. The demographic background, child care arrangement, and employment status of mothers were used most frequently as independent variables in family latchkey studies. Three (Harris 1977; Long & Long 1982; Rowland, Robinson & Coleman 1986) family studies were descriptive and were not concerned with manipulating independent variables.

Dependent Variables. Parental perceptions of child care arrangements, child rearing, and/or employment status were most frequently measured. In addition, Long and Long (1982) addressed parent-child and sibling relationships, and Coleman et al. (1985) studied the differences between families using a latchkey arrangement as opposed to more traditional forms of in-home and out-of-home child care arrangements.

Sampling. Of the five studies listed in appendix 7A, three used nonprobability samples. The two others employed random cluster samples. Random cluster sampling is preferred to nonprobability sampling, although sample clusters are less desirable than simple random sampling from individual members of a population.

Only Coleman et al. (1985) and Rowland, Robinson, and Coleman (1986) recruited large samples. The return rates (78 percent) for both studies were above the acceptable level Gay (1981) reported. The remaining studies recruited relatively small samples. The return rate for the Woods (1972) study was low, and Harris (1977) and Long and Long (1982) did not report their return rates.

The researchers used different family members as study participants. Long and Long (1982) interviewed children about their family relations. Coleman et al. (1985) and Rowland, Robinson, and Coleman (1986) included both mothers and fathers in their studies. Harris (1977) and Woods (1972) included only mothers in their respective studies.

As with the child studies, most family researchers studied children from a range of grade levels, although Harris (1977) did not specify the school grades represented in her study. The family samples also represented a range of geographic locations.

All researchers except Woods (1972) included both single- and two-parent homes, but only Long and Long (1982) made comparisons between the two. Eastern, southern, and western cities were represented, but no rural samples were examined. Similar to child studies, there are no national data on families with latchkey kids.

Methodology. Most of the family researchers used questionnaires or interviews. Only Woods (1972) employed standardized tests. Similar to child studies, no observational methods were used.

Results. The limitations that characterize child research also characterize those of families, although the studies examined suggest that the ecological characteristics of families influence children's and parent's perceptions of a latchkey arrangement. Harris (1977) found that the amount of responsibility given to school-aged children varied according to family size and the parents' age and level of education. Mothers who were younger than 30, had less than a college education, and had three or fewer children were willing to trust a child between the ages of 6 and 9 to go to school on time without assistance. Coleman et al. (1985) suggested that parents turn to a latchkey arrangement for their older children only after their attempts to use more traditional forms of school-age child care fail. These studies lead to the tentative suggestion that certain child and family situations must be present before parents turn to a latchkey arrangement. And even when a latchkey arrangement is adopted, parental ambivalence toward the situation may be characterized by checks and rules that permit them to make the best of an otherwise difficult situation (Rowland, Robinson & Coleman 1986).

Finally, the type of parent-child relationship that results from a latchkey arrangement may relate to family economics and children's perceptions of their mother's employment. Woods (1972) suggests that children from lower socioeconomic families interpret their mother's employment as essential for their family's survival, while children in middle- and upper-class families interpret their mothers' employment as less important to their family's well-being and more as a sign of rejection.

Suggestions for Future Research Studies

Long and Long's (1982) original study of latchkey children in Washington, D.C., first brought attention to latchkey kids. Vandell and Corasaniti (1985) note, however, that Long and Long's study should be accepted with caution: "The procedure for selecting subjects and conducting the interviews was not specified, and no comparable interviews were reported for children who returned home to mother or were in some other form of after school care" (p. 20). The studies we have examined are also original in that they represent the first wave of research to address the latchkey issues Long and Long (1982) ignored.

The sampling and methodological flaws of latchkey studies have gone largely overlooked, in part due to a need for creating a data base. Sampling and methodological specificity will become increasingly important as more researchers begin to study latchkey kids. The purpose of the previous critique was to assess the current status of latchkey research, pointing out some of the sampling and methodological shortcomings that will need to be addressed in future research studies. There are a number of suggestions to be made.

More Research

More empirical research must be conducted. Some of the most frequently cited latchkey studies have dealt with self-care only as a small part of a larger study. The scarcity of empirical studies severely limits the conclusions that can be made about the adjustment of latchkey kids and their families. Clearly researchers must begin to make the latchkey child and family the focal part of their investigations.

Conceptual versus Empirical Work

The lack of empirical research leads to a related suggestion: researchers must also serve as consumer advocates by pointing out when their statements are based on conceptual accounts of the latchkey experience versus research data. This is especially important since a number of conceptual and popular articles have made speculative and contradictory generalizations. For example, Garbarino (1984) has summarized four types of risks he considers to be associated with latchkey kids: they feel badly (rejected and alienated); they act badly (they may be delinquent); they develop badly (for example, they may fail academically); and they are treated badly (they may be victims of accidents or sexual abuse). The implication is that families with latchkey children are in a state of stress. But some empirical studies have not found a link between negative consequences and certain latchkey contexts (specifically safe rural and suburban areas). To prevent confusion, researchers need to make clear the conceptual versus empirical basis of their comments.

Longitudinal Studies

Longitudinal studies are needed to follow latchkey children over time to assess the positive and negative aspects of their development and family relations. For example, the age at which children take care of themselves may be a factor in their adjustment. The adjustment pattern exhibited by latchkey kids of different ages and sexes should be examined in conjunction with related family variables (such as age of parents and siblings and single- versus two-parent homes) that may serve to mitigate negative latchkey experiences. Other longitudinal studies are needed to address the adjustment of latchkey kids who begin attending school-age child care centers, as well as children who are removed from a child-care program and become latchkey kids.

Data Collection

Interviews, questionnaires, rating scales, and standardized tests have served as the basis for data collection on the latchkey issue. All of these techniques are useful, but they also have the potential for bias. Parents may give responses that they think will please the interviewer or that will make them look good. Questionnaire and standardized test items can be misunderstood and supply a limited amount of data since only the information asked for is given.

A multimethod approach to data collection in which observational techniques are used in conjunction with the traditional self-report and interview techniques will yield more sophisticated data and lead to a better understanding of the family dynamics characterizing latchkey arrangements. Videotapes of latchkey kids at home will provide information about their behaviors and the areas of the home that represent comfort or danger to them. Videotapes of parents at home with their child will provide information about the effect of a latchkey arrangement on parent-child relations. Videotapes of spouses will provide information about the marital resources and stresses accompanying a latchkey arrangement.

National Samples

Popular parenting magazines have conducted national polls on the latchkey issue. The data collected, however, are biased since only parents who read the magazines were surveyed. A national study of latchkey kids is clearly needed. Samples drawn from different areas of the United States and Canada allow for only a general inference about the impact of latchkey arrangements. National samples help researchers identify and understand the complexity of demographic variables that have a negative or positive impact on different subgroups of latchkey kids and their families.

We are unaware of any researcher who is conducting, or planning to conduct, a national latchkey study. One issue currently in need of attention through a national sample is the reaction of the public toward public-subsidized or other school-age child care programs. These data would help state and community human service workers plan for programs that would be responsive to the needs of their constituents. Other national studies are needed to develop a description of the characteristics of families with latchkey kids, their needs and resources. Still other national studies need to address school-age child care program elements, including curricula, personnel qualifications, facilities, and parent education programs.

Sample Size

Conclusions drawn about latchkey kids and families are now based on small, isolated samples. To make general statements about latchkey children and families, larger samples randomly drawn from well-defined populations must be recruited. Potential sources for large samples include business and industry, church membership rosters, school systems, and state cooperative extension programs. These agencies have direct contact with almost all children and families.

Defining "Latchkey"

Researchers have not reached a consensual agreement on what defines the latchkey child or latchkey arrangement. In the studies we examined, researchers used a range of ages and grades to define their samples. The lack of specificity in defining the age parameters of latchkey youngsters in part explains why it is difficult to arrive at an agreement on the number of latchkey kids in the United States. The U.S. Department of Commerce (1976) has used the age range 7–13 to estimate that 1.6 million children are without adult supervision before and after school. In contrast, the U.S. Department of Labor (1982) used the age range of 13 and under to arrive at an estimate of 13 million latchkey kids.

Still another problem in defining the latchkey phenomenon is the self-care arrangement. Is the 5-year-old who is left in the care of a 9-year-old sibling a latchkey kid? Must a child spend a certain amount of time home alone each day to be classified as latchkey? Does a latchkey arrangement apply if parents call home once an hour or install a burglar alarm? How do latchkey kids who hang out around a shopping mall differ from those who go home immediately after school and stay there until there parents get home? How are 5-year-old latchkey kids different from 14-year-old latchkey kids?

Researchers have frequently provided their own definition of latchkey arrangements by asking parents, "Is your child in self-care?" In the future, they will need to be more specific in their definitions to prevent subjects from misunderstanding or misrepresenting the extent to which a child is left alone. For example, some parents give qualified and misleading accounts of their child care arrangements. They report that their child is cared for by an older brother or sister when in many cases this older brother or sister is only a year or two older than his or her sibling (Long & Long 1983a; McMurray & Kazanjian 1982). Other parents report that they themselves care for their children when school is not in session, although an increasing number of parents in both single- and two-parent families are working full time (Seligson et al. 1983). Some of the issues that researchers will need to address in order to define latchkey kids include the number of hours that children are totally responsible for their own care, the types of contact children have with neighbors or parents, and the number of days per week children are in a self-care arrangement.

It is possible that research on the different perceptions and definitions given to latchkey arrangements will itself result in the identification of variables mediating the adjustment of latchkey children and families. For example, Trimberger and MacLean (1982) found that children between the ages of 9 and 12 who were unsupervised after school while their mothers worked perceived their mothers to be more interested in them than children who were supervised. In contrast, unsupervised children had more negative attitudes toward their mother's employment than supervised children, although unsupervised children did not feel more negatively affected by their mother's employment than supervised children. These researchers noted that demographic, psychological, and social variables may influence the child's perception of having a working mother. Similarly these variables can also influence the perceptions and behaviors of latchkey kids and their parents. Systems-based studies on the psychological makeup of latchkey children, their siblings, and their parents will provide a better picture of the expectations and feelings that lead to a beneficial versus stressful self-care arrangement.

Family Context

Few research studies have adopted a true ecological perspective of the latchkey phenomenon. Steinberg (1985) found significant differences in children's susceptibility to peer pressure as a function of parenting styles and the degree of adult supervision provided after school. Vandell and Corasaniti (1985) found certain demographic variables to characterize children who returned home to mother after school. When in-home care by mother was eliminated, demographic variables did not influence the types of after-school arrangements families selected. Woods (1972) found that mothers' attitudes toward their employment were related to the adjustment of their daughters. The presence and characteristics of siblings (their ages and sex), family composition (blended, single-parent, or two-parent homes), birth order of children, social demographic characteristics (socioeconomic status, geographic location, and race), family power dynamics, communication styles, and sex-role endorsements are independent variables that will help identify the ecological contexts that distinguish subgroups of latchkey children and families.

Defining Latchkey Studies

Researchers need to define their studies as basic or applied. Clearly evaluative studies are needed to assess existing school-age child care programs. Publication of evaluative research will give direction to other communities interested in establishing their own programs. Staff can use findings to improve programming content, form new partnerships, and redesign their budgets to provide more cost-effective services. Also needed are studies that address the impact of latchkey kids on the community. Teenage pregnancy, delinquency, runaways, emergency hospital admissions, and school dropouts are some problems that might be related to the latchkey phenomenon.

The majority of research published to date can be described as basic research. Many applied researchers, however, use basic research to develop their service-focused projects. Theoretical rationales guide researchers in framing their questions, developing a research design, and formulating conclusions and recommendations. Surprisingly, few researchers have stated the theoretical rationale behind their studies.

Theoretical Guides for Latchkey Research

Latchkey researchers have avoided the use of child and family theories, preferring to use the newness of the issue as justification for their studies. The following theories represent some rationales for guiding latchkey research studies.

Child Development Theories

Child development theories explain or predict the course of growth and development. Two of the most widely used theories in applied and basic childhood research are those by Jean Piaget and Erik Erikson.

Piaget. Piaget's theory describes cognitive growth from birth through adulthood. Briefly, children are active learners who need direct hands-on experiences with their world in order to take in or assimilate new information. When new, more complicated circumstances arise, children as well as adults adapt their learning styles to take in or accommodate still more sophisticated information. Educators use Piaget's theory to design enriching and challenging school curricula.

Piaget's theory suggests some interesting lines of research to expand our understanding of latchkey kids. Does the implied freedom of a latchkey arrangement allow children to expand their formal classroom instruction, or do latchkey kids lack the structure and safety factors necessary to initiate and appreciate self-discoveries when at home alone? Is there a certain stage of cognitive development that must be reached before meaningful self-discovery by children in self-care can take place? Long and Long (1982) found that their all-black sample of latchkey kids in first through sixth grades was better informed about self-care and emergencies than were supervised children, but none of the children in the supervised group reported the high fear levels exhibited by latchkey kids.

Other mediating variables that might relate to the cognitive gains and losses of a latchkey arrangement include the structure of the home situation (safety, enrichment materials), the presence of siblings, the amount of time home alone, the parent-child relationship, and the sex of the child. For example, children at home alone with siblings may serve as cognitive stimulators for each other through their communications, sharing, and even arguments. A certain amount of time alone may serve to increase some children's sense of self-discovery. Still another variable that might influence a latchkey child's cognitive development is his or her social-emotional development.

Erikson. Erikson's theory of psychosocial development addresses the social-emotional aspects of the individual from birth through old age. We each pass through a series of stages during which we must resolve certain social-emotional events. The manner in which we handle these events influences our developing personality. Ideally we move smoothly from one stage to the next. When we are unable to cope with a social-emotional event, our personality is adversely affected. Erikson's theory, like Piaget's, can be described as a systems theory that recognizes the interrelationship between children's natural growth and the environmental forces that influence their development.

Most school-age children are in the psychosocial stage labeled "industry versus inferiority." Children at this stage need positive and constructive feedback about their work and behavior. Condemnation and labeling can lead to feelings of inferiority that carry over into adolescence and adulthood. Children in their preadolescent and adolescent years are in the stage labeled "identity versus role confusion." During this stage adolescents begin to formulate their self-identities, values, and roles they will carry with them into their adult years.

Erikson's theory also allows for the formulation of a number of developmental research studies. Do latchkey kids feel a sense of inferiority due to the lack of adult attention during nonschool hours, or does the implied trust that accompanies a self-care situation lead to feelings of industry? A potential problem that may arise in some homes is the confusing message that the latch-key kid is responsible enough to be left in self-care before and after school but that this responsibility (and implied trust) ends when the parents arrive home. Do preadolescents moving into the identity versus role confusion stage view their latchkey status as an indicator of adult-like responsibility or immaturity? The manner in which parents structure home rules will in part affect preadolescents' identity as a responsible individual. When parents insist on fre-quent check-ins, daily lectures, reminders, and few freedoms outside the home, the preadolescent may adopt poor self-esteem and/or immature identity.

Family Theories

Family theories are concerned with interpersonal relations, family dynamics, and growth within the family system. Structure-functionalism and social ex-change theories are widely used in applied and basic family research.

Structure-Functionalism. The structure-functional theorist is concerned with the interrelationships between social systems and subsystems. The family is portrayed as a network of subsystems (child-parent, husband-wife, brother-sister) that operates as a single system, the family. The family system in turn is interrelated with other social systems (business, religion, school, government). A primary goal of structure-functionalism is to explain the function or role that any structure or subsystem plays in maintaining the stability of the entire system.

What impact do latchkey arrangements have on the stability of the family system? How do different family systems adjust their roles to maintain a stable family life when latchkey kids are present? Do families with latchkey kids make a better adjustment when parents assume traditional sex roles or when they assume egalitarian roles? Do families curtail their involvement in community affairs due to the logistics involved in maintaining a latchkey arrangement, or does a latchkey arrangement allow families to become more involved in com-munity affairs? Do parents benefit more than children from a latchkey arrange-ment, or vice-versa?

Research studies addressing these questions can help human service pro-viders structure support programs that will contribute to the resources and stability of families. A study that finds transportation to be essential for families' utilization of school-age child care programs will have served the needs of the family system by contributing to quality programming. Studies of the stresses of families with latchkey kids will help professionals design parent programs that will allow parents to learn new home management skills, as well as develop new friendships through attending programs.

Social Exchange. A basic principle followed by social exchange theorists is that relationships operate through an exchange of rewards. That is, two or more individuals are continually involved in a process of distributive justice or fair exchange (Eshleman 1981, p. 59) of something that is perceived equivalent to what is given. Children overtly attempt to bargain or exchange their good behavior for special privileges. Spouses overtly and covertly negotiate household chores, family responsibilities, and the budgeting of the family income.

Some would argue that latchkey kids exchange the freedom of childhood for the responsibility of adulthood. The central question in this debate is whether latchkey kids have the developmental capabilities to assume the responsibility of self-care. It would appear that the answer depends on the environmental context within which self-care takes place. Other research questions also would lend themselves to a social exchange rationale. For example, how do latchkey kids use their self-care status as a bargaining chip with their parents? Especially important are the potential sources of family stress that arise when the latchkey kid uses the self-care situation as justification for poor school performance or demands more equality in family decision making. Parents may indeed find it difficult to deny a preadolescent certain social weekend privileges when the child argues that his or her social life is damaged during the weekdays as a result of house rules accompanying a latchkey arrangement.

Ecological Perspective

Bronfenbrenner's (1979) ecological approach to child and family development represents what Garbarino (1982, p. 13) has called the "fourth force" of the social sciences. Interaction between the individual and environment is the major concept underlying the ecological approach. The ecological approach takes a comprehensive view of the whole child interacting with, not just responding to, the surrounding environment. Indeed, children are seen as the bridge between the past and future of a changing society (Garbarino 1982, p. 16) (figure 7–1).

The context issue represents an ecological approach to latchkey research, and the theoretical rationale behind the content and suggestions of this chapter can be described as ecological. Given this perspective, researchers must look beyond isolated samples and independent variables. Multivariate designs with large samples are needed that will address the complexity of environmental, child, and family variables associated with different subtypes of latchkey kids and with different latchkey experiences. Bronfenbrenner's (1979) scheme of social systems can serve as a theoretical rationale for this approach. The quality of life experienced by children is determined by their sociological and physical ecologies. Sometimes children are directly affected by their surrounding ecology (e.g., microsystems and mesosystems). At other times children are indirectly affected by their ecology (e.g., exosystems and macrosystems). In what ways can school-age child care programs improve the ecology and quality of life for children from different backgrounds?

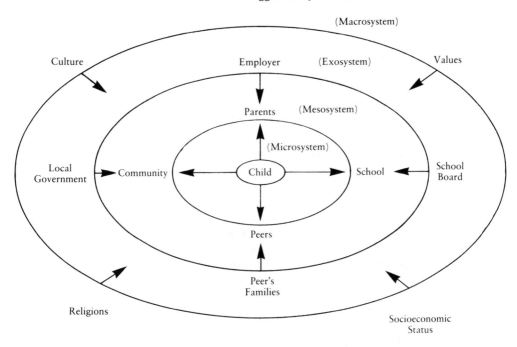

Figure 7–1. An Ecological Approach to the Study of Latchkey Kids

Microsystems. Microsystems are social systems in which the individual is directly involved on a daily basis. The family is the basic microsystem for children. Other childhood microsystems are the school, peer group, and school-age child care program.

Comparisons of the number, types, and quality of microsystems characterizing latchkey versus supervised children will lead to a better understanding of the extent to which a child's social ecology is constricted by a self-care situation. Comparison of latchkey and supervised children's behavior within specified microsystems will contribute to an understanding of the latchkey child's social-emotional development. For example, in a sociometric study of peer groups, will a different network of social relations appear for latchkey versus supervised children? If so, what environmental, child, and family variables might account for the observed differences?

Mesosystems. Mesosystems refer to the relationships among microsystems. The goodness of fit between a family's informal and formal support systems is a family's mesosystem.

An important evaluative contribution researchers can make is to study the strengths and weaknesses of family mesosystems in relation to school-age child care programs. Do these programs contribute to the stability of some families more than others? Are certain programs better able to serve as a conduit through which families are linked to other educational, human service, or informal community support groups? What roles should program staff assume in strengthening the mesosystems of families?

Exosystems. Exosystems are systems that affect the child or family's life but in which the child or family has no direct participation. Administrators of school-age child care programs, local governments, and school boards are examples of exosystems that establish policies affecting the lives of children and families.

There is a need to study the alternatives that might lead to better school-age child care. For example, the parent's workplace in part creates a latchkey situation when work schedules are inflexible. Research into the use of flex-time, job sharing, and employer-sponsored after-school centers may lead to dramatic improvements in the well-being of children, as well as an improvement in work productivity and parental satisfaction. To date, however, these conclusions are not documented.

Macrosystems. Macrosystems refer to cultural and subcultural values. They form the basis on which individuals and families structure their lives. In most instances, families living in middle-class neighborhoods have a different set of ideologies (a different subcultural macrosystem) from families living in a ghetto. Yet certain values are shared by all families.

Many would argue that the latchkey phenomenon reflects an American social value in which family income and pride in one's work is more important than the protection of childhood. But the reality of the latchkey phenomenon is not that simple. Research is needed to investigate the types of parental values and decisions that go into the adoption of a self-care arrangement. At a more abstract level, the social view of childhood is in need of study to determine the extent to which society has adopted the hurried child concept (Elkind 1981). Still another abstract issue in need of study is the values that define the quality and length of childhood. Perhaps more than any other, this issue is most basic to understanding the social implications of the latchkey phenomenon.

References

Baden, R.K.; Genser, A.; Levine, J.A.; & Seligson, M. 1982. *School-age child care: An action manual.* Boston: Auburn.

Bronfenbrenner, U. 1979. *The ecology of human development: Experiences by nature and design.* Cambridge: Harvard University Press.

Chaback, E., & Fortunato, P. 1983 (February). A kid's survival checklist: When you're home alone. *Parents Magazine,* pp. 134–136.

Coleman, M.; Robinson, B.E.; Rowland, B.H.; & Price, S. 1985. Family variables as predictors of three child care arrangements. Unpublished manuscript.

Elkind, D. 1981. *The hurried child*. Reading, Mass.: Addison-Wesley.

Eshleman, J.R. 1981. *The family: An introduction*. 3d ed. Boston: Allyn and Bacon.

Galambos, N.L., & Dixon, R.A. 1984. Toward understanding and caring for latchkey children. *Child Care Quarterly* 13:116–125.

Galambos, N., & Garbarino, J. 1983. Identifying the missing links in the study of latchkey children. *Children Today* 12:2–4.

Galambos, N., & Garbarino, J. 1985. Adjustment of unsupervised children in a rural ecology. *Journal of Genetic Psychology* 146:227–231.

Garbarino, J. 1981. Latchkey children: How much a problem? *Education Digest* 46:14–16.

Garbarino, J. 1982. *Children and families in the social environment*. New York: Aldine.

Garbarino, J. 1984. Can American families afford the luxury of childhood? Unpublished manuscript. University Park: Pennsylvania State University, Department of Individual and Family Studies.

Gay, L.R. 1981 *Educational research: Competencies for analysis and application*. 2d ed. Columbus, Ohio: Charles E. Merrill.

Gold, D., & Andres, D. 1978a. Comparisons of adolescent children with employed and nonemployed mothers. *Merrill-Palmer Quarterly* 24:243–254.

Gold, D., & Andres, D. 1978b. Developmental comparisons between ten-year-old children with employed and nonemployed mothers. *Child Development* 49:75–84.

Harris, O.C. 1977. Day care: Have we forgotten the school-age child? *Child Welfare* 56:440–448.

Hayghe, H. 1982. Weekly family earnings: A quarterly perspective. *Monthly Labor Review* 105:46–49.

Hayghe, H. 1983. Married couples: Work and income patterns. *Monthly Labor Review* 106:26–29.

Iacobucci, K. 1982 (May). After-school alternatives for latchkey kids. *McCalls*, p. 36.

Jones, L.R. 1980. Child care: Who knows? Who cares? *Journal of the Institute for Socioeconomic Studies* 5:55–62.

Klein, D.P. 1983. Trends in employment and unemployment in families. *Monthly Labor Review* 106:21–25.

Levitan, S.A., & Belous, R.S. 1981. Working wives and mothers: What happens to family life? *Monthly Labor Review* 104:26–30.

Long, T., & Long, L. 1982. *Latchkey children: The child's view of self care*. Washington, D.C.: Catholic University. ERIC Document Reproduction Service, ED 211 229.

Long, L., & Long, T. 1983a. *Latchkey children*. Washington, D.C.: Catholic University. ERIC Document Reproduction Service, ED 226 836.

Long, L., & Long, T. 1983b. *The handbook for latchkey children and their parents*. New York: Arbor House.

McMurray, G.L., & Kazanjian, D.P. 1982. *Day care and the working poor: The struggle for self-sufficiency*. New York: Community Service Society of New York.

Rodman, H.; Pratto, D.J.; & Nelson, R.S. 1985. Child care arrangements and children's functioning: A comparison of self-care and adult-care children. *Developmental Psychology* 21:413–418.

Rowland, B.H.; Robinson, B.E.; & Coleman, M. 1986. Parents' perceptions of needs for their latchkey children: A survey. *Pediatric Nursing* 12.

Seligson, M.; Genser, A.; Gannett, E.; & Gray, W. 1983 (December). *School-age child care: A policy report.* Wellesley, Mass.: School-Age Child Care Project, Wellesley College Center for Research on Women.

Steinberg, L. 1985. Latchkey children and susceptibility to peer pressure: An ecological analysis. Unpublished manuscript. Madison: University of Wisconsin-Madison, College of Home Economics.

Stewart, M. 1981. *Children in self-care: An exploratory study.* Greensboro, N.C.: University of North Carolina. ERIC Document Reproduction Service, ED 224 604.

Stroman, S.H., & Duff, R.E. 1982. The latchkey child: Whose responsibility? *Childhood Education* 59:76–79.

Taveggia, T.C., & Thomas, E.M. 1974. Latchkey children. *Pacific Sociological Review* 17:27–34.

Terry, S.L. 1983. Work experience, earnings, and family income in 1981. *Monthly Labor Review* 106:13–20.

Trimberger, R., & MacLean, M.J. 1982. Maternal employment: The child's perspective. *Journal of Marriage and the Family* 44:469–475.

U.S. Department of Commerce. Bureau of the Census. 1976. *Daytime care of children: October 1974 and February 1975.* Current Population Reports Series P-20, no. 298. Washington, D.C.: U.S. Government Printing Office.

U.S. Department of Labor. Women's Bureau. 1982. *Employers and child care: Establishing services through the workplace.* Pamphlet 23. Washington, D.C.: U.S. Government Printing Office.

Vandell, D.L., & Corasaniti, M.A. 1985 (May). After school care: Choices and outcomes for third graders. Paper presented at the meeting of the American Association for the Advancement of Science, Los Angeles.

Woods, M.B. 1972. The unsupervised child of the working mother. *Developmental Psychology* 6:14–25.

Appendix 7A

Table 7–1

Attributes of Studies of Latchkey Kids

Studies	Independent Variables	Dependent Variables	Sampling Procedure	Number in Sample	Return/ Agreeme Rate (%
Galambos & Garbarino 1985	Supervisory status Mother's employment status School grade Child's sex	Academic achievement School adjustment Orientation Fear level	Nonprobability	77	33
Galambos & Garbarino 1983	Supervisory status Mother's employment status School grade Child's sex	Academic achievement School adjustment Orientation	Nonprobability	77	33
Gold & Andres 1978b	Supervisory status	Academic achievement Social adjustment Sex role Personality	Nonprobability	50 (subsample)	58 (total sam
Long & Long 1982	Supervisory status	Fears Home relations	Nonprobability	85	
Rodman, Pratto & Nelson 1985	Supervisory status School grade Child's sex	Self-esteem Social adjustment Locus of control	Nonprobability	96	72 (grade 66 (grade
Trimberger & Maclean 1982	Supervisory status Child's sex Mother's employment (years) Child's position in family Time home alone	Child's feelings about mother's employment	Nonprobability	51	100
Steinberg 1985	Supervisory status School grade Socioeconomic status Mother's employment	Susceptibility to peer pressure Self-reliance Identity Decision making	Random cluster	865	94
Vandell & Corasaniti 1985	Supervisory status Family demographics	Peer relations Academic skills Family relations Self-confidence	Nonprobability	349	
Woods 1972	Supervisory status	Academic achievement Social adjustment Personality Records of accidents, illnesses, and delinquency	Nonprobability	108	

Age or Grade	Family Composition	Geographic Location	Method	Selected Results
Grades 5 & 7	Single- and two-parent homes	Rural eastern	Standardized tests	Unsupervised children did not differ significantly from supervised children
Grades 5 & 7		Rural eastern	Standardized tests	Unsupervised children did not differ significantly from supervised children
9 & 10 years	Two-parent homes	Canadian city suburbs	Standardized tests	Unsupervised boys did not differ significantly from supervised boys except on one sex role subscale (unspecified)
Grades 1–6	Single- and two-parent homes	Eastern city	Interview	Unsupervised children experienced more fear and less flexible home routines
Grades 4 & 7	Single & two-parent homes; grandparent's home	Southern city and suburbs	Standardized tests; teacher ratings	Unsupervised children did not differ significantly from supervised children
9–12 years	Two-parent homes	Canadian city	Standardized tests	Unsupervised children perceived their mother to be more interested in them but had more negative attitudes toward their mothers' employment
				Unsupervised children did not feel significantly more negatively affected by their mother's employment
Grades 5–9	Single- & two-parent homes	Midwestern city suburbs	Standardized tests	Generally unsupervised children did not differ significantly from supervised children
				Specifically children most removed from adult supervision were most susceptible to peer pressure
				Specifically children of authoritative parents were less susceptible to peer pressure
Grade 3	Single- & two-parent homes	Southwestern city suburbs	Sociometric ratings; teacher, parent, and self ratings	Unsupervised children from two-parent and single-parent homes did not receive lower peer, teacher, or parent ratings
Grade 5		Eastern city	Standardized tests; teacher ratings; records	Unsupervised girls had lower academic achievement and social adjustment than supervised girls

Table 7–2
Attributes of Studies of Latchkey Families

Studies	Independent Variables	Dependent Variables	Sampling Procedure	Number in Sample	
Coleman et al. 1985	Child and family variables; Child care variables	Latchkey, in-home, and out-of-home groups	Random cluster	492 parents (subsample)	
Harris 1977	Working mothers from various backgrounds	Attitudes toward child care and child rearing	Nonprobability	66 mothers	
Long & Long 1982	Supervisory status	Parent-child and sibling relations	Nonprobability	85 children	
Rowland, Robinson & Coleman 1986	Parents from various backgrounds using different child care arrangements	Parent's perceptions of school-age child care needs and barriers	Random cluster	1,806 parents	
Woods 1972	Supervisory status	Child care, work experiences, and attitudes	Nonprobability	38 employed mothers	

Age or Grade	Family Composition	Geographic Location	Method	Selected Results
Grades K–9	Single and two-parent homes	Southern city	Questionnaire	Parents were more satisfied than dissatisfied with their respective latchkey, in-home, and out-of home child care arrangement
				Age of children and their time home alone increased across out-of-home, in-home, and latchkey arrangements
	Single- and two-parent homes	Western city	Interview	Mothers were more interested in after-school than before-school child care
				Mothers younger than 30, with less than a college education, and with three or fewer children were willing to trust a child between ages 6 and 9 to go to school on time without supervision
Grades 1–6	Single- and two-parent homes	Eastern city	Interview	latchkey children were closer to the supervisory sibling than parents
				The better the parent-relationship, the less fear was experienced
Grades K–9	Single- and two-parent homes	Southern city	Questionnaire	Cost, transportation, and child's refusal of existing services were most frequent barriers to locating school-age child care
				Parental ambivalence was greatest among parents of children in grades 4–6, who were most frequently left alone
				Parental ambivalence was accompanied by concern and attempts to structure home environments
Grade 5	Single- and two-parent homes	Eastern city	Interviews; standardized tests	Children of full-time employed mothers had the best social adjustment and intelligence scores
				Mothers with the best attitudes toward their work had children with the best social adjustment

8
Public Policy, Advocacy, and Latchkey Kids

At first, the group seemed to be in disagreement. Several people were talking at once. A distinguished-looking woman leafed through a stack of papers and glanced hurriedly around the room. There was an air of excitement and anticipation.

"Looks as if we are all here," she said. "Time to get down to work."

And with that, the first School-Age Child Care Project Oversight Committee meeting began. The group was composed mainly of professionals serving as volunteers who had taken time out from their busy schedules to meet with consultants developing a community-wide before- and after-school program. The project was the outgrowth of several studies conducted by a children's advocacy group and was being designed to respond to child care needs of approximately 6,000 elementary school children.

It was the beginning of the first phase of what was to be a three-year pilot project where options of school-age child care for children of working parents were to be explored. There would be other meetings where decisions would be made in regard to the best action for children in this large metropolitan community. Advocates would work closely with consultants on behalf of the children and youths they had chosen to support.

Child advocacy has been a long, tedious process. In the past, children, perceived as property, were unrepresented outside their families because they had no rights in their communities. The nature of children often has been misunderstood, and efforts to curb their behaviors have at times been cruel and inhumane. Becoming better informed about children's needs through history has increased the many options available to children and their parents. Communities have learned to work together for the improvement of all their citizens, young and old. From bizarre acts of infanticide to sophisticated measures of social research, the quality of children's lives has advanced.

Children and Their Treatment through Time

Demetrius and Melina had looked forward to the birth of their child. They had wished for a son, and the gods had been good to them. Their young son had been born

Case material in this chapter is based on children Dr. Rowland met during visits to Greece, Africa, Morocco, Denmark, and China.

without a problem. Melina had not suffered pain in childbirth, and her mother had helped in the first few weeks after birth. But something was terribly wrong. The infant was fretful. He cried without stopping and seemed to be failing. He would spit up his milk, and his face was taut with pain. The elders had asked to see the child to view his condition. They would decide if he should be reared or suffer the fate of the Apothetal. They would decide if the infant should be brought up or put to death.

Historically children have come a long way from medieval times when infanticide was a common practice. Children who were physically handicapped, frail and small, the wrong sex, or for some other reason labeled unwanted by the community were killed. Throughout the centuries, children have been abandoned, exploited, and oppressed. They have been forced into servitude roles, deemed impulsive and evil, and at times placed in public institutions until they were old enough to make a contribution to their families. For centuries they were viewed as miniature adults and basically lived through two stages of development: infancy (from birth until 4 or 5 years of age) and adulthood (when they were able to work and become productive) (DeMause, 1974).

*Children in the United States at the Beginning
of the Industrial Revolution*

Addie's face was hot, and her mouth was dry. She could see the creek at the back of the mill, and she was yearning to take off her shoes and wade in the cool water. No one would notice if she slipped outside for a few minutes. Addie looked around and moved cautiously toward the door. She jumped down and sank into the cool, wet sand. Off came her shoes, and she splashed into the creek with delight. "Addie, Addie," Uncle Will called. "You get back in here this minute!" Addie turned and saw Uncle Will at the door, scowling. She knew he was angry. She was not allowed to go to the creek alone. And, more important, she had left her job, picking up waste from the mill floor, without permission. The year was 1882, and Addie was 7 years old. (Haynes 1986)

During the early nineteenth century, life in the United States was unpleasant and unpromising for some children. They were left homeless when parents were convicted of criminal charges or declared insane. Being poor was just cause for sending adults away from a thriving community and leaving children in the hands of strangers. Children as young as 4 years of age without protective parents were used as laborers. They were leased to textile mills and worked sixteen to eighteen hours a day. Older children of 6 or 7 worked on looms and in spinning rooms. They received harsh treatment when they fell asleep on the job or left their appointed place (Westman 1979). Even when loved, they were perceived as little adults and were expected to supplement family incomes.

Efforts to Improve the Lives of Children

Efforts to improve children's lives have come and gone. Reform movements and special interest groups have sprung up in response to concerns and problems. In 1875, the New York Society for the Prevention of Cruelty to Children was formed to "rescue children from bad situations" (Westman 1979, p. 33).

In the 1880s G. Stanley Hall led a child study movement that "revolutionized ideas about childhood" (Westman 1979, p. 33). He believed that children grow and develop in predictable, sequential stages. In 1923 Lawrence Frank advocated a systematic and intensive study of child development. He was interested in the whole child, the influence of the community and its agencies on the child, and the role of parents.

The federal government began to study the needs of children and held the first White House Conference on Children in 1909, which focused on the care of dependent children. Each ten years since, conferences have provided an arena for experts and parents to analyze and evaluate the social, emotional, and educational measures that benefit children. Some conference outcomes have been preventive; others have been descriptive. Some have worked; others have not. But most have been unrealistic in terms of interventions and outcomes.

The mid-century White House Conference (1950), for example, was concerned with the development of a healthy personality with basic foundations stemming from interactions in early childhood. In 1960 teenage marriages and lack of training for parenthood were emphasized. Concern also was expressed over free public education for kindergarten children. At the 1970 White House Conference, participants were divided into two groups: one addressing young children's needs and the other older youth. The 1980 conference moved to the state and local levels and searched for ways for private and public sectors to work together for children and youth. Problems began to take on a more community-wide orientation, and advocacy groups began to emerge.

State of the Child Today

Today children are found in mixed circumstances. We have a better understanding of children's growth and developmental needs. Special resources and agencies operate with the blessings of both private and public sectors. Public policy has begun to focus on helping children and their families by improving their quality of life and ensuring proper nutrition, housing, education, and care. Leagues and advocacy groups work to sensitize individuals and groups to unmet needs. Roundtable discussions are held with business and community leaders to apprise them of the impact of federal cuts in health and welfare aid to children.

In the past these groups dealt mainly with crisis situations and reacted with what Rhodes (1972) described as "recoil" solutions. Energies directed toward remedial intervention have achieved only temporary results and have not prevented reoccurrence. For example, children had to be developmentally delayed or suffer severe physical or emotional problems before they gained the public's attention.

Long-range planning was viewed as too expensive and unpalatable for society's short-range orientation. Political leaders have been slow to develop public policy that views children's needs as a priority. Prevention has been beyond reach. "As a result, services that support and strengthen families are underdeveloped or nonexistent" (Westman 1979, p. 39). Lack of continuity and fragmentation of available services have resulted in some misdirection of funds and in many instances a sense of turf building. Agencies sometimes battle one another for funding and do not cooperate to serve children's needs more efficiently.

Emphasis on Prevention

Today advocates are reevaluating their approaches. The current climate and the societal trends have created a need for a new form of advocacy, one that will affect the legislative process, alert the community to gaps in services, promote institutional change, and revitalize childhood. Sentiment is growing for preventing problems before children become teenagers and adults. An increase in school-age child care projects across the country reflects an awareness of the importance of providing safe and stimulating experiences for children during the out-of-school hours. Reports of long-term effects of self-care and the development of a variety of options for children and youth are evidence of this new emphasis.

Redirection of programs and services is needed to ensure and protect the rights of children and to remind the community of its responsibilities to their growth. In the recent past, services for children often have been carried out to serve the interests and needs of adults. For example, some industry has developed day care without taking children's needs into account. Parents leave their children with untrained workers or alone at home while they work. Many adults are preoccupied with new careers and preserving their own youth. Some people constantly face unemployment and family breakdown. Loss of government funds threatens health and nutritional programs for children. When funds are tightened and programs cut, children carry more than their share of the burden (Children's Defense Fund 1985).

Cultural Context of Children

American children have few functions and make minor, if any, contributions to their family's welfare. They can easily be swept aside or ignored. The result is that society has dehumanized children. Unrealistic expectations and pressures to accelerate their natural development are outgrowths of this attitude. Children are put on display and shown off in superficial ways. A recent beauty contest produced a wall of tears when 3-year-olds competed for the title of "Little Miss Wee One." Most of the tears were in the eyes of the losing parents or on the faces of very tired children. David Elkind eloquently describes the dilemmas of children in *The Hurried Child* (1981) and *All Grown Up and No Place to Go* (1984).

American children have not been included in the total life and concerns of their society. In other parts of the world, children have fared better, perhaps because of centuries of tradition or specific beliefs and values. In some places respect for children is mandated by law. In other societies high regard prevails for the advancement of the total population and a realization that children's early years are the foundations for later life. A man living in an Israel kibbutz once said to one of the authors, "We consider the kibbutz as the extended family—everyone responsible for the children and everyone overtly caring. We cannot afford to waste a life."

Consider the children described in the next section. Their culture perceives them as valuable, and they are given consideration in every realm of decision making. Although we may not agree with certain child-rearing practices, we cannot argue with the importance some cultures place on their young.

Children around the World

Chigozie is 8 years old and spends part of each day fishing in the streams near his home in the green and fertile delta region of Nigeria. Along with his brothers and sisters, he is responsible for bringing food home for the evening meals. He learned to spear fish from watching his father. His mother taught him to clean fish and wrap them in leaves to cook over hot coals. His practical schooling includes lessons in daily living. A more formal education would require him to venture to a faraway city at the mouth of the Niger River. When he is older, he will attend a boarding school and experience a more worldly curriculum, but for now, his education consists of the life he lives. He experiences childhood as his tribe conceives it, and his activities and roles are clearly defined.

Saturday is a special day for wrestling in the village grove. Chigozie wishes he were old enough to join the fun, but for now he must be content to climb with his friends to the top of a huge tree and watch. He knows his turn at wrestling will come when he is older and able to do things young men do. He can depend on village elders to continue the traditions and rituals associated with approaching manhood.

Shi Kai, a 10-year-old Chinese girl, lives in the same house as her parents, grandparents, and her older brother. It is a simple home with a small herb garden joining two stone and cement buildings. She goes to school in the people's commune, and her teachers drill her in ways of self-control. She is very proud to be Chinese and always wants to obey her parents. In the summers, she attends a work camp where all school-age children wear blue and white uniforms. Despite the fun she has, Shi Kai knows the importance of learning how to be productive and of helping her mother and father. When children are good in China, everyone is pleased.

Fifteen-year-old Alaribi has never attended school, but his father taught him to read and write. Alaribi earns money by leading tourists through the small, narrow streets in the medina of Marrakesh, Morocco. He has always run free in the medina. The merchants, workers, and older children keep a watchful eye on the younger ones. In practice adults function as a community of care givers. There is no sense of danger, and the children are safe. Alaribi was born without one arm and was, according to custom, designated for vocational work instead of academics. His culture practices the teachings of Mohammed, which emphasize the importance of a sound body and mind. He speaks several languages, a skill he has picked up through his streetwise education. He has a winsome personality and an inquiring mind. He values his faith and relies heavily on his people's customs.

In modernized countries, responsibility for children shifts from families to specialized child care systems. Denmark, for instance, has an orderly and deliberate process through which comprehensive welfare services are provided at all ages. The country enjoys a high standard of living; taxes are high, and extremes of wealth and poverty have been eliminated. Parents are active in decisions that affect child care and education.

Mete is 10 years old and lives in Lungby, Denmark, about one hour's train ride from Copenhagen. She lives with her mother in a small stone house next to the local bakery. She rides her bicycle to school each day. Her best friend, Leif, joins her daily for the journey on the bicycle path. Mete has lived with her mother, a single parent, since she was a baby. At birth the government paid Mete's mother a stipend so that she could remain at home to care for her child. Mete was enrolled in a day care center a few blocks from her home when she was 1. The carefully designed day care center employed professionally trained staff and maintained a small staff-child ratio, allowing Mete to receive care from warm, trusting adults. In the summertime, Mete will go to a camp in the country and will be able to pursue her newly found interest in computers. Mete's mother works a shared schedule and greets her child when she comes home from school. Leif is enrolled in the leisure after-school program run by the community recreation center. At times Mete goes with him to the center for special events.

In the United States modernization has been quite rapid and sometimes disorderly. The large population and the diversified areas of the country have prohibited needed social changes from becoming widespread. Children do not get the high priority children do in Denmark. Instead they get public attention only when things go wrong. American society has focused on delinquency, runaways, and dropouts. Currently Americans are waging a war on child abusers. We do not imply that we should deny the urgent nature of this terrible injustice to children—children are stolen, are missing, and molested—but can this blatant disregard for youngsters be traced to inadequate support for families in changing times?

To be a parent and rear a child is a never-ending process. Adults must make arrangements for child care, carefully plan education and social development, and assure protection and supervision of their offspring under the best of circumstances. Parents can provide most of the necessary services for their children by negotiating with child-serving institutions for special needs and programs. Support services are essential to guarantee child care, and parents are dependent on the community's commitment in providing these services. What are the necessary steps for initiating changes in communities to meet children's needs? Answers to these questions lie in the advocacy movement.

Advocacy Movement

We can give many reasons for the advocacy movement unfolding in the United States. One major cause is the shifting of authority in decision making from the service deliverer to the service consumer. As campaigns mount for rights of minorities, women, and the disabled, attention has focused on accountable service delivery systems. Consumers have spoken out, and, in the case of children, individuals and groups have joined forces emphasizing children's rights to develop their fullest potential.

Advocacy reflects society's obligations to its citizens. It also recognizes the built-in impersonal nature of delivery systems. Advocacy provides a check system to ensure that people get needed services. Advocacy provides a voice for children who, as a group, are vulnerable and powerless (Paul, Rosenthal & Adams 1976).

To carry out the process of child advocacy, citizens work together to ensure that basic health, housing, nutritional, educational, and clothing needs are met. Child advocates study children's issues and strive to seek new or improved services to help growth and development. Advocates follow a task-oriented process, staying involved with problems only long enough to see that they are rectified. The activities therefore reflect the purpose of acting on behalf of children to ensure and protect their rights and to remind the community of its responsibilities (Council for Children 1985).

Child advocates can be individuals, parents, professional workers, neighbors, volunteers, or groups of people who intervene on behalf of a single child or group of children. Alone or in concert, they work to mobilize individual and group efforts toward common actions or goals. Child advocates are not service providers, nor do they attempt to build relationships with children just for therapeutic benefit. Instead, child advocates work to enable parents to help children get services they need.

Case and Class Advocacy

Advocacy relationships are structured in several ways. Paul, Rosenthal, and Adams (1976) at the Frank Porter Graham Child Development Center, University of North Carolina, Chapel Hill, suggest a variety of combinations. Individuals have been known to advocate for an entire category of persons such as the retarded, the poor, or the oppressed. Ghandi, for example, was an individual advocate.

Collective or corporate advocacy involves a group of individuals forming an association to represent the interests of an entire category of persons. The Council for Children, Charlotte, North Carolina, and the Children's Defense Fund, Washington, D.C., are two examples. Special demonstration projects are potential outgrowths of association advocacy. In Charlotte, the school-age child care project sponsored by the Council for Children gave direction to the local YMCA, the parks and recreation department, the public schools, and a family day care homes system coordinator. The council provides resources, public education and awareness efforts, and a project coordinator. The Children's Defense Fund provides a strong and effective voice for children, who cannot vote, lobby, or speak for themselves. These advocates pay particular attention to the needs of poor, minority, and handicapped children. The Children's Defense Fund provides information, technical assistance, and support to local child advocate organizations such as the Council for Children.

Group advocacy is a more formal approach and involves specific groups of people, such as the elderly or disabled being adopted by a church group or woman's club. Families can advocate for other families. Teenagers can select other teens for whom they provide support and friendship. Self-advocacy exists when citizens work to improve their own conditions. Child advocacy groups take steps to promote and protect the developmental needs of both an individual child and children in general. The former is defined as individual case advocacy and the latter class advocacy.

Class Advocacy

Class advocacy, the essential background for individual case advocacy, promotes the general interests of children through remedial or preventive intervention. It can be an attempt to change program policies, ensure adequate appropriations for children's services, initiate new or expanded services, or promote new legislation or changes in existing laws. Class advocacy is based on thorough study and planning and cannot depend on simplistic, quick solutions to problems. Knowledge of how social policy is formed is essential, and ways for translating social policy into public policy are the backbone of class advocacy. Overall class advocacy concentrates on needed changes in policies, law, procedures, personnel, rules, funding, and budgets.

Class advocacy efforts for latchkey children have changed governmental policies at local and state levels. Funds for programs have become available in recent years. In North Carolina, the Children's Trust Fund provided financial support to groups seeking ways of preventing child abuse and neglect through out-of-school care.

Social Policy and Public Policy Defined

Social policy—the way society expresses its aims and purposes—guides the government's public policies and society's customs and traditions. Social policy determines the priorities of society by changing with the times, admittedly sometimes slowly. Policymakers determine how public resources will be allocated by setting goals and developing logical processes to reach goals. The philosophy behind Lyndon Johnson's Great Society is an example of social policy at work. Striving to create equal opportunity and release from poverty, the Department of Health, Education and Welfare was created to serve people and their problems.

In order for an issue to become public policy, an ensuing theme is implemented at the national, state, or community level. Policy can be expressed through funding, legislative change, and service delivery as part of the human services systems. A recent public policy that covers national, state, and local levels is the fight against drunk drivers. Examples are Mothers Against Drunk Drivers and Students Against Drunk Drivers and the laws enacted as a result of the efforts of these advocacy groups.

Role of Advocacy

The role of advocacy becomes one of urging the creation of social policy that recognizes children as the nation's future. Advocates must challenge compromises and discrepancies and force attention on the long-range benefits that result from a good childhood. A crucial contribution can be the sustained evaluation of the way child care systems and services work. In providing programs and options for school-age children, advocates keep the issue before the public as solutions are tried and evaluated. As a school-age child care program develops, advocates gather data and disseminate information on the project's effects on children.

Case Advocacy

The case advocacy mode takes the form of remedial or preventive intervention to help a specific child or family in locating a service to meet particular needs. Correcting a situation where an agency is not fulfilling its responsibilities to on individual child is one illustration. Specific outreach efforts can be designated to target categories of children such as those with health problems or school dropouts, who may be in need of case advocacy services but not aware of them. Case advocacy serves as a major source for advocacy groups to identify gaps in services and policy issues that need to be addressed on a class advocacy basis.

Tools of Advocacy

Child advocacy groups work to increase public understanding, support, maintenance, and development of high-quality children's services. They facilitate interagency cooperation and communication. In a sense they become a hub for all child-serving agencies in the community. They research and assess children's needs and available resources. When necessary, they make recommendations to appropriate bodies on ways to improve services for children. As they work to strengthen the community's preventive investment in children, they provide a long-range and systematic voice on children's behalf.

In Kansas City, Missouri, school-age child care was considered a community problem. Using funds from a midwestern foundation, the Family Living Center, a nonprofit community services organization, requested proposals from individuals and groups who wished to establish before- and after-school programs. Recreation centers, scout groups, the Ys, Girl Guides, and others responded with interest to the proposals. Applications for start-up funds were filed, and many programs were funded. The Family Living Center established and coordinated a coalition of care givers who facilitated the development of new programs. Agencies exchanged valuable information and expertise. As other community groups who provided school-age child care were allowed to join the coalition, standards for all programs improved.

Advocates use a variety of strategies to make children's issues and concerns known. Patricia Lloyd (1984), director of the Council for Children, has identified the tools of advocacy:

1. *Collecting information.* An advocacy program must be able to develop, organize, and disseminate knowledge on needs, resources, issues, and problems related to children and their families. Data should be collected and continuously updated regarding children's needs and services. Information is gained through research projects, needs assessments, case histories, study of laws and policies, documentation of events, and identifying community citizens to oversee responsibilities for the well-being of children.

The Charlotte, North Carolina, SACC Project was an outgrowth of two social research projects. In 1980 a day care committee, appointed by the Council for Children, conducted a survey of child care needs in Mecklenburg County and identified over 5,400 latchkey youngsters in need of some type of before- or after-school supervision. In 1984, a second survey asked school-age children, their parents, and service providers questions about care needs, types of care being used, problems experienced, and kinds of care desired. At a conference held to review the findings, community leaders made recommendations and suggestions based on identified needs. The outcome was the School-Age Child Care Task Force, which designed a pilot project of four child care models offering a variety of care options and utilizing existing community resources.

2. *Organizing and coalition building.* For advocacy to work effectively, coalition building and networking are essential. Power exists in numbers, and when an issue is affected at the local, state, and national levels, everyone listens. A second advantage of coalition building is the elimination of unnecessary duplication. Pooling resources increases the potential power of groups. As the Mecklenburg County School-Age Child Care project develops, a strong coalition of service providers is evolving. Monthly meetings are held to exchange ideas. Public education efforts that will benefit each model program are being developed. A steering committee identifies key issues and concerns and sets the agenda. The Council for Children will continue to coordinate the project during the pilot years. Areas of expertise are exchanged, and an attitude of helping each program achieve its best prevails. This type of networking helps to maintain high standards and keeps program philosophies intact.

3. *Influencing legislative and political decisions.* Legislators should be held accountable for their views. At the same time, they should be properly informed and receive the results of social research. Advocates work to elect people who support children's issues. They stay in touch with their legislators, analyze voting records, and monitor meetings of child-serving agencies. Local, state, and national representatives hold roundtable discussions for public review of children's issues. City and county government officials are informed of identified needs and issues.

4. *Educating the public.* Advocates inform citizens of children's needs and how public policy can be changed to satisfy unmet needs. They make presentations to community groups to persuade them of the importance of children's lives to the rest of society. They use a variety of media—pamphlets, public forums, speaker's bureau, radio and television talk shows, newsletters, letters to newspaper editors, advertising, recruitment of volunteers, and advocacy membership groups—to promote advocacy and raise community awareness on children's issues.

School-age child care projects throughout the nation have received media attention. Advocacy councils use newsletters to highlight their work for latchkey kids. Local, state, and national conferences have received television coverage and attention from magazine feature writers. The project in Mecklenburg County was featured in the Council for Children's newsletter, in the daily newspaper, and on television talk shows. A media blitz is planned for the second phase of the project. Presentations to community groups by council members on a regular basis keep the public informed on this and other children's issues. Such a forum will keep the school-age child visible as the project gains momentum and credibility.

5. *Influencing appointments to advisory boards.* Advocates make suggestions for membership to community, state, and national appointed boards and task forces. They strive to place a child advocate on all important policymaking boards. Appointments can help to fill neglected viewpoints and priorities.

6. *Evaluating and influencing the use of tax dollars.* The Children's Defense Fund, based in Washington, D.C., prepares a budget that reflects children's needs and gaps. They analyze the federal budget and highlight excessive use of monies for nonessential causes. Advocacy groups use the same strategies for scrutinizing local and state budgets. They make suggestions for spending and carefully evaluate returns on money invested in children's programs. The focus is on programs that work for children and the wise use of funds.

7. *Using other tools.* Advocacy groups develop position papers and take public stands. They hold public hearings and invite public comment on proposed changes and regulations.

8. *Ensuring due process.* Advocates work to ensure due process for children in the judicial system so that children are protected from abuse by the courts. They seek procedures to ensure the rights of children and families.

9. *Taking legal action.* Children who come into court without protective parents need a voice. Advocacy takes several forms of representation of children. In many cases children have complex and demanding problems, which demand special training and skills. Sometimes advocates will take action or threaten action against the government. Effective results are achieved when the court system is used against private corporations, organizations, and individuals.

Initiating Community Change for Latchkey Kids: An Eight-Step Plan

Table 8–1 contains an eight-step plan that we have devised for initiating community change for latchkey kids.

Step 1

The first step is to help community citizens understand and respond to factors that contribute to quality child and family relationships. Social and economic changes have left many gaps in children's lives. The influx of mothers into the labor force, the rise of single-parent households, and increases in poverty have led to new conditions in which children live. These conditions can become formidable barriers to children's healthy development. Thus the first step is to determine children's unmet needs and provide a comprehensive picture of their well-being in the community. Careful documentation of problems, as well as reliable reports of conditions, trends, and levels of services for children, can be provided through surveys, compiling key statistics, talking with professionals,

Table 8–1
Eight Steps for Initiating Community Change for Latchkey Kids

Step 1: Determine unmet needs of school-age children and provide a comprehensive view of their well-being in the community

Step 2: Bring the latchkey issue to the attention of the public

Step 3: Plan and recommend priorities for action based on significant statistics and documentation of the latchkey problem

Step 4: Establish committees to follow up initial plans and recommendations

Step 5: Develop an intervention plan, with goals and time-tables

Step 6: Sell the plan to the community

Step 7: Implement the plan by putting ideas to work and producing concrete results

Step 8: Evaluate the outcomes by determining what has been accomplished and how latchkey kids have been served

and interviewing children and their families. Impetus for change can come from such sources as a desperate parent, a report of abuse, new knowledge about children's circumstances, and social research findings.

Step 2

Now it is time to raise the public's awareness of the latchkey problem. Convening agencies, organizations, and individuals concerned with children and families to develop strategies for addressing the problem is one way. Holding conferences to disseminate information and utilizing the media are others. Publications and printed materials are effective means for maintaining high visibility.

Step 3

The third step is to plan for action. Working groups recommend priorities for community action based on significant statistics and documentation. The important component at this time is the identification of groups and the formation of networks that will promote policies and programs to benefit latchkey children. Suggested questions from the Council for Children (1984) include the following:

1. How can the community organize and develop support for the latchkey problem?
2. What are the policy issues?
3. What are the best approaches for using community resources?
4. What are possible funding sources for school-age child care programs?

5. What successful remedial or preventive models are available in other communities?

6. How can parents become involved from the beginning?

Step 4

The fourth step is to establish a special committee to follow up initial recommendations and plans. This can be accomplished by coordinating with selected organizations and individuals, depending on which aspect of the latchkey problem is being addressed. This special group identifies important details, such as confirming numbers of children and families affected by the problem. This is also the time for hunting for ideas and brainstorming methods of intervention. The ability to amass as many ideas and approaches as possible makes change more likely. Use of consultants for ideas at this stage can be valuable.

Step 5

The fifth step is the time to develop the intervention plan that tells who will do what and when. Objectives are set and time-tables proposed. Efforts should be made to maximize the use of existing community resources for real change to occur. Options for collaboration between the public and private sectors are explored. Those who will put the plan into effect are identified. Now is the time to use good judgment and to select the best options for action.

Step 6

The sixth step, the execution phase, is the time to sell the plan. Reasons for the plan and what the plan will utlimately mean to both community and children must be explained. Advocates should be prepared for disagreement and resistance while stressing the plan's preventive and cost-effective advantages. They should have alternative suggestions, keep their enthusiasm high, and be willing to give a little.

Step 7

During the seventh step, the implementation phase, the plan becomes a reality. Ideas are put to work, and intentions are put to the test. All forces are gathered to improve or solve the problem. Depending on the plan, implementation takes many forms. Specific actions produce concrete results. Methods vary but can include the following:

1. Duplicating models that have proved successful for similar kinds of problems.

2. Developing community education programs to increase an awareness and value of the plan.

3. Placing volunteers in strategic spots to carry out the program objectives.

4. Making a time-task graph to guide workers through the implementation stage.

5. Considering all possible combinations of the specifics of the plan. When one does not work, another should be tried.

Step 8

The eighth step is the time for evaluation—a time to determine what has been accomplished and to what degree latchkey children have been served. The quantity and quality of the outcomes must be measured. Special attention should be given to examining changes in services and attitudes over time. Self-criticism and careful reviewing are important for planning appropriately for the next advocacy venture. The process of initiating change is nothing more than good problem solving. The evaluation process is cumulative as we learn from our experiences and build on them for future successes.

Putting the Steps into Action

The School-Age Child Care Program (SACC) in Charlotte, North Carolina, was conceived through these steps. This section shows how the authors, working under the umbrella of the Council for Children, put these eight steps into action.

Step 1

The Council for Children convened a task force and charged it with conducting a survey of 1,806 parents and children and 188 service providers and to develop a report of its findings regarding the latchkey problem in Mecklenburg County. We conducted the surveys in the fall of 1983. Results of the surveys were printed as the *Latchkey Study Report* and distributed to community leaders in the spring of 1984 (Council for Children 1984).

Step 2

The council convened a planning conference consisting of agencies and individuals concerned with children and youth and charged them with developing strategies for addressing the latchkey issue in the county. The *Latchkey Study Report* and national conference speakers provided a working platform. Newspaper and radio coverage of the conference gave visibility and information on the community needs of latchkey kids.

Step 3

Conference participants divided into five work groups and made priority recommendations based on the *Latchkey Study Report* and speaker presentations. They recommended that existing community resources and programs be expanded and that existing parks, playgrounds, and community facilities be used in new ways to help latchkey kids. Collaboraton between public and private sectors was emphasized. These recommendations led to step 4.

Step 4

The School-Age Child Care Task Force was appointed by the Council for Children in the fall of 1984 to design four model programs to deliver services to latchkey kids:

1. Extended-day programs in the Charlotte-Mecklenburg school system,
2. After-school programs through the parks and recreation department,
3. Out-of-school programs offered by the YMCA,
4. After-school care offered by private day care home providers.

Consultants were hired to design the programs and to match needs with program possibilities through the use of existing community facilities.

Step 5

Consultants, working with the School-Age Child Care Task Force, developed an intervention plan. The plan consisted of an administrative structure, timetables for implementation, and evaluation criteria.

Step 6

Consultants met with the School-Age Child Care Task Force to present the plan for approval. Once the plan was approved, consultants met with community individuals and groups to sell the plan and form networks for service delivery.

Step 7

State funds were allocated for a school-age child care coordinator's position and for money to launch the four model programs. A training package also was developed for training SACC staff and volunteers. The SACC project was launched in the fall of 1985. Although the project is still in the implementation stage, all four programs appear to be running smoothly.

Step 8

At year's end, each model program will conduct annual programmatic, performance, and outcome evaluations. Feedback will be assessed from participating parents, children, and SACC staff. In addition, the Council for Children will conduct an overall administrative evaluation of the SACC project in terms of cost per child effectiveness, additional resources needed, and program continuation. Once complete, these evaluation reports will be presented to concerned community groups and published in agency newsletters and local newspapers.

Conclusion

Children and families require attention from many people. Any concerned citizen—educators, professionals, social workers, nurses, doctors, attorneys, judges, police officers, parents, students—can be an advocate for children.

Advocacy efforts are underway in many communities as latchkey kids get well-deserved attention. Some advocates suggest these children are targets of abuse and neglect and become delinquent. In the spring of 1986 concerned citizens of Houston, Texas, expressed alarm over a rash of unrelated incidents in which six unattended children, playing with guns, were accidentally shot and killed. Latchkey programs with different magnitudes and unique solutions are addressing such genuine concerns. In chapter 9 we will discuss some of these intervention programs and describe their components for change. These program components, combined with steps for initiating community change, represent the key to opening doors for latchkey kids.

References

Aries, P. 1962. *Centuries of childhood.* New York: Knopf.
Childen's Defense Fund. 1985. *Children's defense budget report.* Washington, D.C.: Children's Defense Fund.
Council for Children. 1984. *Taking action for latchkey children.* Charlotte, N.C.: Council for Children.
Council for Children. 1985. *Membership brochure.* Charlotte, N.C.: Council for Children.
DeMause, L. 1974. *History of childhood.* New York: Psychohistory Press.
Elkind, D. 1981. *The hurried child.* Reading, Mass.: Addison-Wesley.
Elkind, D. 1984. *All grown up and no place to go.* Reading, Mass.: Addison-Wesley.
Haynes, E. 1986. Living history report. Personal communication.
Koberg, D., & Bagnall, J. 1976. *The universal traveler.* Los Altos, Calif.: William Kaufmann.

Lloyd, P. 1984. Seminar on child advocacy. Charlotte, N.C.: University of North Carolina.

Paul, J.; Rosenthal, S.; & Adams, J. 1976. *Advocacy: Resources and approaches.* Developmental Disabilities Technical Assistance System. Chapel Hill, N.C.: Frank Porter Graham Child Development Center, University of North Carolina.

Phillips, M. N.d. *Statement of child advocacy.* New York: Child Welfare League of America.

Rhodes, W.C. 1972. *Behavior threat and community response.* New York: Behavioral Publications.

Westman, J.C. 1979. *Child advocacy.* New York: Free Press.

White House Conference on Children and Youth. 1950. *Midcentury conference proceedings.* Washington, D.C.: U.S. Government Printing Office.

White House Conference on Children and Youth. 1960. *Conference proceedings.* Washington, D.C.: U.S. Government Printing Office.

White House Conference on Children and Youth. 1970. *Report to the President.* Washington, D.C.: U.S. Government Printing Office.

9
Program Development for School-Age Children

June Kirby of Live Oak, Florida, tried several after-school arrangements before settling on her current one. Her 14-year-old son can take care of himself, but leaving 8-year-old Nickey in his charge did not work out because of constant squabbling between the two.

June tried picking Nickey up after school and taking her to a day care center and then racing back to her job as a bank officer. That arrangement was also short-lived when Nickey complained that the owner made her change the younger children's diapers and give them their snacks.

"I thought she was too mature to be in a day care center (her friends called her 'baby')," complained June. "There were no kids there her age, and she was being used to take care of the other children. Still, she was too young to stay home alone. And unfortunately, no school-age programs are available in this area."

Having exhausted all other possibilities, June now picks up her daughter after school and takes her back to the bank where she works. Nickey does not mind too much. "It's sorta fun," she says. "I go back and draw and help my mom put things in envelopes, but I wish I could go home and play with my friends."

Kathleen Wilmore of Charlotte, North Carolina, was worried about adequate after-school care now that her 5-year-old son had begun kindergarten. William was lucky enough to attend one of the more than one hundred elementary schools in this country that offer extended-day programs. Such programs are designed to provide before- and after-school care for children in kindergarten through fifth grade of single and working parents.

"William loves the program because there's so much to do, and he can play with his friends!" exclaims Kathleen. "I like it because I know he's learning and having fun in a well-supervised program. There are benefits for me too. He stays at school, which eliminates any transportation hassles, and I'm more productive in my work because my mind is at ease."

At a recent program meeting of a Virginia cooperative extension district, a home economist began by noting, "I am already training leader volunteers to conduct the Survival Skills Program. I need to reach parents, not the kids." Another home economist agreed: "I get a number of requests for school-age child care services, but no one wants to manage a program or staff. Everyone is afraid their idea will flop. I think we need to direct our efforts toward getting parents involved."

Suggestions for the approach to take with parents varied. One home economist shared her experience in conducting parent discussion groups. "Working parents just do not come to discussion groups," she stated. "I have tried it, and they are too tired to attend night meetings." Joining in was a home economist from the

Washington, D.C., area: "Perhaps a series of radio public service announcements for parents commuting to and from work is needed or a series of informational cassettes." Another participant from a more rural area thought public service announcements were not practical: "I don't think radio stations will schedule public service announcements during prime time. I think we need to work on reaching parents within their homes. Our program needs to be brought to parents and not forced on them." Most agents agreed, but a few had still other suggestions. Church programs, parent worksheets, and a PhoneFriend line were all discussed prior to taking a vote.

The home economists voted to pursue three school-age child care programming efforts: a series of public service announcements, a parenting newsletter targeted for parents of school-aged children, and a parent home-based study program. Foreseeing the need to continue the networking and sharing process, the district home economist leader ended the meeting by directing, "We need to divide into three groups and work on the specifics of each program area. Remember, there are different needs within each of your counties, and we need to talk with each other as we work on our programs. Good luck, and keep in touch!" The participants agreed that they had a better sense of purpose and direction. "I'm excited," noted one participant. "I think our programs are going to meet a real need in my county."

The diversity of family forms and life-styles make school-age child care (SACC) a difficult issue to resolve. Mothers traditionally assumed responsibility for the supervision of their school-age children. By 1980, however, 62 percent of married mothers with children between the ages of 6 and 17 had entered the work force (U.S. Department of Commerce 1981). As the opening cases illustrate, many communities lack SACC programs, and there are few referral agencies (Divine-Hawkins 1983). Many families cannot afford the cost of SACC programs, and other families, like June Kirby, have difficulty finding available programs or arranging transportation to and from programs. These problems are especially troublesome for single parents. Finally, older school-age children, like Nickey, often reject SACC programs, viewing themselves as too old for child care (Long & Long 1983a; McMurray & Kazanjian 1982).

Creative staffing, financing, and program operation are keys to developing innovative SACC programs. Most innovative programs today can best be described as partnership models, and for good reason. Resources shared among community agencies result in comprehensive services that benefit parents, children, and the cooperating agencies themselves.

Some partnership SACC programs feature a limited sharing of space, staff, or activities. In other cases, the programs include a coalition in which a governing body oversees the operation of different types of programs that are jointly operated by two or more community groups. Regardless of their particular structure or operation, all SACC programs are primarily concerned with meeting the increased demand for a safe and enriching environment for children when school is not in session. Currently a number of programs contribute to the social, emotional, and physical growth of children. In this chapter, the different types of partnership programs are reviewed. A detailed step-by-step account of the process for developing and implementing one specific partnership SACC program is also presented in this chapter to point out some of the issues and barriers that may be faced during the development of programs. A discussion of some key logistical issues in developing a partnerhip SACC program is presented in appendix 9A.

Review of SACC Programs

Community SACC Programs

One of the first responses to the need for SACC programming was the expansion of existing child care centers, youth service agencies, business, and church programs to include school-age children. National concern over the potential dangers facing latchkey kids and parental requests for community-based school-age child care, led to the development of the following types of SACC programs.

Day Care Centers. Many day care centers have expanded their programs to include before- and after-school care. Private SACC programs also exist that are nonprofit, parent-owned, cooperative ventures.

The quality of day-care SACC programs depends on state and local licensing requirements, as well as the philosophies of operators. Day care programs vary in relation to staff training, curriculum, hours of operation, transportation services, cost, and degree of parent involvement. Day care centers also provide services during nonschool days, such as school holidays, when other SACC programs are closed.

Many staff members recognize that the needs of school-age children are different from those of preschoolers. The Reston Children's Center in Virginia is a private, nonprofit, parent-owned center serving children between 3 months and 14 years of age. Operation of the center is based on meeting the developmental needs of children and serving as a family support system. Before- and after-school care is offered at the center and in a network of family satellite homes. Home providers are carefully selected, trained, and supervised by the Reston center staff. Special enrichment and recreational activities are provided at the center and in a summer camp.

Parent involvement is high. Parents serve on the board of directors and work in the center itself. Seminars and workshops on child development and family life are conducted in addition to family outings and dinners. Information bulletins and a monthly newsletter keep parents informed about the activities of the center.

Financial support for the center comes from tuition payments and fund raising. Financial aid is available through Title XX and the Kerry Helmuth Memorial Scholarship Fund. The Reston center also participates in the U.S.

Department of Agriculture's Child Care Food Program, which reimburses the center for serving nutritious snacks and meals to children of low- and moderate-income families.

Family Day Care Homes. For some parents the homes of neighbors, relatives, and friends represent a valuable source of school-age child care. Licensing and registration requirements for family day care homes are different from day care centers. In some instances, family day care homes register with state or local offices, but no licensing is required.

Some communities have a private agency that brings together a network of family day care homes to offer quality school-age child care. For example, the Child Care Assurance Plan of Tidewater, Virginia, serves as a clearinghouse for parents seeking child care in a home setting (Fooner 1985). Referrals are made for families with preschoolers, special needs children, sick children, and school-age children. Services include registration of the family day care homes under state licensing regulations, a training program for providers, a twenty-four-hour answering service to help parents locate substitute care, toy and equipment loans, insurance, and a monitoring program to ensure that high-quality care is maintained.

Block Parents. Some communities have block parents who care for children within their own neighborhood and in the providers' homes. Neighborhood friends and activities are more accessible to children, and parents have less difficulty with transportation.

Block parent programs take a number of forms. In Reston, Virginia, the Reston Children's Center Senior Satellite Program sponsors a check-in program for upper elementary and junior high school students (McKnight & Shelsby 1984). Children are assigned to a trained neighborhood family day care provider who carries out a contract developed by the children, their parents, the Reston center, and the providers. Each contract is different. Some children use their neighborhood provider's home as a check-in point before attending an after-school activity. Others spend most of their after-school time in the home of the provider.

The Reston check-in program is a good example of a developmentally sound program that provides child care while recognizing the developmental needs of preadolescents. As McKnight and Shelsby (1984) note, "By early adolescence, children have developed their own interests and are capable, to a large degree, of self-care. However, when parents are not accessible or available, they still need to have a responsible adult available."

A somewhat different type of block parent arrangement is found in Orlando, Florida, where the Community Coordinated Child Care for Central Florida, a private nonprofit organization, operates the Home Based Child Care Program. Before- and after-school care is provided in the homes of certified, insured, and trained providers. Children are cared for within a safe, supervised home environment where they enjoy books and toys supplied through a resource library, do homework under adult supervision, and participate in youth programs and activities.

Youth Service Agencies. During recent years, youth service agencies have implemented SACC programs. These agencies display an exceptional ability to form partnerships and to conduct SACC programs within a variety of settings.

The recreational and enrichment curricula offered by youth service agencies are so attractive that getting children to attend these programs is rarely a problem. Youth service agencies also have staff trained for working with school-age children. For example, the YMCA (YMCA School-Age Child Care Manual 1985) and Virginia Cooperative Extension and 4-H (*Survival Skills for Kids* 1984) have developed SACC training manuals that are used to instruct staff members and volunteer leaders in conducting developmentally appropriate SACC programs.

A comprehensive youth service SACC program exists in Sioux Falls, South Dakota. According to Barnett (1985), KARE-4 coordinator, "The purpose of KARE–4 [Kids After-School Recreation and Enrichment–4—the four agencies are the Girls Club, Boys Club, YMCA, and YWCA] is to provide after-school transportation and recreation for dual-career and single employed families in the Sioux Falls area." Transportation is provided from school to SACC centers by city and agency vehicles. Activities include supervised free play and structured classes in crafts, cooking, and other areas.

Funding and registration are especially unique features of the KARE-4 project. Start-up money was donated by the Gannett Foundation. United Way, parents' fees, contributions, and grants provide additional funds. Barnett reports that advance registration is used to develop transportation routes and as a means of conducting a daily check on children who are enrolled. Parents are called when an enrolled child is not present.

In Miami, 142 of the 175 elementary schools contain SACC programs. According to Joseph Mathos, supervisor of adult and community education, and Barbara Frances, educational specialist (personal correspondence, November 1985), "Some programs are offered directed by the school system through its community schools, others are offered by school-allied organizations such as the YMCA or YWCA." All school-allied organizations must complete annually an agreement for their use of Dade County school facilities to operate a before- and after-school care program.

Mathos and Frances report that principals select the types of programs that best meet their communities' school-age child care needs. All programs must meet safety, health, facility, and enrollment standards.

All staff positions in the Miami program carry certain responsibilities, duties, and qualifications. In-service training is provided for employees. Parents are encouraged to become involved in the program through making activity materials, assisting in the library, organizing community activities, or bringing resource people or materials to the class. Parent fees, Title XX, and United Way provide funding for the program.

Church-Sponsored SACC. Church-sponsored school-age child care programs are sometimes preferred by parents not only because they are safe but also because they provide a religious atmosphere that contributes to their child's moral development. A major advantage of church-sponsored programs is that many support systems are already in place. Young adults, parents, and high school and college students serve as care providers. Financial support is drawn from the congregation, as well as from community fund drives. Many churches have buildings for conducting youth programs, and with some planning these buildings are made available for school-age child care.

Two different church-based SACC programs exist in the Kansas City metropolitan area, each working in cooperation with a different community group. The Kansas City YWCA conducts one of its SACC programs in cooperation with the Covenant Presbyterian Church (*New Program for School Age Children* 1984). The church congregation volunteered to help clean, paint, and modify a building for use by the SACC program. In Mission, Kansas, a suburb of Kansas City, the St. Michael and All Angels Episcopal Church, in cooperation with the Sante Fe Trail Elementary School, provides after-school and vacation enrichment activities for school-aged children (*New Program for School Age Children* 1984). This partnership SACC program is staffed by certified teachers who are assisted by church volunteers. The program was made possible by two grants, one from the Kansas City Living Center for Family Enrichment and the other from the Diocese of Kansas Episcopal Churches Venture in Missions (Local Churches Respond to Special Needs, 1984).

Employer-sponsored SACC. The three o'clock syndrome describes the slowdown in work productivity at 3 P.M. when parents call home to check on their latchkey kids. As a result, employers are becoming involved in school-age child care. A survey conducted by the National Employer-Supported Child Care Project (Divine-Hawkins 1983) found that 40 percent of 211 companies in the survey providing on-site or near-site child care centers offered programming for school-age children.

As the demand for SACC increases, employers will become increasingly more interested in this kind of care. Divine-Hawkins (1983) suggests some trends that will characterize future employer-supported child care. First, more partnerships will exist among the public, private, and voluntary sectors. Second, employers will begin offering more flexible working arrangements in the form of flextime, leave policies, part-time work, job sharing, and at-home work. Third, employee benefits will expand to include child care services. Fourth, the federal government will continue to offer financial incentives for employer-supported child care programs.

An example of a partnership that already exists between two Arizona industries and a nonprofit agency is found in Tucson, Arizona. Two electronic industries share the cost of a sick child care home health care program with their employees (Anderson 1984). This service saves the companies money by allowing their employees to work. The companies also support the program as a way of demonstrating loyalty to their employees.

The Schools

The public school is the most common institution to which families turn for their children's welfare, so it comes as no surprise that a number of school systems have responded to the need for school-age child care through cooperative partnerships with other community groups.

Extended-Day Programs. Perhaps the most common type of school-age child care provided by schools is the extended-day program. These programs operate before school, after school, during school holidays, on teacher work days, and on inclement weather days. Primary focus is the after-school program. Time is allotted for arts and crafts, homework, snacks, and free play. Most programs also have special enrichment activities. Transportation services, fees, and staffing characteristics vary. Regular school teachers staff some programs; other programs train and employ high school students, volunteers, parents, or aides.

Sometimes funding for extended day programs is based solely on parents' fees. In other instances, funds come from many sources. Some programs have a special scholarship fund or implement a tuition exchange program in which a scholarship is provided in exchange for the parent's providing some type of service to the extended-day program. In the Phillips Magnet School in Raleigh, North Carolina, a child's scholarship is provided in exchange for the parent's providing ten volunteer hours each week (Mayesky 1979). Some parents teach special activities or assist in the classroom. Others help prepare activity materials or do clerical work.

The Phillips Extended Day Magnet in Raleigh was designed as the first licensed day care magnet in the Southeast (Mayesky 1980). Mayesky summarizes three goals of the program: "to provide quality extended day care for elementary children"; "to design a program that would expand and enrich the 'regular' [academic day] curriculum"; and "to draw white children into a formerly black elementary school in Raleigh by the strength of this extended day program." The achievement of these goals is a result of effective planning and programming.

The Phillips extended-day curriculum contributes to children's cognitive, affective, and psychomotor development. Activities include weaving, dance, drama, karate, and wrestling. All activities include hands-on experiences and are supervised by a large, specialized staff.

Teachers are selected for their experience and ability to individualize activities to meet the needs of all children. Assisting teachers are aides, student teachers, high school assistants, and parent volunteers. Mayesky (1980) views the nonthreatening environment and small teacher-pupil ratio as two factors contributing to the success of the Phillips program. She states, "If, for instance, a child's first attempt at constructing an electrical circuit is not successful, there is no strict classroom time limit on a lesson to curtail further attempts. And the smaller teacher-child ratio naturally allows more 'turns' than in a regular classroom."

Fooner (1985) lists the After School Day Care Association (ASDCA) of Madison, Wisconsin, as operating one of the most successful after-school programs in the country. This nonprofit organization rents nonclassroom space from elementary schools to provide after-school services for more than 350 children aged 5–11. After-school activities include relaxation time, snacks, cooking, crafts, gymnastics, and field trips. Three full-time and thirty part-time staff supervise groups of ten children. Volunteers provide additional assistance. In addition to the after-school program, ASDCA operates a day camp during the summer vacation months.

After-School Learning Centers. Some school systems offer special after-school learning centers for children who are educationally at risk. The Charlotte-Mecklenburg school system, for example, has designed a series of after-school learning centers for Chapter 1–eligible students in grades K–6. The program focus is on improving academic skills and providing enrichment activities. Certified teachers, instructional assistants, and community resource persons staff the centers. Free transportation is provided through the school system. Workshops and special family nights are held to encourge parents to take an active role in the centers.

Special Programs

Parents seeking school-age child care for their children with special physical, emotional, and cognitive needs are faced with a number of problems. With the passage of the Handicapped Children's Act of 1975, increased attention is being given to mainstreaming special needs children into regular classrooms and providing enrichment programs for at-risk children residing in disadvantaged environments.

Guidance Centers. Guidance centers offer after-school programs in which children with learning disabilities or emotional and behavior problems engage in activities that contribute to their social growth. For example, the Manville

School in Boston, a division of the Judge Baker Guidance Center, serves children ages 8–16 who have been referred from public schools because of emotional and interpersonal problems. Suzanne Bram (1985), the after-school coordinator, reports that twelve children are currently enrolled in the after-school component of the Manville School. The activities, which promote group interaction and socialization skills, include work on group projects, field trips, and a series of choice group activities, such as cooking, drama, and puppets. Pair therapy is also used; two children are paired with one therapist who helps the children negotiate and work through problems.

Bram further reports, "We have worked hard to help foster the communication between our [after-school] program and the day school." The after-school staff members attend conferences conducted by the staff and counselors of the day school. One counselor serves as a liaison, sharing information between the day and after-school programs. The after-school staff members write daily notes on each child, and the day staff members review them each morning.

Funding for the Manville after-school program comes from a federal grant and private sources. Discarded musical equipment, a juke box, and a video game were donated by a local hospital.

Summer Programs. Special-needs children have had difficulty entering regular summer camp programs, but some summer camps now include these children. Programs are staffed by specially trained teenage counselors and professional staff. Camp activities include arts, crafts, and sports. Financial support comes through a combination of community fund drives, parents' fees, and volunteer staff.

An example of a summer camp in which special-needs children are mainstreamed is the Playing and Learning in Adaptable Environments (Project PLAE) in Berkeley, California. This project began as a community effort to remove an asphalt school yard and to construct an environmental yard on a half acre of land (Goltsman, Moore & Iacofano 1982). Today that land includes a miniature forest, two ponds, grassy meadows, streams and garden plots, play equipment, sand areas, climbing structures, a stage, and large open areas. The guiding principle in designing the environmental yard was to develop a space that would challenge children to learn and play together rather than be segregated into "special" and "regular" facilities. The environmental yard is perceived as a flexible space that is accessible to both able-bodied and handicapped children.

During the summer, a series of week-long PLAE workshops are conducted. Each workshop includes an average of twenty children aged 6–16. Each PLAE workshop provides a combination of artistic expression and physical activity. For example, "Do-It-Yourself Circus" involves a week of mime, mask construction, and makeup. The week culminates with a circus production based on scripts written by the children. Other artistic-physical workshops include

"Adventure Village" and "Voyage to the Bottom of the Sea." Funding for PLAE comes from parent fees and fund raising.

Community Enrichment Programs. Children residing in economically disadvantaged areas are at risk in their physical, social, and emotional development. SACC enrichment programs contribute to these children's development in many ways. The Gethsemane Enrichment Program, a nonprofit organization in Charlotte, North Carolina, serves more than 400 disadvantaged children in grades K–6 (Battle, Hunt & Robinson 1985). After-school and summer programs are conducted in several satellite locations. Prior to entering the Gethsemane Program, children are screened for academic strengths and weaknesses. Program activities focus on educational and cultural experiences. Students receive help with their homework to improve their study skills. Field trips include drama, ice shows, museum visits, and dance recitals. The Gethsemane Program also includes a parenting component, which promotes better communication between home and school.

The Citizens Advisory Board works in conjunction with the Charlotte Community Development Program and the Charlotte-Mecklenburg School System to manage the Gethsemane Program. Funding is provided by Mecklenburg County and the Community Development Department of the City of Charlotte.

Another enrichment center, the Carole Robertson Center for Learning in Chicago, offers academic enrichment, arts and crafts, recreation, classes for parents, and social service and health care referrals. The Robertson Center serves school-age children up to 14 years of age who reside in a tenement neighborhood that is being disrupted by expansion of a hospital complex. Activities are conducted during after-school hours, the summer months, and on days when schools are closed. Parents, who make up 60 percent of the governing board, take an active role in the center. They also serve on the personnel board, whose function is to interview candidates for employment at the center.

Sick Care. Most schools and child centers have strict health and safety guidelines. When children become ill, working parents often have no option other than to stay home.

In Tucson, Arizona, the Sick Child Home Health Care Program helps working parents with sick children (Anderson 1984). This nonprofit program provides on-call, in-home health care for children from birth through high school. Children with common illnesses, such as flu, or who have been in accidents are cared for, as well as some critically or terminally ill children. In emergencies, such as an ill parent, home care is sometimes provided for children who are not sick.

Health care aides are carefully screened and trained. Ongoing in-service training, supervision, consultation, and evaluation also are conducted to ensure quality care. Funding comes from a variety of sources. Parents pay according to a sliding scale fee, although the Tucson chapter of Altrusa, a women's service organization, has established a fund for families who are unable to pay. The program also has received a grant from the Brewster Foundation for training and child care subsidies. Additional funds come from United Way and the City of Tucson.

Unique to this program are the two electronic industries, Unitronics and Burr-Brown, which share the cost of aides with their employees. According to Anderson (1984), these companies "find that the service saves [them] money that would otherwise be lost when a parent misses work to care for the child, and that it enhances employee loyalty. They also see this arrangement as an appropriate and caring response to the needs of their employees, their families and the community."

TenderCare for Kids of St. Paul-Minneapolis, Minnesota, is another in-home sick child care program that operates twenty-four hours a day, seven days a week. The program was developed by Home Health Plus, a full-service home care agency. Children in infancy through adolescence who are mildly ill are eligible for services. The staff members of TenderCare are child care workers who have training in childhood illnesses, child development, cardiopulmonary resuscitation, infection control, and first aid. Both individual families and companies may purchase the services of TenderCare.

Indirect Services

A number of services provide indirect school-age child care. The services supplied by these programs also benefit latchkey kids and their families.

Handbooks. A number of handbooks for children (Chaback & Fortunato 1981; Kyte 1983) and parents (Long & Long 1983b; Pfafflin 1982) have appeared on the market. These books offer suggestions that make latchkey situations safer and more pleasant. Information for children ranges from safety rules to after-school activities. Information for parents ranges from factual information about the latchkey experience to tips on arranging for a safe home environment. The Appendix at the end of this book presents a comprehensive list of these sources.

Help Lines. Help lines focus on providing emotional support for children who are scared or who just need to talk with someone. Services include supplying information on how to handle minor problems and referral for circumstances that require special expertise. Volunteers are trained to staff help lines and work under the guidance of a professional staff.

The PhoneFriend help line in Kansas City is unique in that it is operated jointly by KCTV-5 and the Family and Children Services, a United Way agency. Funding for this project is made possible by the Missouri Children's Trust Fund.

The Kansas City PhoneFriend program supplies support and information for children at home alone. The program operates from 3–6 P.M. during weekdays. Other hours of operation include teacher in-service days, inclement weather days when schools are closed, and vacation days. Volunteers, trained by mental health professionals, develop listening and communication skills that help children feel reassured.

When answering calls, a PhoneFriend volunteer first asks the child's name, age, and the school he or she attends. This information helps the volunteer build rapport with the child and respond at an appropriate level. Children call PhoneFriend for a number of reasons. Some are bored or fearful. Others are lonely, and still others need help in making a decision or simply need to share information.

A similar operation in State College, Pennsylvania, is operated by two women's groups (Guerney & Moore 1983). Hours of operation are from 2:30–5:30 P.M. during school days and 9:00 A.M. to 5:30 P.M. on days when school is not in session because of teacher in-service training or adverse weather conditions. Mothers or students with some background in the helping professions serve as volunteers. All volunteers receive training in listening and communication skills, responding to emergency situations, and making referrals to other sources.

The goals of the State College PhoneFriend are similar to those of Kansas City. Guerney and Moore (1983) list three: "to create a helping network to provide information and support for children at home without adult supervision after school hours," "to help these children help themselves," and "to increase community awareness of the children's needs." A sampling of calls from September 1982–May 1983 showed that most calls (33 percent) were made by 8- and 9-year-olds, followed by 6- and 7-year-olds (19 percent), 10- and 11-year-olds (17 percent), 3- to 5-year-olds (14 percent), and 12- and 13-year-olds (7 percent) (Soto & Guerney 1984). Topics in order of frequency were "just want to talk" (448), "bored" (371), "lonely" (258), "scared" (95), and "curious about PhoneFriend" (94) (Soto & Guerney 1984).

Educational Programs. Community agencies provide safety lessons for children who must care for themselves when not in school. Lessons are conducted within the school or as part of a community awareness program. "I'm In Charge" is conducted by the Family and Children Services of Kansas City. Trained facilitators conduct classes that help parents determine when self-care is appropriate and improve their self-care arrangements. Parents are taught how to structure and monitor a self-care situation. Children are instructed in safety skills, emergency responses, and the care of younger siblings. Parents and their children receive lessons in communication skills and rule setting.

Other educational programs for children in self-care are conducted by the Virginia Cooperative Extension Service (Survival Skills for Kids 1984) and the

Boy Scouts of America (Prepared for Today 1982). The Virginia survival skills program focuses on safety, nutrition, self-entertainment, and the care of younger siblings. Trained volunteers conduct the program with assistance from community service workers, such as police officers, who instruct children in special areas. The "Prepared for Today" program helps children follow safety rules, respond to emergencies, care for younger siblings, plan meals, learn about their neighborhood, and solve problems.

Developing an SACC Program

In 1985, the authors, working with the Council for Children in Charlotte, North Carolina, initiated a SACC project based on a needs assessment study conducted the previous year (Council for Children 1984). The program components involved in this project are summarized in figure 9–1.

Needs Assessment

The Charlotte-Mecklenburg, North Carolina, community experienced rapid growth during the past decade. Its school system is today the thirtieth largest system in the country, with a student population of approximately 80,000 (Council for Children 1985). Thirty-four languages are represented in the school's bilingual education program. Whites make up the largest percentage (59 percent) of the student population, with a smaller percentage of blacks (39 percent) and other ethnic minorities (2 percent).

The diversity of families represented in this heterogenous school population indicated that no single SACC program would suffice. As a result, a needs assessment was conducted to determine what program options would best fit community needs.

A random sample of eighty-five classes was drawn from the five school districts of the Charlotte-Mecklenburg School System. The eighty-five classes consisted of two classes from grades K–6 and one class from grades 7–9 from each of the districts.

A total of 2,371 parent or guardian questionnaires were sent home, and 1,842 were returned, yielding a return rate of 78 percent. Thirty-six questionnaires were unusable because of incomplete data. The final sample consisted of 1,806 parents or guardians who had 842 children in grades K–3, 703 children in grades 4–6, and 261 children in grades 7–9.

The questionnaire consisted of twenty-seven self-administered items that focused on four areas of school-age child care: the demographic background of the families, the child care arrangements being used by the parents and their attitudes toward these arrangements, barriers that parents perceived to their use of existing SACC programs, and the school-age child care needs of the parents.

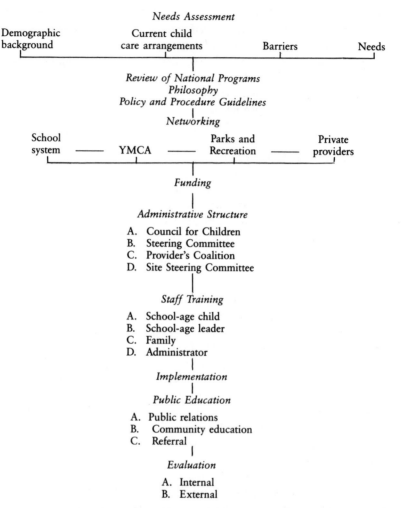

Needs Assessment

Demographic
background
Current child
care arrangements
Barriers
Needs

Review of National Programs
Philosophy
Policy and Procedure Guidelines

Networking

School
system — YMCA — Parks and
Recreation — Private
providers

Funding

Administrative Structure

A. Council for Children
B. Steering Committee
C. Provider's Coalition
D. Site Steering Committee

Staff Training

A. School-age child
B. School-age leader
C. Family
D. Administrator

Implementation

Public Education

A. Public relations
B. Community education
C. Referral

Evaluation

A. Internal
B. External

Figure 9–1. SACC Project Development, 1984–1985

An equal number of male and female children were represented in the 1,806 families. Most of the respondents were women (82 percent) between the ages of 30 and 39 (56 percent). The families were otherwise diverse in their race, marital status, level of education, work status, and incomes.

Across all families, the child care arrangements used most frequently were direct parent care (35 percent) and the child in self-care (20 percent). Thirteen percent of the parents or guardians reported that a younger child was left in the care of an older brother or sister. This finding suggests that the percentage of children in self-care situations may actually be closer to 33 percent since researchers have found that older brother or sister caretakers are frequently only a year or two older than the younger sibling who has been left in their charge (Long & Long 1983a; McMurray & Kazanjian 1982). The incidence of self-care was related to the grade level of the child. A greater percentage of older children in grades 5–9 were in self-care than parent care; the reverse was true for children in grades K–4 (Rowland, Robinson & Coleman 1986).

Across all families, the most frequently reported barriers to the use of existing SACC programs were cost of programs (28 percent), transportation problems (19 percent), and difficulty in getting children to accept existing programs (17 percent). The most frequently reported SACC needs were summer care (27 percent) and after-school care (22 percent). A sizable percentage of parents or guardians needed holiday care (14 percent) and emergency care (11 percent).

As a result of the needs assessment, two questions were raised: What type of SACC program could meet the identified needs of such a diverse population? How could the identified barriers be overcome? For assistance in addressing these questions, the SACC project entered its next phase.

Review of National Programs, Philosophy, and Guidelines

We reviewed different SACC programs from around the country and found a range of structures and philosophies. Based upon this review, along with the needs assessment, a philosophy statement was developed focusing on a child-centered enrichment SACC program (appendix 9B). Policy and procedure guidelines were developed that focused on a flexible program to meet the needs of families from different backgrounds and a curriculum to meet the needs of different aged children (appendix 9c).

Together the philosophy statement and policy and procedure guidelines indicated that a partnership program was in order. The next phase of the SACC project was to identify community groups that could form a strong network of SACC programs.

Networking

Four agencies were selected for the SACC project: the Charlotte-Mecklenburg school system, the Charlotte Department of Parks and Recreation, the YMCA, and a coalition of private day care home providers. Three criteria were used in selecting these agencies, all of which fulfilled the philosophy statement and policy and procedure guidelines:

1. The different agencies would provide program options for families and children to choose from.

2. All agencies had more than one site already established, and three of the agencies had sites scattered demographically throughout the Charlotte-Mecklenburg community. This made it easier for children to attend SACC programs located close to their homes.

3. All programs were already providing services to children from diverse backgrounds or had the potential to do so.

The logistics of the networking process was not easy. Some of the agencies began with fewer program sites than originally planned. Space and staff will not be shared initially. As the SACC project grows, additional sites will be added, and it is anticipated that the agencies will display greater cooperation in their programming efforts.

The networking process, however, was successful. Outside start-up funds were sought and received. These funds helped each agency establish its program sites. The school system agreed to provide transportation to SACC programs that could feasibly be worked into existing bus routes. All agencies agreed to provide developmentally appropriate programs for children between the ages of 5 and 12. Finally, all agencies adopted a common sliding-scale fee schedule not to exceed $20 per week. One agency was able to offer the program on a nonfee basis by utilizing ongoing funding that required only supplemental income for snacks and materials.

The networking process will continue as the SACC project expands and the participating community agencies begin to share their resources. Certainly the importance of the networking phase paid off in setting the groundwork for the remaining components of the SACC project.

Administrative Structure

A four-tier administrative structure oversees the operation of the SACC project. The responsibility of the Council for Children is to oversee the general management and coordination of the entire project. A half-time SACC project coordinator spearheads this top administrative level.

The SACC project steering committee serves as a conduit for program information flow among the SACC programs. This administrative level ensures continuity of programming throughout the project.

The SACC project providers' coalition provides direct management and guidance for their respective SACC program site. The sharing of new resources and enrichment activities takes place at this administrative level.

Finally, the SACC site steering committee conducts a grass-roots campaign to receive advice on program development from those individuals having daily contact with SACC programs: staff and volunteers working within the programs and parents with enrolled children.

The SACC administrative structure ensures shared community responsibility for a community problem. In short, the four-tier structure provides the checks and balances needed for a SACC quality assurance component.

Staff Training

SACC workers need to be well informed of child and family development principles, as well as applied programming issues. A staff training package was developed to prepare workers and administrators for their roles in the Charlotte SACC project (Rowland, Coleman & Robinson 1986).

The staff training package focuses on three issues. First, the package is self-administering, allowing training to take place in different-sized groups with minimum direction. Second, the format is both didactic and experiential. Four modules separately address the school-age child, the school-age child care leader, the family, and the school-age child care administrator. Forty topic papers are accompanied by twelve discussion guides and thirty-seven activities that allow participants to work with, and thereby better understand, the material. Four videotapes accompany the training package.

Implementation and Public Education

The SACC program sites were initially planned to be implemented at the same time; however, delays and setbacks in some agencies led to a redesign of program plans to allow each agency to implement its program sites when staffing, space, and program content were in place.

With the implementation of all SACC programs, a public education campaign involves ongoing contacts with the community media. Educational programs will address child and family issues. A referral service will direct parents to the program sites that best meet their needs. As with the other SACC components, the public education campaign is expected to expand its services over time. Indeed, as the SACC project grows, this component will become an important outreach program serving the community and state.

Evaluation

The goal of the evaluation component is to document project successes and give direction for improvement. Internal evaluations consist of evaluations by staff of their training, annual staff performance evaluations by supervisors, and annual program operation evaluations by site directors. External evaluations include parent evaluations of the SACC project and evaluations of the social and academic gains made by enrolled children.

Summary

The focus of this chapter was on developing SACC programs in which maximum use is made of existing community resources. No one formula ensures a high-quality SACC partnership program, but the information in this chapter can assist parents and community groups in thinking about the steps to take in creating a quality program. These steps are an assessment of commmunity school-age child care needs, followed by the development of policy and procedure guidelines and a SACC philosophy. Networking among existing community agencies can ensure efficient use of community resources. An administrative structure provides guidance to program operation, and a training component results in competent child care providers. Public education is important in publicizing the program. Finally, an evaluation program documents program successes and identifies areas that need improvement.

A knowledge of SACC program development is important for program developers and parents. Program developers need guidance in planning SACC programs. Parents need to know the questions to ask in order to be good consumers of SACC services. A checklist of SACC programming issues is presented in appendix 9D. Program developers can use the checklist to plan and assess their SACC programs. Parents can use the checklist to be good consumers of SACC services.

References

Anderson, J.S. 1984. Who's minding the sick children? *Children Today* 13:2–5.

Barnett, S. 1985 (December). Personal communication.

Battle, G.E.; Hunt, A.H.; & Robinson, B.B. 1985. *Giant steps: An instructional guide for tutoring.* Charlotte, N.C.: Batts and Associates.

Bram, S. 1985 (December). Personal communication.

Chaback, E., & Fortunato, P. 1981. *The official kids' survival kit: How to do things on your own.* Boston: Little, Brown.

Council for Children. 1984. *Taking action for latchkey children.* Charlotte, N.C.: Author.

Council for Children. 1985. *The state of the child in Mecklenburg County.* Charlotte, N.C.: Author.

Divine-Hawkins, P. 1983. *Employer supported child care: Where are we and where are we going?* Washington, D.C.: Administration for Children, Youth, and Families. ERIC Document Reproduction Service, ED 246 988.

Fooner, A. 1985 (October). Six good solutions for child care. *Working Woman*, pp. 173, 174.

Lefstein, L. 1982 (January). *Common Focus.* Carrboro, N.C.: Center for Early Adolescence.

Goltsman, S.M.; Moore, R.C.; & Iacofano, D.S. 1982 (May). *Newsletter of the International Association for the Child's Right to Play.* Available from Project PLAE, 2390 Woosley Avenue, Berkley, California 94705.

Guerney, L., & Moore, L. 1983. PhoneFriend: A prevention-oriented service for latchkey children. *Children Today* 12:5–10.

Kyte, K. 1983. *In charge: A complete handbook for kids with working parents.* New York: Knopf.

Local churches respond to special needs of latchkey kids. 1984 (August). *Sun Newspapers,* p. 3A.

Long, L., & Long, T. 1983a. *Latchkey children.* Washington, D.C.: Catholic University of America. ERIC Document Reproduction Service, ED 226 836.

Long, L., & Long, T. 1983b. *The handbook for latchkey children and their parents: A complete guide for latchkey kids and their working parents.* New York: Arbor House.

McMurray, G.L., & Kazanjian, D.P. 1982. *Day care and the working poor: The struggle for self-sufficiency.* New York: Community Service Society of New York. ERIC Document Reproduction Service, ED 221 266.

McKnight, J., & Shelsby, B. 1984. Checking in: An alternative for latchkey kids. *Children Today* 13:23–25.

Mathos, J., & Frances, B. 1985 (November). Personal communication.

Mayesky, M.E. 1979. Extended day program in a public elementary school. *Children Today* 8:6–9.

Mayesky, M.E. 1980. Phillips extended day magnet: A successful blend of day care and academics. *Educational Horizons* 58:178–183.

New program for school age child care. 1984 (August). Kansas City: Living Center.

Pfafflin, N. 1982. *Survival skills for kids.* Blacksburg, Va.: Polytechnic Institute and State University.

Prepared for today. 1982. Irving, Texas: Boy Scouts of America.

Rowland, B.H.; Robinson, B.E.; & Coleman, M. 1986. Parents' perceptions of needs for their latchkey children: A survey. *Pediatric Nursing* 12.

Soto, L.D., & Guerney, L. 1984. Latchkey children count on PhoneFriend. *Educational Horizons* 62:105.

Survival skills for kids. 1984. Blacksburg, Va.: Virginia Cooperative Extension Service, Virginia Polytechnic Institute and State University.

U.S. Department of Commerce. Bureau of the Census. 1981. *Population profile of the United States: 1980 population characteristics.* Current Population Reports, Series P-20, No. 363. Washington, D.C.: U.S. Government Printing Office.

YMCA school-age child care manual. Champaign, Ill.: YMCA of the USA.

Appendix 9A:
Logistical Issues in Developing a
Partnership SACC Program

Administration

When two or more community groups work together in providing school-age child care, administrative responsibilities take a number of forms. In some cases, all groups take equal responsibility, and in other cases administrative duties are assigned based on the unique characteristics of each group. For example, in a coalition between the county government and a network of churches, budgeting and financial matters are handled by the government and staffing and curriculum matters by the churches.

In other cases a group simply provides space for a SACC program while allowing another group to administer the program. This type of situation is most frequently found in coalitions between boys' and girls' clubs that administer and operate SACC programs within school classrooms or other facilities that have been provided as an in-kind service.

In still other cases, schools administer a SACC program but use neighborhood block mothers or community physical facilities as placement sites. Finally, parent boards sometimes administer SACC programs that are conducted within school classrooms or other community facilities.

Administration of SACC programs is dependent on the unique resources and networks within the community. A successful program in one community may fail in another. Administrative responsibilities must be clearly established if the SACC program is to operate smoothly and succeed.

Staffing

Some partnership models share staff. Staff members with specialized training provide in-service workshops or help create and implement a specific program component. Community groups not directly involved in administering a SACC program provide support staff. Senior citizen centers, high school civic groups, fraternities and sororities, and college and community groups are potential sources from which volunteers are recruited and trained for work in SACC programs.

Funding

Financial stability is a major concern for all SACC programs. Operating costs are usually reduced when two or more groups share their resources. In some instances, a network of day care centers rents out empty classroom space to operate their SACC program. In a school system with a declining enrollment, this arrangement contributes to the financial needs of the school without interfering with the regular school program. Renting of school space is less costly and logistically more feasible for day care providers than building a new site located away from the school.

In many communities, operational costs are supported from a range of sources. Community groups band together to engage in fund raising, local or state governments pay a percentage of operational expenses, funds are directly obtained from various foundations and businesses, and in-kind services are supplied by community groups. Examples of in-kind services that are often supplied include transportation, in-service training, custodial assistance, staff, and space.

Optional Programs

A partnership SACC program can lead to program options that would not otherwise be possible. For example, in a coalition between a school system and a network of day care centers, parents are provided with options between a school-based extended-day SACC program and a day care–based program. The two programs work together in providing transportation, arranging field trips, staff, space, equipment, and other programming features. The practicality of maximizing existing community resources to provide a comprehensive SACC program makes a partnership model equally relevant to rural and urban areas.

Appendix 9B:
SACC Project Philosophy

School-age child care (SACC) can be defined as any program that provides child care for elementary school children during the hours that school is not in session. Generally included are before- and after-school care, snow days, school vacations, and school holidays.

This type of program is usually designed around the needs of the children of working parents in a dual- or single-parent family. Typical SACC programs include activities such as arts, crafts, sports, field trips, supplemental learning experiences, self-care skills, club membership, quiet time, and time for homework.

The uniqueness of a good SACC program is its design to meet the developmental needs of children ages 5–12 through recreational and educational activities. The format for such a program allows for an informal, relaxing environment in which a child can make activity choices within a structured framework.

The philosophy of the SACC project is reflected in its policy guidelines and procedures. The need for a varied enrichment program of activities that meet the needs and interests of children of different ages, from different backgrounds, and with different capabilities is stressed throughout the SACC project. The theme of the uniqueness and worth of the individual child is intended to focus attention on the belief that children can best identify and develop their physical, cognitive and social-emotional strengths within a safe, supportive, and enriched environment.

Appendix 9C:
Policy and Procedure Guidelines

1. Each model program shall be approved initially by the Council for Children Board of Directors.

2. Each model program must forward a balanced budget to be approved by the Council for Children to include the expenditures of any seed monies.

3. Each model program shall be responsible for establishing its own tuition rates and selecting its own staff subject to the following:

   a. Tuition rates and a yearly financial statement shall be filed with the Council for Children each year of the pilot project.

   b. All staff shall meet minimum requirements as outlined in the personnel descriptions and qualifications section of the project outline.

4. Each model program must participate in the project evaluation plan.

5. Each model program must:

   a. Develop policies that address health and safety regulations.

   b. Maintain records on enrolled children to include the name of parent or guardian, address, fee payments, and emergency medical information.

6. Each model program shall comply with regulations regarding the following:

   a. Staff: child ratio not to exceed 1:15.

   b. Sliding fee scale to be used with a maximum fee of $20 per week.

   c. State and local licensing requirements.

   d. Appropriate liability insurance.

7. Each model program is expected to become totally self-supporting within the three years of the pilot project.

8. Each model program must:

   a. Encourage parent involvement and participation.

   b. Distribute program policies and procedures concerning children's behavior and discipline.

c. Design a program of curriculum and activities that speaks to the differences of children's ages from 5–12 years.

d. Include basic program elements that:

Capitalize on the interests of the children.

Consider the expansion possibilities of activities and projects.

Use the community resources and events as much as possible.

Capitalize on the many opportunities that present themselves for informal, social learning.

Build upon the special talents and interests of the staff.

Allow for spontaneity and flexibility.

Agree upon and communicate clear, consistent expectations and limits to children.

Use an integrated approach to planning and implementing activities.

Balance the day's activities to include formal and informal times, teacher-directed and child-initiated experiences, and a wide range of activities.

10. All program staff must:

a. Participate in preservice and in-service training.

b. Be trained in first aid and CPR.

11. Each program site must:

a. Develop an advisory steering committee as outlined in the administrative structure section of the project outline.

b. Serve as a model SACC site that can be studied and used for high school, college and university interns and community volunteers.

Appendix 9D:
SACC Programming: A Checklist for Program Developers and Parents

This checklist can be used for program developers to plan an efficient SACC program. Parents can use the checklist to assess the quality of SACC programs.

Needs Assessment

_____ The need for SACC programs in the community is documented.
_____ The types of SACC services needed in the community are documented.
_____ The barriers to implementing SACC programs in the community are documented.
_____ The community resources (money, agencies, staffing) available to overcome barriers and maintain SACC services are documented.

Philosophy

_____ The broad goals of the SACC program are clearly stated (such as, "To ensure the safety of school-age children").
_____ The specific objectives that fall under each goal are clearly stated (such as, "To offer after-school care between 3 and 7 P.M." and "To offer a survival skills class").
_____ The strategies to accomplish each objective are clearly stated (such as, network with school system or have county extension agent conduct survival skills class).
_____ An evaluation tool to assess the success of the SACC program is developed (for example, by a survey of the number of in-home accidents or children's knowledge of how to respond to an emergency).

Staffing

_____ The regular, part-time, and/or volunteer staff who will conduct the SACC program are identified.

_____ The SACC staff training program is identified.
_____ All SACC staff have completed the training program.
_____ A listing of staff work roles and schedules is posted.

Funding

_____ Direct funding sources are identified (for example, tuition, contributions, grants, budget).
_____ Indirect funding sources are identified (for example, in-kind services such as space, facility maintenance, staffing, and materials).
_____ A plan for long-term financial support of the SACC program is developed.

Space

_____ Space for conducting SACC activities is identified.
_____ The identified space is safe and meets state standards.
_____ The identified space is appropriate for the age group served.
_____ A schedule for use of space shared with another program is developed.

Administration

_____ An administrative structure to manage each SACC program site is developed.
_____ An administrative structure to manage the entire SACC program is developed.
_____ The role for each administrative structure is specified.
_____ Policies regarding sick children and medical emergencies are developed.

Activities

_____ An activity schedule is developed.
_____ A variety of activities are scheduled.
_____ Each activity is appropriate for the age group served.
_____ Each activity meets at least one of the SACC objectives.
_____ All activities are safe.
_____ All activities are conducted with appropriate adult supervision.

Appendix:
Resources on Latchkey Children
and Their Families

This appendix contains annotations of books for adults and children, organizations, periodicals, audiovisuals, unpublished research reports, model programs, and publications for researchers, program developers, parents, teachers, and other human service workers—all pertaining to school-age children, school-age child care, and latchkey arrangements.

Books for Adults

School-Age Child Care Programs

Bacchus, Joan, & Hurst, Marsha. 1983. *After school.* New York: Resourceful Family. Includes descriptions of children's programs available in Manhattan during school-day afternoons.

Baden, Ruth; Genser, Andrea; Levine, James; & Seligson, Michelle. 1982. *School-age child care: An action manual.* Boston: Auburn House. A comprehensive guide on how to set up school-age child programs. Information is given for parents, program staff, and administrators in one of the best available books on this topic.

Bender, Judith; Schuyler-Haas Elder, Barbara; & Flatter, Charles. 1984. *Half a childhood: Time for school-age child care.* Nashville, Tenn.: School Age Notes. Discusses types of school-age child care programs, what to look for, types of families seeking care, the school-age child's needs, curriculum and planning ideas, and training considerations for staff.

Bergstrom, Joan. 1984. *School's out—now what? Creative choices for your child.* Berkeley, Calif.: Ten Speed Press. Presents ways for parents to provide practical help and guidance for their school-age children for afternoons, weekends, and vacations. Gives resources, checklists, and ideas for busy parents to use with their school-age children.

Blau, R.; Brady, E.; Bucher, I.; Hiteshaw, B.; Zavitkovsky, A.; & Zavitkovsky, D. 1977. *Activities for school-age child care*. Washington, D.C.: National Association for the Education of Young Children. Provides an array of ideas for the child care curriculum—from puppets to gardening—for children between 3 and 7 years.

Cohen, Abby. 1985. *School-age child care: A legal manual for public school administrators*. Wellesley, Mass.: Center for Research on Women. Offers legal guidance to public school officials who wish to establish school-age child care programs in their areas. This readable book is an invaluable resource for those who want to operate their own programs or provide space for other outside agencies for program operations. Topics such as lease agreements, contracts, liability, and other relevant considerations are covered.

Dorman, Gayle. 1985. *3:00 to 6:00 P.M.: Planning programs for young adolescents*. Chapel Hill, N.C.: Center for Early Adolescence. A comprehensive curriculum designed to help youth-serving agencies improve services for 10 to 15 year olds, this book provides eight instructional modules to teach youth workers and administrators what young adolescents want and need in program development.

Forman, George, & Hill, Fleet. 1986. *Constructive play*. St. Paul, Minn.: Toys N' Things. Includes over 100 games developed from Piaget's theory of child development that allow children to design their own rules and play at their own pace.

Hawkins, Melba, & Vandergriff, Barbara. 1986. *Caring for school-age children*. Nashville, Tenn.: Convention Press. A guidebook for planning weekday programs for children in grades 1–6. Suggested helps and activities are given for before-school, after-school, and school holiday care.

Hendon, K.; Grace, J.; Adams, D.; & Strapp, A. 1977. *The after school day care handbook: How to start an after-school program for school-age children*. Madison, Wis.: Community Coordinated Child Care 4-C in Dane County. Order from: 4C in Dane County, 3200 Monroe Street, Madison, Wisconsin 53711.

High/Scope Consultants. 1985. *Hands-on after-school day care activities for 5 to 9 year olds*. Ypsilanti, Mich.: High/Scope Press. A series of five books to help children generate their own projects and activities after school: *Learning through sewing and pattern design* (making and using patterns to create toys, puppets, and clothes); *Learning through construction* (building with wood); *Children as music makers* (writing and reading stories and plays, writing plans for activities); *Writing and reading* (writing and reading stories and plays, writing plans for activities); *Daily routine: Small group time* (100 child-tested activities in art, drama, sewing, construction, music, movement, math, writing, reading, classification, seriation, space and time). Order From: High/Scope Press, 600 North River Street, Ypsilanti, Michigan 48198.

Lefstein, Leah, & Lipsitz, Joan. 1983. *3:00 to 6:00 P.M.: Programs for Young Adolescents.* For youth workers, directors of youth-serving organizations, and planners of community services for young people; describes twenty-four after-school programs around the United States that are especially effective in serving the needs of young adolescents.

Marzollo, Jean. 1986. *Superkids: Creative activities for Children 5–15.* St. Paul, Minn.: Toys N' Things. Activities especially for school-age kids include making movies, planning parties, baking bread, planting gardens, and building birdhouses. A good resource for school-age child care teachers.

Nall, Susan, & Switzer, Stephen. 1984. *Extended day programs in independent schools.* Boston: National Association of Independent Schools. Presents the survey results of extended day programs in private schools; also provides program descriptions of a few of the participating schools.

Oregson, Bob. 1986. *The incredible indoor games book.* St. Paul, Minn.: Toys N' Things. An unlimited resource for games and activities that require little preparation and are designed for children between the ages of 6 and 16.

Rosenzweig, Susan. 1986. *Resources for youth workers and program planners.* Carroboro, N.C.: Center for Early Adolescence. Describes resources helpful to those who work with 10 to 15 year olds in out-of-school settings, such as churches, recreation departments, community education programs, youth organizations, libraries, museums, clubs, and volunteer programs. Topics covered include program development and implementation, model programs, funding, youth participation, community collaboration, social trends and public policy, racial, ethnic, and gender differences, and promoting physical and emotional health.

Seaver, Judith, & Cartwright, Carol. 1986. *Child care administration.* Belmont, Calif.: Wadsworth. An excellent book on planning programs, designing environment, materials and equipment, program and personnel management, and parental relationships in child care programs. Also provides information on characteristics and program implementation of school-age child care programs.

Seligson, Michelle; Genser, Andrea; Gannett, Ellen; & Gray, Wendy. 1983. *School-age child care: A policy report.* Wellesley, Mass.: Wellesley College Center for Research on Women. Addressed to policymakers and those who wish to influence policies in their respective communities. Surveys the research and provides a brief history of school-age child care in the United States. Special sections examine the role of the public schools, financing, regulation, and recommendations for policymakers.

Latchkey Kids

Center for Early Adolescence. 1985. *Setting policy for young adolescents in the after-school hours.* Carroboro, N.C.: Center for Early Adolescence. Proceedings of a national conference at the Wingspread Conference Center sponsored by the Center for Early Adolescence and the Johnson Foundation. Identifies program initiatives and policy barriers to increasing and improving opportunities for 10 to 15 year olds when school is out and recommends policies and strategies for reducing risks and increasing opportunities for young adolescents.

Coolsen, Peter; Seligson, Michelle; & Garbarino, James. 1985. *When school's out and nobody's home.* Chicago: National Committee for Prevention of Child Abuse. Gives information on children in self-care, supervised alternatives to self-care, and excellent resources on national educational programs, community help lines, check-in programs, sick care programs, and employer-based programs. Provides names of programs and addresses, educational materials, names of orgnaizations, and sources of technical assistance.

Grollman, Earl, & Sweder, Gerri. 1986. *The working parent dilemma.* Boston: Beacon Press. More than a thousand kids of working parents were interviewed by the authors. Their creative tips to problems of having working parents comprise the book's content. Some of the children were latchkey kids and some were not, but their messages are interesting, clear, and worth hearing.

Kraizer, Sherryll. 1985. *The safe child book.* New York: Dell Publishers. Describes for parents a comprehensive program on developing prevention of abduction and sexual abuse of children as well as safety training. The approach taken stresses that children can be taught to protect themselves without making them fearful. The author takes the point of view that children can make judgments, speak up for themselves, and play a major role in being responsible for their own well-being.

Lefstein, Leah; Kerewsky, William; Medrich, Elliott; & Frank. Carol. 1982. *Young adolescents at home and in the community.* Carroboro, N.C.: Center for Early Adolescence. Examines the developmental needs of young adolescents and how these needs can be best met in the out-of-school hours.

Lipsitz, Joan. 1986. *After-school: Young adolescents on their own.* Carroboro, N.C.: Center for Early Adolescence. A comprehensive report that discusses the effects of the so-called latchkey problem on the early adolescent age group, public policy initiatives that have addressed public responsibility for adolescent socialization, current municipal, state, and federal policies that either help or impede health growth of young adolescents, and possible options for the future.

Long, Lynette, and Long, Thomas. 1983. *The handbook for latchkey children and their parents: A complete guide for latchkey kids and their working parents.*

New York: Arbor House. Based on five hundred interviews, describes the positive and negative aspects of latchkey arrangements and projected consequences. Includes suggestions for parents and survival skills for children.

Medrich, Elliott; Roizen, Judith; Rubin, Victor; & Buckley, Stuart. 1982. *The serious business of growing up: A study of children's lives outside of school.* Los Angeles: University of California Press. Looks at how 11- and 12-year-olds spend their time when not in school. Based on a five-year research project in Oakland, California.

Growth and Development of School-Age Children

Collins, W.A. (ed.). 1984. *Development during middle childhood: The years from six to twelve.* Washington, D.C.: National Academy Press. Assesses the status of knowledge on middle childhood within the framework of three areas: the distinctive developmental characteristics of school-age children, the influence of new settings and changing relationships during the elementary years, and the long-term implications of developmental difficulties experienced during middle childhood.

Elkind, David. 1981. *The hurried child.* Reading, Mass.: Addison-Wesley. Describes how society is pushing children to grow up before they are developmentally ready and offers insights, advice, and hope for solving these problems.

Elkind, David. 1984. *All grown up and no place to go.* Reading, Mass.: Addison-Wesley. A sequel to *The hurried child* that focuses on the problems youth face as a result of being hurried.

Farel, Anita. 1982. *Early adolescence: What parents need to know.* Carroboro, N.C.: Center for Early Adolescence. An easy-to-read handbook for parents seeking to understand the rapid physical, emotional, intellectual, and social changes their 10- to 15-year-old children are experiencing.

Flake-Hobson, Carol; Robinson, Bryan; & Skeen, Patsy. 1983. *Child development and relationships.* Reading, Mass.: Addison-Wesley. Provides a comprehensive coverage of growth and development from conception to adolescence. Special chapters are included on the school-age child's physical, cognitive, and social-emotional development.

Hill, John. 1980. *Understanding early adolescence: A framework.* Carroboro, N.C.: Center for Early Adolescence. A comprehensive examination of early adolescent development for professionals, parents, volunteers, and policymakers.

Minuchin, Patricia. 1977. *The middle years of childhood.* Monterey, Calif.: Brooks/Cole. Summarizes theory and research pertaining to the four major aspects of development: cognitive, social, and individual development, and the school as a context for growth during the school-age years.

Strommen, Ellen; McKinney, John; & Fitzgerald, Hiram. 1983. *Developmental psychology: The school-aged child*. Homewood, Ill.: Dorsey Press. Presents an overview of the growth and development of school-age children. Developmental areas include physical, cognitive, personality, and moral. Special chapters are included on children and schools, families, friends and peer relationships, and attitudes, values, and society.

Williams, Joyce, & Stith, Marjorie. 1980. *Middle childhood: Behavior and development*. 2d ed. New York: Macmillan. A practical and readable examination of development during the middle years. This book is more applied than most others and includes special sections on the family, school, peers, and guidance of the school-age child.

Worell, J. (ed.). 1982. *Psychological development in the elementary years*. New York: Academic Press. An excellent book for graduate students and researchers that addresses specific concerns for relating current theory and research on psychological development of school-age children to educational practice. Reviews of literature include sex roles, peer relations, aggression, self-control, learning and achievement, developmental problems, family influences, and school context.

General Interest

Aitken, Margaret. 1972. *Play environments for children*. Bellingham, Wash.: Educational Designs and Consultants. Aimed at improving play environments for children by providing recommendations for constructing facilities for physical education in the elementary school, along with teaching child-centered elementary physical education. Chapters focus on the importance of play, indoor and outdoor play settings, and sources of equipment, supplies, and teaching aids.

Gorelick, Byrna. 1986. *The working parent's guide to child care*. St. Paul, Minn.: Toys n' Things. Covers the pros and cons of in-home care, family day care, and center care. Drawing on latest research, important issues such as interviewing care givers, evaluating settings, contracts, adjustment to day care, and costs are addressed.

Hechinger, Grace. 1984. *How to raise a street-smart child: Complete parent's guide to safety on the street and at home*. New York: Facts on File Publications. Attempts to give children a sense of personal security and safety by teaching them to take reasonable precautions. Topics include safety in traffic, risks at home, sexual abuse, missing children, muggings, and gangs and bullies.

Rauch, Gay, & Schmitt, Gretchen. 1986. *Single parenting*. St. Paul, Minn.: Toys n' Things. Describes a course to help parents meet the demands of their special roles as single parents. Handouts, bibliographies, and exercises for participants make this a complete and easily adopted curriculum.

Toys n' Things. 1986. *Health, safety and first aid.* St. Paul, Minn.: Toys n' Things Press. Covers emergency first aid procedures, accident prevention, children's illnesses, health practices, and helping children learn safety and good health habits. Tips for teachers on how to make this topic fun and interesting are included. Especially written for care-giver trainers.

Books for Children

A number of books have been written specifically for school-age children. Most of these books furnish safety tips and constructive ways of occupying time while children are in self-care. They can serve as a basis for starting a lending library in classrooms or used for reading enjoyment at home or school.

Chaback, Elaine, & Fortunato, Pat. 1981. *The official kid's survival kit: How to do things on your own.* Boston: Little, Brown.

Clifton, L. 1975. *My brother fine with me.* New York: Holt, Rinehart, & Winston.

Freeman, Lori. 1985. *A kid's guide to first aid: What would you do if . . .* Nashville, Tenn.: School-Age Notes.

Kyte, Kathy. 1983. *Play it safe.* New York: Alfred Knopf.

Long, Lynette. 1984. *The kids' self-care book: On my own.* Washington, D.C.: Acropolis Books.

Long, Thomas. 1985. *Safe at home, safe alone.* Alexandria, Va.: Miles River Press.

Pfafflin, N. 1982. *Survival skills for kids.* Blacksburg, Va.: Polytechnic Institute and State University.

Skurzynski, G. 1979. *Martin by himself.* Boston: Houghton Mifflin.

Swan, Helen, & Houston, Victoria. 1985. *Alone after school.* Englewood Cliffs, N.J.: Prentice-Hall.

The telephoto book: The emergency phone book for kids. Pasadena, Calif.: Mother Goose Distributing Company.

Wolff, Margaret. 1985. *The kid's after school activity book.* Belmont, Calif.: David S. Lake Publishers.

Organizations

This section details the major organizations concerned with school-age and latchkey children. We have subdivided the organizations into two types: assistance organizations and professional organizations. Assistance organizations provide such services as dissemination of resources on latchkey and other school-age children, materials for replicating model school-age child care programs, and other types of technical assistance in the area of latchkey situations. Professional organizations are national associations of professionals dedicated to the improvement of those who work with school-age children. These organizations generally charge membership dues, publish journals, and sponsor an annual meeting where members gather for seminars, speeches, and workshops.

Assistance Organizations

Boy Scouts of America. 1325 Walnut Hill Lane, Irving, Texas 75062. Publishes training manuals for staff in school-age child care programs and for children in self-care. Its training program is titled "Prepared for Today."

Camp Fire, Inc. 4601 Madison Avenue, Kansas City, Missouri 64112. Has published a self-reliance program for latchkey kids in second through fourth grades. The program, "I Can Do It," is available from Camp Fire.

Center for Early Adolescence. Suite 223, Carr Mill Mall, Carroboro, North Carolina 27510. As part of the Department of Maternal and Child Health at the University of North Carolina at Chapel Hill, the center disseminates information such as resource lists and bibliographies that deal with school-age and early adolescent children. The center's quarterly newsletter is filled with valuable resources such as programs, research, books, films, and conferences for professionals who work with 10–15 year olds.

Child Care Action Campaign. 99 Hudson Street, New York, New York 10013. A national advocacy organization committed to establishing high-quality child care and providing a national network for child advocates.

Child Care Law Project. 625 Market Street, Suite 815, San Francisco, California 94105. Serves as a legal resource for local, state, and national child care communities. Its purpose is to foster the development of high-quality, affordable child care programs. The project's services are available to parents, attorneys, child care centers, family day care providers, policymakers, governmental and community agencies, unions, and employers. Its publications provide preventive law information to the child care community and inform the legal community of legal issues in child care.

Children's Defense Fund. 122 C Street, N.W., Washington, D.C. 20001. Publishes information on prevention problems, issues, and news regarding children of all ages. A newsletter and booklets are available for child advocates, community leaders, public health workers, and others interested in improving the lives of children.

Day Care and Child Development Council of America. 711 Fourteenth Street, N.W., Suite 507, Washington, D.C. 20005. Offers information and technical assistance on all types of day care, including after-school care for school-age youngsters. A newsletter, *Voices for Children,* is also sponsored by the council.

Family Day Care Check-in Project. Fairfax County Office for Children, 10396 Democracy Lane, Fairfax, Virginia 22030. Provides a comprehensive package of materials for agencies and organizations interested in adapting the Family Day Care Check-in Project in their communities. The package contains step-by-step procedures for starting up, administering, supervising, and evaluating a program. In addition to addressing such issues as licensing, zoning, and liability, the materials include a section on community outreach, describing methods of educating the community about the needs and problems of unsupervised young adolescents and procedures for recruiting day care providers and families.

Girl Scouts of America. 830 Third Avenue, New York, New York 10022. Publishes training manuals for staff in school-age child care programs and for children in self-care. Its training program is titled "Safe and Sound at Home Alone."

National Crime Prevention Council. Woodward Building, 733 Fifteenth Street, N.W., Washington, D.C. 20005. Publishes a kit for safety in self-care, *Keeping Kids Safe: Kids Keeping Safe.* The packet includes the *Play it Safe* coloring book and topics on babysitting and bicycle safety.

PhoneFriend. P.O. Box 735, State College, Pennsylvania 16804. An after-school telephone help line for children at home without adult supervision. It is a community service project and operated by the State College, Pennsylvania, branch of the American Association of University Women in cooperation with the State College Women's Resource Center. The goals of PhoneFriend are to create a helping network to provide information and support for children at home without adult supervision after school hours, to help these children help themselves, and to increase community awareness of the children's needs. A PhoneFriend replication packet giving information and instruction on how to establish and operate a help line for children is available.

School-Age Child Care Project. Center for Research on Women, Wellesley College, 828 Washington Street, Wellesley, Massachusetts 02181. A national information and technical assistance resource started in 1979 and committed to promoting the development of programs and services for children between the ages of 5 and 12, before and after school at such times when there is a need for care and supervision. Offers technical assistance throughout the country regarding the design and implementation of school-age child care programs, publishes a newsletter, and acts as a clearinghouse for national programs and publications on latchkey children and school-age child care.

Professional Organizations

Association for Childhood Education International. 11141 Georgia Avenue, Suite 200, Wheaton, Maryland 20902. A professional medium for those concerned with the education and well-being of children from infancy through early adolescence: classroom teachers, teachers in training, teacher educators, parents, day care workers, librarians, supervisors, administrators, and other practitioners.

Child Study Association of America. 9 East Eighty-ninth Street, New York, New York 10028. Concerned with the study and development of young children and the environments that affect them.

Child Welfare League of America. 67 Irving Place, New York, New York 10003. Concerned with any facet of social policy that bears on the welfare of children and their families. Its membership is composed of professionals who work for child and family welfare through administration, supervision, casework, group work, community organization, teaching, or research.

National Association for the Education of Young Children. 1834 Connecticut Avenue, N.W., Washington, D.C. 20009. A professional organization for teachers, parents, and other practitioners who work with children from birth to 8 years of age.

National Center for Youth Law (NCYL). 1663 Mission Street, San Francisco, California 94103. Devoted to improving the lives of poor children in the United States by providing advice and technical assistance to legal services attorneys regarding the law affecting poor children and adolescents.

National Middle School Association. P.O. Box 14882, Columbus, Ohio 43214. Designed to improve intermediate education. Membership is composed of teachers, administrators, parents, teacher educators, counselors, curriculum directors, and college students.

National PTA. 700 North Rush Street, Chicago, Illinois 60611. A professional organization for parents, teachers, and others concerned with bridging the gap between home and school for the welfare of the nation's children.

Society for Research in Child Development. 5801 Ellis Avenue, Chicago, Illinois 60637. A professional platform for researchers and theoreticians interested in the study and development of children from infancy to adolescence.

Periodicals

This section highlights the major periodicals in the field that publish articles pertaining to latchkey kids, school-age child care, and elementary school youngsters in general. The periodicals list is classified in three types: professional journals, popular magazines, and newsletters. Professional journals are usually, but not always, sponsored by a professional organization and refereed by experts in the field; their content tends to be academic and research based in nature. Popular magazines are generally written for the layperson in a casual style and sometimes lack a sound scientific basis. Nevertheless, many of the magazines listed here publish articles by top experts in the field. Newsletters are published by assistance organizations that keep readers up to date.

Professional Journals

Child Care Information Exchange. Child Care Information Exchange, P.O. Box 2890, Redmond, Washington 98073. For child care directors with an abundance of information on school-age child care. Bimonthly.

Child Care Quarterly. Human Sciences Press, 72 Fifth Avenue, New York, New York 10011. Committed to the improvement of child care practices in a variety of day and residential settings. Designed for child care practitioners, their supervisors, and other personnel in the child care field. Quarterly.

Child Development. SRCD, 570 Ellis Avenue, Chicago, Illinois 60637. A research journal citing findings on all aspects of development including school-age children. Published by the University of Chicago Press and sponsored by the Society for Research in Child Development.

Child Study Journal. Child Study Journal, State University College of New York at Buffalo, 1300 Elmwood Avenue, Buffalo, New York 14222. Publishes theory and research on child and adolescent development. Particular attention is given to articles devoted to the educational and psychological aspects of development. Published by the Faculty of Applied and Professional Studies, State University of New York at Buffalo.

Child Welfare. Child Welfare League of America Inc., 67 Irving Place, New York, New York 10003. Extends knowledge in any child-family welfare or related service on any aspect of administration, supervision, casework, group work, community organization, teaching, research, interpretation, or any facet of interdisciplinary approaches to the field or on issues of social policy that bear on the welfare of children and their families. Sponsored by the Child Welfare League of America, Inc.

Childhood Education. ACEI, 11141 Georgia Avenue, Suite 200, Wheaton, Maryland 20902. A journal for professionals of school-age children. Includes essays and research studies dealing with development and curriculum concerns. Sponsored by the Association for Childhood Education International.

Children and Youth Services Review. Pergamon Press, Inc., Maxwell House, Fairview Park, Elmsford, New York 10523. A journal concerned with fostering knowledge in the field of children and youth services and improving the quality of effectiveness of services to children.

Children's Environments Quarterly. Center for Human Environments, Graduate Center of the City University of New York, 33 West Forty-Second Street, New York, New York 10036. Designed to improve understanding of the relationship of children to the physical environment. A broad range of theoretical and research papers are included as they apply to the planning, design, and management of children's environments. Quarterly.

Children Today. Room 356-G, 200 Independence Avenue, S.W., Washington, D.C. 20201. Deals with social problems, social policy, and government-related services and issues and child care. Published by the Office of Human Development Services, Department of Health and Human Services.

Elementary School Journal. University of Chicago Press, Journals Division, P.O. Box 37005, Chicago, Illinois 60637. Publishes original studies, reviews of research, and conceptual analyses for researchers and practitioners in the field of elementary schooling. Sponsored by the Center for Research in Social Behavior.

Journal of Research in Childhood Education. ACEI, 11141 Georgia Avenue, Suite 200, Wheaton, Maryland 20902. Publishes articles that advance knowledge and theory of the education of children, infancy through adolescence. Sponsored by the Association for Childhood Education International.

Merrill-Palmer Quarterly. Journals Department, Wayne State University Press, Detroit, Michigan 48202. Publishes articles from a variety of disciplines that bear on human development.

PTA Today. National PTA, Program Department, 700 North Rush Street, Chicago, Illinois 60611. Publishes articles that are the mutual concern of parents, teachers, and other school personnel. Reprints of numerous articles on latchkey kids and school-age child care are available from the National PTA Organization.

Young Children. NAEYC, 1834 Connecticut Avenue, N.W., Washington, D.C. 20009. A journal for teachers, parents, and professionals who work with children from birth to 8 years. Articles include reviews of research and timely topics on developmental issues as well as curriculum concerns. Sponsored by the National Association for the Education of Young Children.

Popular Magazines

Family Circle, 488 Madison Avenue, New York, New York 10022.

Lady's Circle, 105 East Thirty-fifth Street, New York, New York 10016.

Mothers Today, 441 Lexington Avenue, New York, New York 10017.

Parents Magazine, 685 Third Avenue, New York, New York 10017.

Woman's Day, 1515 Broadway, New York, New York 10036.

Working Mother, 230 Park Avenue, New York, New York 10169.

Working Parents, 441 Lexington Avenue, New York, New York 10017.

Working Woman, 342 Madison Avenue, New York, New York 10173.

Newsletters

Center for Early Adolescence Newsletter. Center for Early Adolescence, Suite 223, Carr Mill Mall, Carroboro, North Carolina 27510. Contains valuable resources for professionals who work with children between 10 and 15 years old. Quarterly.

Children's Defense Fund Reports. Children's Defense Fund, 122C Street, N.W., Washington, D.C. 20001. Includes news and issues in federal, state, and local initiatives for children. Monthly.

First Teacher. P.O. Box 29, Bridgeport, Connecticut 06602. Designed like a newspaper and filled with excellent curriculum activities appropriate for younger school-age children. Monthly except July and August.

PhoneFriend Newsletter. PhoneFriend, P.O. Box 735, State College, Pennsylvania 16804. Gives information on funding, new programs, facts and articles on latchkey issues, suggested resources, news from other warm lines across the country, and a column, "PhoneFriend Childspeak," which contains quotes from children's telephone calls. Quarterly.

School-Age Child Care Project Newsletter. Center for Research on Women, Wellesley College, Wellesley, Massachusetts 02181. Details upcoming national events, important legislation, new publications and audiovisuals, and other actions being taken on behalf of school-age children around the country. Three issues a year.

School Age Notes. P.O. Box 120674, Nashville, Tennessee 37212. Provides tips for school-age child care workers and administrators on planning activities, staffing, and program management. Six issues per year.

Voices for Children. Day Care and Child Development Council of America, 711 Fourteenth Street, N.W., Suite 507, Washington, D.C. 20005. The newsletter of the Day Care and Child Development Council of America.

Youth Law News. National Center for Youth Law, 1663 Mission Street, Fifth Floor, San Francisco, California 94103. Six issues per year.

Audiovisuals

The audiovisuals section is perhaps the least comprehensive because very little in the way of media has been developed on latchkey children. Still, there are a number of good resources that we have included here and have organized by type of audiovisual.

16 MM Films

Better Safe Than Sorry. FilmFair Communications, 10900 Ventura Boulevard, Studio City, California, 91604. Presents a series of vignettes on children encountering strangers under potentially dangerous circumstances—for example, when children walk home alone from school or a stranger comes to their door. The film has three versions, each for a different age level: (I) For primary and elementary children; (II) For kindergarten and primary children; (III) For adolescents. Dramatized examples are followed by commonsense rules for personal safety and avoidance to match age levels.

In Charge at Home (Latchkey Children). FilmFair Communications, 10900 Ventura Boulevard, Studio City, California 91604. A 1985 release that presents vignettes of children coping on their own at home. Includes what to do if a key is lost, checking in with a parent upon arrival at home, how to answer the door and telephone, and other responsibilities that latchkey children must assume. Also available in videocassette (any size).

Lord of the Locks. Living Center for Family Enrichment, 3515 Broadway, Kansas City, Missouri 64111. A twenty-eight-minute film that highlights the seriousness of self-care and the need for responsible actions by both parent and child. Through two magical characters, the humorous story illustrates possible self-care dangers, the feelings of parents and children, and appropriate child-parent response.

What Ever Happened to Childhood? Churchill Films, 662 North Robertson Boulevard, Los Angeles, California 90069. A forty-five-minute film that portrays the rush children are in to grow up and as part of its documentary highlights latchkey children and their problems. Suggests that childhood as we know it may no longer exist for many children. Interviews older latchkey kids responsible for younger siblings while parents work.

Work and Family: Walking the Tightrope. Bureau of National Affairs, Customer Service, 9435 Key West Avenue, Rockville, Maryland 20850. This thirty-minute film explores how employers and unions are responding to the needs of the new generation of workers walking the tightrope between demands of jobs and family. Child care options for working parents, maternity, paternity, adoption-leave policies, alternative work schedules, and assistance programs are discussed.

Videotapes

Business of Caring. Women's Bureau, U.S. Department of Labor, 200 Constitution Avenue, N.W., Room S3305, Washington, D.C. 20210. A twenty-three-minute videotape that examines employer-sponsored child care programs and services.

Children and Working Parents. Education Center of Sheppard Pratt, 6501 North Charles Street, Towson, Maryland 21204. A twenty-minute videotape that presents seven parents who discuss their own career circumstances and child care problems after viewing a dramatized latchkey episode. Topics include quality parenting, job demands, and responsibilities. A leader's guide contains target lead questions and specific issues from the video. An accompanying packet, "Juggling," contains individual sheets showing self-help skills and solutions for many of the situations raised by the discussion.

Friends: How They Help . . . How They Hurt. Sunburst Communications, Room Q 7575, 39 Washington Avenue, Pleasantville, New York 10570. Examines for fifth through ninth graders the meaning of friendship during the difficult transition from childhood to adolescence. Open-ended dramatizations encourage discussion and provide a nonthreatening forum in which children can gain practice in solving their own problems with friendships.

The Group and You: Handling the Pressures. Sunburst Communications, Room Q 7575, 39 Washington Avenue, Pleasantville, New York 10570. Designed for grades 5 through 9, this film helps children understand the ways groups exert pressure on their members. Stresses that the more young people know about how groups work, the better they will be able to resist group pressure that could cause them to act against their own best interests.

Nutrition on the Run: Snacks and Fast Foods. Sunburst Communications, Room Q 7575, 39 Washington Avenue, Pleasantville, New York 10570. Especially helpful for latchkey kids who prepare their own snacks when in self-care. Encourages teens to question the nutritional quality of the food they buy and consume by examining their own eating habits.

Santa Monica Children's Centers: An Introduction. SACC Project, Center for Research on Women, Wellesley College, Wellesley, Massachusetts 02181. Portrays a typical day in a school-age care program, showing the daily curriculum and the philosophy behind the program. Twelve minutes; available on 1/2 or 3/4 inch.

Santa Monica Children's Centers: The Making of Snow White. SACC Project, Center for Research on Women, Wellesley College, Wellesley, Massachusetts 02181. Shows the re-creation of a play of *Snow White* by a group of children in a summer school-age program in Santa Monica, California. Emphasis is on the curriculum planning for staff. Fifteen minutes; available on 1/2 or 3/4 inch.

School-Age Child Care Training Package. Council for Children, 229 South Brevard Street, Suite 202, Charlotte, North Carolina, 28202. A training package for school-age child care personnel that contains four videotapes and four written modules that accompany the videos on the following topics: (1) focus on the SACC leader, (2) the SACC curriculum, (3) the SACC administrator, and (4) parent education. The modules contain forty papers on a variety of topics centered around the four modules. A pretest, activities, discussion, and suggestions for further reading are also included.

Slide-Tapes

Fairfax County Office for Children School-Age Child Care Program. SACC Project, Center for Research on Women, Wellesley College, Wellesley, Massachusetts 02181. Details the startup of the school-age child care program in Fairfax County, Virginia. Twenty minutes.

Filmstrips/Cassettes

Adventures in Learning. Toys N' Things, 906 North Dale Street, St. Paul, Minnesota 55103. Helps teachers make the best of the teachable moment by showing how to make field trips exciting adventures in learning. Trip sites and the mechanics of planning are included.

Choosing Child Care. Toys N' Things, 906 North Dale Street, St. Paul, Minnesota, 55103. Outlines all child care options and provides parents with guidelines. Excellent for use by social service agencies, pediatricians, health organizations, referral agencies, and child care providers. Filmstrip.

Planning After-School Programs for Young Adolescents: What Works and Why. Center for Early Adolescence, University of North Carolina at Chapel Hill, Suite 223, Carr Mill Mall, Carroboro, North Carolina 27510. Explains the characteristics of effective programs, shows several examples of popular activities, and offers a model for successful planning. Filmstrip.

You and Your Parents: Making it Through the Tough Years. Parts I and II. Sunburst Communications, Room H6262, 39 Washington Avenue, Pleasantville, New York 10570-9971. Designed for children between fifth and ninth grades to help them understand and cope with the tensions in parent-child relationships that often accompany the developmental years between 10 and 14. Part I shows the years between 10 and 14 and times of physical and emotional change that can trouble parents and children. Notes that conflict is normal and that there are techniques for handling it. Part II outlines a simple version for better communication and includes an introduction to the skills of negotiation as a method for resolving conflict. Two filmstrips and two cassettes with teacher guide.

Unpublished Research Reports

This section includes local and state research reports that have relevance for program developers, child advocates, researchers, and practitioners nationwide. Because they are unpublished, it was difficult to locate a comprehensive annotation of research reports, but this list is a good sampling of what is available across the country.

Belle, D. In progress. Social support processes among latchkey and adult supervised children. Deborah Belle, Department of Psychology, 64 Cummington Street, Boston University, Boston, Massachusetts 02215. Dr. Belle is conducting a four-year longitudinal study comparing children in adult-supervised care, children in self-care, and children in the care of underage siblings on numerous factors.

Coleman, T.M. 1984. Families with latchkey children: A study with implications for service delivery. Ph.D. dissertation, University of Georgia. Mick Coleman, Cooperative Extension Program, Virginia State University, Petersburg, Virginia 23803. Investigates the possibility of using selected family variables to predict differences between families using different types of child care arrangements in order to offer suggestions regarding service delivery for families with latchkey children.

Committee on School Age Child Care. 1979. The choice is ours: A report on the latchkey child. Arlington, Va.: Virginia Health and Welfare Council.

Council for Children. 1984. Taking action for latchkey children. Council for Children, 229 South Brevard Street, Suite 202, Charlotte, North Carolina 28202. Presents the results of a survey of 1,806 parents and 188 service providers regarding the latchkey problem in Charlotte, North Carolina. Focuses on what children do before and after school and during school holidays and vacations; what their child care arrangements are; the resources that are available for children; the problems related to utilization of current resources; the degree of satisfaction of parents with current arrangements; and gaps in services.

Entwisle, B. 1976. The impact of school age day care upon achievement. Paper presented at the Annual Meeting of the American Sociological Association, New York. Barbara Entwisle, Carolina Population Center, University of North Carolina at Chapel Hill, University Square 300A, Chapel Hill, North Carolina 27514. Presents the results of how a school-age day care program in Baltimore, Maryland, influenced participants in positive ways.

Hawkins, Melba. 1984. Programming for kindergarten through grade 3 (K–3) children in after-school care: A literature related guide. Master's thesis, University of North Carolina at Greensboro. Melba Hawkins, College of Education, University of North Carolina at Greensboro, Greensboro, North Carolina 27712.

Addresses programming needs and models of after-school care programs. A compendium of ideas of children's literature-related activities for school-age children also is presented in the following areas: Let's Create, Let's Pretend, Let's Make Music, Let's Cook, and Let's Celebrate.

Hedin, Diane. In progress. The family's view of after-school time. Diane Hedin, Center for Youth Development, 386 McNeal Hall, 1985 Buford Avenue, University of Minnesota, St. Paul, Minnesota 55108. Dr. Hedin is studying how children between the ages of 5 and 13 spend their summer and after-school time. She is also looking at children's preferences for how they would like to use time, compared to their parents' preferences.

Kersten, Elisabeth. 1983. Who's watching our children? The latchkey child phenomenon. Elisabeth Kersten, Director of Senate Office of Research, 1100 J Street, Suite 650, Sacramento, California 95814. Documents the expanding occurrence of the latchkey kids in California. Explores the latchkey dilemma and reviews the possible effects the problem may have on the physical and psychological well-being of the latchkey children.

Rodman, H. 1981 (January). Children in child care arrangements. Hyman Rodman, Child Survey, University of North Carolina at Greensboro, Greensboro, North Carolina 27712. Prepared for the Ford Foundation based on a summary of questionnaires mailed to readers of *Working Mother*.

Rodman, H. 1986. From latchkey stereotypes to self-care realities. Paper presented at the First National Conference on Latchkey Children. Hyman Rodman, Department of Child Development and Family Relations, University of North Carolina at Greensboro, Greensboro, North Carolina 27712. Deals with the perpetuation of negative stereotypes of latchkey kids by the media.

Sparks, S. 1983. Latchkey Children. Thesis, University of North Carolina. Sandra Sparks, Ashley Park Elementary School, 3128 Belfast Drive, Charlotte, North Carolina 28208. Reports the results of a survey conducted at the author's school regarding parents' needs and wishes for their latchkey children.

Steinberg, L. 1985. Latchkey children and susceptibility to peer pressure: An ecological analysis. Laurence Steinberg, Child and Family Studies, 1430 Linden Drive, University of Wisconsin, Madison, Wisconsin 53706. Compares 865 fifth through ninth graders in different kinds of self-care situations with those who are supervised by adults after school.

Vandell, D.L., & Corasaniti, M.A. 1985 (May 27). After-school care: Choices and outcomes for third graders. Paper presented at the Annual Meeting of the American Association for the Advancement of Science, Los Angeles, California. Deborah Lowe Vandell, Department of Psychology, Box 688, University of Texas at Dallas, Richardson, Texas 75080. Dr. Vandell studied 349 children from a relatively affluent, well-educated suburb. Four types of after-school care were contrasted: children who spent afternoons at home with mothers; those in self-care either alone or with a sibling; those who went to a day care center or community center after school; and those who stayed with a babysitter.

Programs for Latchkey Kids

School-age child care programs continue to develop throughout the United States. Individuals and advocacy groups work together to muster community resources to help bridge the ever-increasing gaps between needs and services. Some selected persons and addresses of existing programs are included in this section. This list of models represents a variety of collaborative efforts among government, schools, parents, community agencies, business and industry, and advocacy groups.

Patricia Rowland, Coordinator
Arlington Public Schools
Extended Day Program
1426 North Quincy Street
Arlington, Virginia 22207

Janet Larson Braun
Home Health Plus
TenderCare for Kids
825 South Eighth Street,
Suite M-50
Minneapolis, Minnesota 55404

Suzanne Bram, Coordinator
Manville After-School Program
Judge Baker Guidance Center
295 Longwood Avenue
Boston, Massachusetts 02115

Pheobe Carpenter, Director
Home Based Child Care Program
816 Broadway
Orlando, Florida 32803

Susan Goltsman, Director
Project P.L.A.E., Inc.
1824 A Fourth Street
Berkeley, California 94710

Barbara Keelan, Coordinator
After-school Enrichment Program
Charlotte-Mecklenburg Schools
Box 30035
Charlotte, North Carolina 28230

Joan Israelite, Coordinator
School-Age Child Care Project
Living Center for Family
  Enrichment
3515 Broadway, Suite 203
Kansas City, Missouri 64111

Janice Stroud, Coordinator
School-Age Child Care Project
Council for Children, Suite 202
229 South Brevard Street
Charlotte, North Carolina 28202

Julia McKnight, Director
Family Day Care Check-In Project
Fairfax County Office for Children
Fairfax, Virginia 22030

Paulette Bomberger, SACC
  Coordinator
Newport News Park & Recreation
  Program
2400 Washington Avenue
Newport News, Virginia 23607

Henry Daniels, Director
Joseph Mathos, Supervisor
Barbara Frances, Educational
  Specialist
After-School Care Program
Dade County Public Schools
1450 Northeast Second Avenue
  Room 814
Miami, Florida 33132

Kathy Hermes
Family and Children Services
"I'm In Charge Program"
3217 Broadway, Suite 500
Kansas City, Missouri 64111

Sheryl Barnett
KARE-4 Project Coordinator
304 South Phillips Avenue
Suite 310
Sioux Falls, South Dakota 57102

Christine M. Todd, Extension
  Specialist
"Key Kits" Program
Illinois Cooperative Extension
  Service
University of Illinois
Urbana-Champaign, Illinois 61801

Nancy Pfafflin, Extension Agent
"Survival Skills" Program
Virginia Cooperative Extension
Alexandria, Virginia 22313

Donna Kesler, Director
Reston Children's Center
School-Age Child Care Program
11825 Olde Crafts Drive
Reston, Virginia 22091

Professional Bibliography

This section provides an extensive bibliography of further readings for professionals in the field who wish to pursue their study in more detail. The bibliography that follows is drawn from professional journals and ERIC Documents and is subdivided into four interest groups: Researchers, Program Developers, Teachers and Administrators, and Parents.

Researchers

Chawla, L. 1986. Children in self-care: Latchkey children in their environments. *Children's Environments Quarterly. A special issue on latchkey children.*

Fosarelli, P.D. 1985. *Children left alone: Latchkey problems—Future research questions and interventions.* ERIC Documents. ED 255 313.

Galambos, N.L., & Dixon, R.A. 1984. Toward understanding and caring for latchkey children. *Child Care Quarterly* 13:116–125.

Galambos, N.L., & Garbarino, J. 1983. Identifying the missing links in the study of latchkey children. *Children Today* 12:2–4, 40.

Galambos, N.L., & Garbarino, J. 1985 Adjustment of unsupervised children in a rural ecology. *Journal of Genetic Psychology* 146:227–231.

Harris, O.C. 1977. Day Care: Have we forgotten the school-age child? *Child Welfare* 56:440–448.

Long, T., & Long, L. 1981. *Latchkey children: The child's view of self-care.* ERIC Documents, ED 211 229.

Long, T., & Long, L. 1983. *Latchkey children.* ERIC Documents. ED 226 836.

Mayesky, M.E. 1980a. Phillips extended day magnet: A successful blend of day care and academics. *Educational Digest* 58:178–183.

Mayesky, M.E. 1980b. A study of academic effectiveness in a public school day care program. *Phi Delta Kappan* 62:284–285.

Mayesky, M.E. 1980c. *Differences in reading and math—Grades 1–3,* as measured in Phillips Extended Day. ERIC Documents. ED 184 675.

Peterson, L. 1984. Teaching home safety and survival skills to latchkey children: A comparison of two manuals and methods. *Journal of Applied Behavior Analysis* 17:279–293.

Peterson, L. In Press. The "safe-at-home" game: Training comprehensive safety skills in latchkey children. *Behavior Modification.*

Robinson, B.E.; Coleman, M.; & Rowland, B.H. 1986. The after-school ecologies of latchkey children. *Children's Environments Quarterly.*

Rodman, H.; Pratto, D.J.; & Nelson, R.S. 1985. Child care arrangements and children's functioning: A comparison of self-care and adult-care children. *Developmental Psychology* 21:413–418.

Rowland, B.H.; Robinson, B.E.; & Coleman, M. 1986. Parents' perceptions of needs for their latchkey children: A survey. *Pediatric Nursing* 12.

Stewart, M. 1981. *Children in self-care: An exploratory study.* ERIC Documents. ED 224 604.

Taveggia, T.C., & Thomas, E.M. 1974. Latchkey children. *Pacific Sociological Review* 17:27–34.

Trimberger, R., & MacLean, M.J. 1982. Maternal employment. The child's perspective. *Journal of Marriage and the Family* 44:469–475.

Woods, M.B. 1972. The unsupervised child of the working mother. *Developmental Psychology* 6:14–25.

Program Developers

Adams, D., & Strupp, R. 1984. *School-age child care parent survey final report.* ERIC Documents. ED 251 180.

Auerbach, S. 1975. Child care and the public schools: An interview with Albert Shanks. *Day Care and Early Education* 3:18–19, 53–55.

Baumgartner, U., & Hammond, J. 1982. Extended day care: A school system. *Social Work in Education* 4:53–58.

Caldwell, B. 1981. Day care and the schools. *Theory into Practice* 20:121–129.

Core, M. 1978 (December). When school's out and nobody's home. *Record,* pp. 2–6.

Ellis, J.B. 1972. Love to share: A community project tailored by oldsters for latchkey children. *American Journal of Orthopsychiatry* 42:249–250.

Genser, A., & Baden, C. 1980. *School-age child care: Programs and issues.* ERIC Documents. ED 196 543.

Gilbert, R., & Price, A. 1981. Is the school day long enough? *Phi Delta Kappan* 62:524.

Guerney, L., & Moore, L. 1983. PhoneFriend: A prevention-oriented service for latchkey children. *Children Today* 12:5–10.

Levine, J.A. 1978. Day care and the public schools: Profiles of five communities. *Day Care and Early Education* 6:15–19.

Levine, J.A. 1979. Day care and public schools: Current models and future directions. *Urban and Social Change Review* 12:17–21.

Long, T. 1984. So who cares if I'm home? *Educational Horizons* 62:60–64.

Mayesky, M.E. 1979. Extended day care in a public elementary school. *Children Today* 8:6–9.

McKnight, J., & Shelsby, B. 1984. Checking in: An alternative for latchkey kids. *Children Today* 13:23–25.

Merrow, J. 1985. Viewpoint: Self-care. *Young Children* 40:8.

Mills, B.C., & Cooke, E. 1983. Extended day programs—a place for the latchkey child. *Early Child Development and Care* 12:143–151.

Morgan, G. 1979. *Putting it together: Some program and policy issues on school-age day care.* ERIC Documents. ED 192 902.

Nengebauer, R. 1979 (November). School age day care: Getting it off the ground. *Child Care Information Exchange,* pp. 9–15.

Pierce, J.W. 1978. Before and after school day care—Parent's evaluation. *Illinois School Research and Development* 14:123–126.

Rosalind, S. 1977. Extended day. *Journal of Home Economics* 69:7–10.

Seltzer, M. 1981. Planning school-age child care in public schools. *Education Digest* 46:17–20.

Stickney, F. 1981. *Latchkey Cares for kids: A guide for a successful child development program.* ERIC Documents. ED 013 355.

Teachers and Administrators

Campbell, L.P. & Flake, A.E. 1985. Latchkey children—What is the answer? *Clearing House* 58:381–383.

Carter, D. 1985. The crisis in school-age child care: What you should know: What you can do. *PTA Today* 10:4–8.

Coleman, T.; Robinson, B.E.; & Rowland, B.H. 1984. Latchkey children and their families. *Dimensions* 13:23–24.

Garbarino, J. 1980. Latchkey children: Getting the short end of the stick? *Vital Issues* 30.

Garbarino, J. 1981. Latchkey children: How much a problem? *Education Digest* 46:14–16.

Long, L. 1985. (February). Safe at home. *Instructor,* pp. 64–70.

McCurdy, J. 1985. Schools respond to latchkey children. *School Administrator* 42:16–18.

McNairy, M.R. 1984. School-age child care: Program and policy issues. *Educational Horizons* 62:64–67.

Nieting, P.L. 1983. School-age child care: In support of development and learning. *Childhood Education* 60:6–11.

Pecoraro, A.; Theriot, J.; & Lafont, P. 1984. What home economists should know about latchkey children. *Journal of Home Economics* 76:20–22.

Robinson, B.E.; Rowland, B.H.; & Coleman, M. 1986. Taking action for latchkey children and their families. *Family Relations* 35.

Scherer, M. 1982. The loneliness of the latchkey child. *Instructor* 101:38–41.

Seltzer, M.S. 1979. *Family day care and the school-age child.* ERIC Documents. ED 192 901.

Stroman, S.H., & Duff, E. 1982. The latchkey child: Whose responsibility? *Childhood Education* 59:76–79.

Strother, D.B. 1984. Latchkey children: The fastest-growing special interest group in the schools. *Phi Delta Kappan* 66:290–293.

Parents

Behan, R.A. 1985. Should Johnny or Janet "sit" themselves? *PTA Today* 10:27–28

Chaback, E., & Fortunato, P. 1983 (February). A kid's survival checklist: When you're home alone. *Parents magazine*, pp. 134–136.

Clements, C. 1983 (February). Lessons for latchkey kids. *Ladies' Home Journal*, p. 50.

Grollman, E.A., & Sweder, G.L. 1986 (March). Preparing your child to be home alone. *Working Woman*, pp. 154–156.

Grollman, E.A., & Sweder, G.L. 1986 (February). Tips for working parents from kids. *Reader's Digest*, pp. 107–110.

Hagan, S. 1981 (October). Setting up an after-school program. *Parents Magazine*, pp. 44, 48, 50–54.

Huff, K. 1982 (September 20). In their own words. *People*, pp. 83–84, 87–88.

Iacobucci, K. 1982 (May). After-school alternatives for latchkey kids. *McCall's Magazine*, p. 36.

Kieffer, E. 1981 (February 24). The latchkey kids—How are they doing? *Family Circle*, pp. 28–35.

Langway, L. 1981 (February 16). The latchkey children. *Newsweek*, pp. 96–97.

Lapinski, S. 1982 (September 12). Latchkey blues: When kids come home. *Family Weekly*, pp. 22–23.

Latchkey kids speak their minds. 1982 (April 26). *Day Care U.S.A.*, p. 34.

Leishman, K. 1980 (November). When kids are home alone—How mothers make sure they're safe. *Working Mother*, pp. 21–22, 25.

Levine, J., & Seltzer, M. 1980 (September). Why are these children staying after school? (And why are they so happy about it?). *Redbook Magazine*, pp. 23, 158, 160, 163–166.

Long, L., & Long, T. 1982 (March). What to do when children are home alone. *Essence*, pp. 38–41.

Long, L., & Long, T. 1982 (May). The unspoken fears of latchkey kids. *Working Mother*, pp. 88–90.

Long, L., & Long, T. 1982 (September 20). The lonely life of latchkey children. *People Magazine*, pp. 63–65.

Raymond, B.B. 1985 (September). And they said kindergarten would be easier! At least day care lasted the whole day. *Working Mother*, pp. 118–120.

Robinson, B.E. 1986 (July). Where do the children go? *Lady's Circle Magazine,* pp. 22–24.

Rodman, H. 1980 (July). How children take care of themselves. *Working Mother,* pp. 61–63.

Survival training for latchkey kids. 1980 (October 6). *Newsweek,* p. 100.

Wellborn, S.N. 1981 (September 14). When school kids come home to an empty house. *U.S. News & World Report,* pp. 42, 47.

Whitbread, J. 1979 (February 20). Who's taking care of the children? *Family Circle,* pp. 88, 89, 102–103.

Name Index

Adams, J., 145, 146, *156*
Anderson, J.S., 163, 166, 167, *174*
Andres, D., 18, 24, 32n, *34*, 113, 115, 116, 117, 119, *131*
Aries, P., *155*

Baden, R.K., 30, *33*, 112, *130*
Bagnall, J., *155*
Bandura, A., 49, 50, *54*
Barnett, S., 161, *174*
Barnhart, D., 52, *55*
Battle, G.E., 166, *174*
Behan, R.A., 7, *13*
Belle, D., 4, *13*
Belous, R.S., 113, *131*
Bernstein-Tarrow, N.B., 40, *55*
Binet, A., 41
Bram, S., 165, *174*
Bronfenbrenner, U., 128, *130*
Brouwer, R., 9, *15*

Caldwell, B., 30, *33*
Campbell, L.P., 29, *33*, 107, *109*
Carter, D., 108, *109*
Castelli, J., 20, *33*
Chaback, E., 10, *13*, 19, *33*, 112, *130*, 167, *174*
Chapman, J.E., 29, *33*
Charles, C., 52, *55*
Charlesworth, R., 46, *54*
Children's Defense Fund, 142, *155*
Coleman, M., 4, *15*, 17–18, 26, 27, 28, 29, *33, 35*, 118, 119, 120, *131*, 171, 173, *175*
Cooke, E., 30, *35*
Coolsen, P., 3, *13*
Coopersmith, S., 46, *54*
Corasaniti, M.A., 21, 24, 26, 29, 31, 32, 33, *36*, 114, 116, 117, 119, 121, 124, *132*

Core, M., 30, *34*
Council for Children, 28, *34*, 145, 151, 153, *155*, 169, *174*
Creedon, D.L., 9, *15*

Davidson, E.S., 50, *54*
Davis, J., 29, *34*
DeMause, L., 140, *155*
Dion, K., 39, *54*
Divine-Hawkins, P., 158, 162, *174*
Dixon, R.A., 20, *34*, 111, 113, *131*
Drabman, R.S., 9, *15*
Drizid, T., *54*
Duff, E., 8, *15*, 18, 30, *35*

Elkind, D., *131*, 8, 11, *14*, 50, *54*, 91, 93, 130, *132*, 143, *155*
Entwisle, B., 31, 32n, *34*
Erikson, E.H., 8, 45, *54*, 126
Eshleman, J.R., 128, *131*
Evette, L., 86, *93*

Flake, A.E., 29, *33*, 107, *109*
Flake-Hobson, C., 30, *34*, 39, 40, 46, 48, *54*, 58, 76
Flavell, J.H., 43, *54*
Fooner, A., 160, 164, *174*
Fortunato, P., 10, *13*, 19, *33*, 112, *130*, 167, *174*
Fosarelli, P.D., 6, *14*, 18, *34*
Furth, H., 51, *54*

Galambos, N.L., 2, 5, *14*, 20, 25, 32n, *34*, 111, 113, 115, 116, 117, 119, *131*
Gannett, E., *15, 35*, 132
Garbarino, J., 2, 3, 5, 8, 11, 12, *13, 14*, 23, 25, 32n, *34*, 112, 113, 115, 116, 117, 119, 121, 128, *131*

Note: Page numbers followed by *n* indicate material in footnotes; italicized page numbers indicate full references.

Gay, L.R., 116, 120, *131*
Genser, A., *15, 33, 35, 130, 132*
Gold, D., 18, 24, 32n, *34,* 113, 115, 116, 117, 119, *131*
Goltsman, S.M., 165, *174*
Gray, W., *15, 35, 132*
Grollman, E.A., 92, *93*
Grossman, A.S., 2, *14*
Gruvaeus, G., 23, *36*
Guerney, L., 47, *55,* 168, *175*

Hall, J.M., 107, *109*
Hamill, P., 40, *54*
Haney, J.I., 9, *14*
Harris, L., 8, 9, *14*
Harris, O.C., 27, 29, *34,* 119, 120, *131*
Hartup, W., 46, 47, *54*
Hayghe, H., 113, *131*
Haynes, E., 140, *155*
Hedin, D., 4, *14*
Hite, R.L., 18, *36*
Hoffman, L.W., 18, *34*
Huff, K., 19, *34*
Hunsinger, S., 30, *36*
Hunt, A.H., 166, *174*
Hurst, M., 18, *36*
Hyman, I., 50, *54*

Iacobucci, K., 112, *131*
Iacofano, D.S., 165, *174*

Johnson, B.L., 2, *14*
Johnson, C., *54*
Jones, L.R., 112, *131*
Jones, R.T., 9, *14*

Kamii, C., 51, *54*
Kazanjian, D.P., 4, 6, *14,* 28, *35,* 118, 124, *131,* 158, 171, *175*
Kazdin, A.E., 9, *14*
Kieffer, E., 9, *14,* 19, 20, *34*
Klein, D.P., 113, *131*
Koberg, D., *155*
Kyte, K., *175*

Lafont, P., 28, *35,* 98, 101, *109*
Langway, L., 19, *34*
Lazar, J.B., 29, *33*
Lefstein, L., *174*
Leishman, K., 19, *34*
Lerner, J., 39, *54*
Lerner, R., 39, *54*
Levine, J.A., *33, 130*
Levitan, S.A., 113, *131*
Library Hotline, 6, *14*
Liebert, R.M., 50, *54*
Lipinski, S., 20, *34*
Lloyd, P., 148, *156*

Local Churches Respond to Special Needs of Latchkey Kids, 162, *175*
Long, L., 4, *5,* 6, 8, 10, 12, *14,* 20, 21–22, 23, 24, *25,* 27, 32n, *34,* 96, 101, 102, *109,* 112, 114, 116, 117, 118, 119, 120, 121, 124, 126, *131,* 158, 167, 171, *175*
Long, T.J., 4, *5,* 6, 7, 8, 9, 11, 12, *14,* 20, 21–22, 23, 24, *25,* 27, 32n, *34,* 50, *55,* 105, 106, *109,* 112, 114, 116, 117, 118, 119, 120, 121, 124, 126, *131,* 158, 167, 171, *175*
Lowrey, G.H., 38, *55*
Lundsteen, S.W., 40, *55*

Maccoby, E.E., 40, *55*
McGurdy, J., 13, *14,* 30, *35*
McKnight, J., 108, *109,* 160, *175*
MacLean, M.J., 23, 24, 32n, *35,* 116, 117, 119, 124, *132*
McMurray, G.L., 4, 6, *14,* 28, *35,* 118, 124, *131,* 158, 171, *175*
McNairy, M.R., 106, *109*
Mathos, J., 161, *175*
Maxim, G.W., 39, 42, *55*
Mayesky, M.E., 31, 32n, *35,* 163, 164, *175*
Medrich, E., 6, *14*
Melizzi, M.A., 38, 47, *55*
Merrow, J., 10, *14*
Mills, B.C., 30, *35*
Moore, L.C., 29, *35,* 168, *175*
Moore, R.C., 165, *174*
Moore, S.G., 18, *35*
Mount, R., 9, *14*
Murray, J.P., *55*

Nelson, R.S., *5, 15,* 25, *35,* 112, 116, 117, 119, *131*
New Program for School Age Child Care, 162, *175*
Newsweek, 10, *15,* 19, *35*
Nieting, P.L., 13, *15,* 30, *35*

Paul, J., 145, 146, *156*
Pecoraro, A., 28, *35,* 98, 101, *109*
Peterson, J., 9, *15*
Pfafflin, N., 167, *175*
Phillips, M., *156*
Piaget, J., 8, 41, *55,* 125
Poche, C., 9, *15*
Pratto, D.J., 3, *5, 15,* 25, *35,* 112, 116, 117, 119, *131*
Prepared for Today, 169, *175*
Price, S., *33, 131*

Rhodes, W.C., 142, *156*
Ried, R., *54*

Robinson, B.B., 166, *174*
Robinson, B.E., 4, *15,* 17–18, 22, 28, 29, 30, *33, 34, 35,* 39, 40, 46, 48, *54, 58, 76, 118,* 120, *131,* 171, 173, *175*
Roche, A., *54*
Rodes, T.W., 29, *35*
Rodman, H., 3, *5, 15,* 20, 21, 25, 27, *35,* 112, 116, 117, 119, *131*
Rosalind, S., 30, *35*
Rosenbaum, M.S., 9, *15*
Rosenthal, S., 145, 146, *156*
Rowland, B.H., 4, *15,* 17–18, 22, 28, 29, 32n, *33, 35,* 118, 120, *131,* 171, 173, *175*

Samples, B., 52, *55*
Scherer, M., 96, 101, 103, *109*
Seligson, M., 3, 8, *13, 15,* 29, 30, *33, 35,* 124, *130, 132*
Sheldon, H.H., 39, *55*
Shelsby, B., 108, *109,* 160, *175*
Sherman, D., *5, 14*
Skeen, P., 30, *34, 39,* 40, 46, 48, *54, 58, 76*
Smith, K., 9, *14*
Solomon, P., 29, *34*
Soto, L.D., 47, *55,* 168, *175*
Sparks, S., 27, *35, 76,* 99, 104, *109*
Spock, B., 51, *55*
Sprafkin, J.N., 50, *54*
Steinberg, L., 5, 6, *15,* 25, 26, 32n, *35,* 113, 114, 115, 116, 117, 118, 119, 124, *132*
Stewart, M., 27, *35,* 113, *132*
Stith, M., 50, *55*
Stroman, S.H., 8, *15,* 18, 30, *35,* 112, *132*
Strother, D.B., 101, 106, *109*
Survival Skills for Kids, 168, *175*

Swearingen, M., 9, *15*
Sweder, G.L., 92, *93*

Tanner, J.M., 40, *55*
Taveggia, T.C., 18, *35,* 112, *132*
Terry, S.L., 113, *132*
Theriot, J., 28, *35,* 98, 101, *109*
Thomas, E.M., 18, *35,* 112, *132*
Trimberger, R., 23, 24, 32n, *35,* 116, 117, 119, 124, *132*
Turkington, C., 13, *15,* 24, *36*

U.S. Department of Commerce, 4, *15,* 123, *132, 158, 175*
U.S. Department of Labor, 4, *15,* 123, *132*

Vandell, D.L., 21, 24, 26, 29, 31, 32, 33, *36,* 114, 116, 117, 119, 121, 124, *132*

Wachs, H., 51, *54*
Waldman, E., 2, *14*
Wellborn, S.N., 19, 30, *36*
Westman, J.C., 140, 141, 142, *156*
Whitbread, J., 13, *15,* 29, *36*
White House Conference on Children and Youth, 141, *156*
Williams, J.W., 50, *55*
Wolff, M., 2, 3, 10, *15*
Woods, M.B., 8, *15,* 22, 32n, *36,* 114, 115, 116, 117, 118, 119, 120, 125, *132*
Woyshner, K., 23, *36*

Yawkey, T.D., 38, 47, *55*

Zambrana, R.E., 18, *36*
Zigler, E., 30, *36*
Zill, N., 23, 32n, *36*
Zucker, H.L., 2, *15*

Subject Index

Acceptance of self-care, 72–73
Achievement: as dependent variable in child studies, 115; parental view of, 11; school-age child care and, 31; among suburban and rural latchkey kids, 24, 25
Action for Children's Television (ACT), 50
Activities: cognitive development and, 43–45; to disbel boredom, 98–101; physical growth and development and, 40–41; in school-age child care programs, 182; social-emotional development and, 47–48; on weekends, 83
Adjustment to self-care, 57–76; age of children and, 19, 59–60; degree of supervision and, 26; as dependent variable in child studies, 115; geographic location and, 118–119; maturity and, 26; among suburban and rural latchkey kids, 24–25
Administrative structure: for school-age child care programs, 172–173, 176, 182
Adult(s): "latchkey syndrome" among, 24; responses to attractiveness of children, 39. See also Parent(s); Teacher(s)
Advocacy, 145–150; case and class, 146–148; tools of, 148–150
Advocates: influence on children, 49; school officials as, 106–107
After School Day Care Association (ASDCA), 164
After-school learning centers, 161–162, 164
After-school playground programs, 107, 161–162
Age: adjustment to self-care and, 59–60; of children with working mothers, 18–19; safety and, 80–81; at which self-care can begin, 6–8
Aggression: television violence and, 50

Ambivalence: of parents toward self-care, 27–28
Anxieties: of middle childhood, 50–51. See also Fear(s)
Appreciation: as level of adjustment to self-care, 73–75
ASDCA. See After School Day Care Association
Assistance organizations, 190–191
Attitude(s): of children toward maternal employment, 120–121, 124; of employers, 118; maternal, toward employment, 125; parental, adjustment to self-care and, 62–63; school-age child care and, 31; sex role, 19
Authoritativeness: susceptibility to peer pressure and, 118

Behavioral characteristics: safety and, 80–81
Block parents, 108, 160–161
Body build, of school-age children, 39
Boredom: in children, 23; strategies for reducing, 98–101
Boy Scouts of America: survival skills program of, 9, 85, 169
Burr-Brown: involvement in school-age child care program, 167

Camp Fire, Inc.: survival skills program of, 9, 85
Carole Robertson Center for Learning, 166
Checking in, 83; programs for, 160
Child abuse, 50–51
Child Care Assurance Plan of Tidewater, Virginia, 160
Child development theories: of Erikson, 46, 126–127; latchkey research and, 125–127; of Piaget, 41–43, 125–126
Child labor, 140

Children: cultural context of, 142–145; historical treatment of, 139–142; hurried, 11–13; instruction and guidance for, 67, 69, 71, 73, 75; prevention of problems for, 142. See also Latchkey kids

Children's Defense Fund, 142, 146, 155

Children's Trust Fund, 147

Child studies, 113–119; attributes of, 134–135; dependent variables in, 115; independent variables in, 113–115; methodologies of, 117–118; results of, 118–119; sampling in, 115–117

Churches: ability to assist with latchkey problems, 89; school-age child care provided by, 162

Classification, 43

Cognitive development, 41–45; ability to handle self-care and, 8; implications for activities, 43–45; latchkey research and, 125–126; Piaget's theory of, 41–43, 125–126

Community change: eight-step plan for, 150–153; putting plan into action, 153–155

Community Coordinated Child Care for Central Florida, 160–161

Community enrichment programs, 166

Community leaders: cooperation with schools, 107; development of self-reliance and, 58–59; influence on children, 48–49

Community organizations, 48, 49; adjustment to self-care and, 62; location of, 78, 85; programs assisting with latchkey problems sponsored by, 89–90; school-age child care provided by, 159–163, 176–177; survival skills programs of, 9–10, 85, 161, 168, 169

Community strategies, 87–90; agencies and, 89–90; church and, 89; employers and, 89; networking and, 87; publicity and, 87

Competence: sense of, 43

Concrete operations, 41, 42–43

Confinement: environmental context and, 25; imposed by self-care, 23

Conflict: in social-emotional development, 45–46

Consequences: logical, 50

Conservation, 43

Context: in research, 113. See also Ecological context

Cost: as obstacle to child care, 28, 171

Council for Children, 146; Charlotte, North Carolina, SACC Project and, 148, 149, 153–155, 169–173

Creativity, 43

Crime rate: adjustment to self-care and, 5, 62; influence on outcome of self-care, 25; parental assessment of, 78

Culture: influence on children, 142–145

Curricula: for latchkey kids, 98–105; for school-age child care programs, 51–52; for teaching of self-reliance skills, 10

Day care centers: school-age child care provided by, 159–160, 177

Decision making: development of, 58

Demographics: of family, 4, 113

Dependent variables: in child studies, 115; in family studies, 119

Development: cognitive, 41–45; implications for school-age child care programs, 51–52; matching supervision with, 52–53; physical, 38–41; resources on, 187–188; social-emotional, 45–48. See also Maturity

Diet, 50

Disabled children: school-age child care programs for, 164–165

Discipline, 50

Ecological approach: to research, 128–130

Ecological context, 5–6, 22–26. See also Environment; Neighborhood(s)

Ectomorphs, 39

Educational programs, 168–169. See also Curricula; Public education

Egocentrism: shift to relativism, 42

Emergencies: contacting parents in, 106; procedures for, 85–86; telephone numbers for, 103

Emotion(s): observation by teacher, 102–103

Emotional development. See Social-emotional development

Employers: assistance to parents by, 89; in child studies, 118; involvement in school-age child care programs, 162–163, 167

Employment: maternal. See Maternal employment

Endomorphs, 39

Enrichment programs, 161–162, 166

Environment: adjustment to self-care and, 61–62; child outcomes related to, 32; interaction between individual and, 128; suburban and rural, 24–26; urban, 22–24. See also Ecological context; Neighborhood(s)

Equilibration: cognitive development and, 42

Erickson, Erik: latchkey research and, 126–127

Evaluation: of school-age child care programs, 173
Exosystems: 129–130
Experience: cognitive development and, 42
Extended-day programs, 163–164, 177

Family: building strengths in, 91–92; changes in, 2; childhood stress and, 90–91; composition of, 116–117; demographic differences among, 4, 113; social climate of, 8; stress on, 11, 118
Family and Children Services: survival skill training provided by, 168
Family day care homes: school-age child care provided by, 160
Family Living Center, 148
Family studies, 119–121; attributes of, 136–137; dependent variables in, 119; independent variables in, 119; methodology of, 120; results of, 120–121; sampling for, 119–120
Family theories: latchkey research and, 127–128
Fear(s), 23, 63–65; grade level and, 22–23; of middle childhood, 50–51; parental attitudes and, 62–63; presented by popular press, 21
FHA. *See* Future Homemakers of America
Financial support, 177, 182; in a day care center, 159–160
Frank, Lawrence, 141
Future Homemakers of America (FHA): school-age child care provided by, 107

Geographic location: adjustment and, 118–119
Gethsemane Enrichment Program, 166
Girl Scouts of America: survival training program developed by, 9
Grade level: child care arrangement and, 7; of children in self-care, 5; fear and, 22–23; as independent variable in child studies, 114–115; onset of self-care and, 8
Growth. *See* Physical development
Guidance. *See* Instruction and guidance
Guidance centers: school-age child care provided by, 164–165
Guilt: parental, 63

Hall, G. Stanley, 141
Handbooks, 167
Help lines, 103, 167–168; social-emotional development and, 47
High school students: school-age child care provided by, 107

Home: assessing safety of, 79–81; safety in, 82–86, 104–105
Home Based Child Care Program, 160–161
Home Health Plus, 167
Homework assignments, 101
House key. *See* Key
"Hurried" children, 11–13

Independence: promotion by self-care, 9
Independent variables: in child studies, 113–115; in family studies, 119
Industrial Revolution: children at time of, 140–141
Industry versus inferiority, 46; latchkey research and, 126–127
Infanticide: medieval, 140
Inferiority versus industry, 46; latchkey research and, 126–127
Information processing, 43
In-service training: for school personnel, 106
Instruction and guidance: for children, 67, 69, 71, 73, 75; for parents, 67, 69, 71–72, 73, 75; for safety, 102
Interaction between individual and environment, 128
Isolation: environmental context and, 25; imposed by self-care, 23

Kansas Committee for Prevention of Child Abuse: survival training program developed by, 9
KARE–4 (Kids After-School Recreation and Enrichment–4), 161–162
Key, house: care of, 101–102; safety strategies for, 82

Latchkey arrangements: definition of, 123–124; differences among, 25–26
Latchkey ecologies, 5–6
Latchkey kids: emergence of, 2; grade-level differences among, 5; increases expected in, 13; myths about, 2–4; resources on, 186–187; use of term, 3–4, 123–124
"Latchkeyphobia": in popular press, 19–20
Latchkey risk quotient (LRQ), 97–98; computation of, 97 f
"Latchkey syndrome," 24
Laterality: maturation of, 40
Learning: cognitive development and, 42, 44
Learning centers: after-school, 161–162, 164
Learning disabled children: school-age child care programs for, 164–165
Logical consequences, 50
Logical reasoning, 43
Loneliness: in children, 23
Longitudinal studies: need for, 122

Macrosystems, 129–130

Map: of location of service agencies, 78, 85

Maternal employment, 2; children's attitudes toward, 23–24, 120–121, 124; definition of, 114; growth of, 158; influence on children, 18–19; mothers' attitudes toward, 125

Maturity: adjustment and, 26; adjustment to self-care and, 60; cognitive development and, 42; evaluation of, 7; necessary for self-care, 6–8; parental view of, 11. *See also* Development

Media: advocacy and, 149

Memory, 43

Mesomorphs, 39

Mesosystems, 129–130

Microsystems, 129

Middle Ages: children during, 140

Middle childhood, 49–51

Mother(s). *See* Maternal employment; Parent(s)

Multimethod approach: need for, 122

National Crime Prevention Center: emergency recommendations of, 85, 86

Needs assessment: for school-age child care programs, 108, 169–171, 181

Neighbor(s): adjustment to self-care and, 62

Neighborhood(s): assessing safety of, 78–79; high- and low-risk, 5. *See also* Ecological context; Environment

Nervous system: maturation of, 40

Networking: among parents, 87; for school-age child care programs, 171–172

New York Society for the Prevention of Cruelty to Children, 141

Nutrition, 50

Observational techniques, need for, 122

Orientation: as level of adjustment to self-care, 65–67

Pair therapy, 165

Parent(s), 26–28; ambivalence of, 27–28; approach to children by, 92; assessment of safety buffer and, 78–82; association of maturity with achievement by, 11; attitudes of, 19, 62–63; in block parent programs, 108, 160–161; building family life and, 91–92; checking in with, 83; childhood stress and, 90–91; in child studies, 118; community strategies and, 87–90; contacting in emergencies, 106; development of self-reliance and, 58; family climate and, 90–91; importance to social-emotional development, 45;

in-home safety and, 82–86; instruction and guidance for, 67, 69, 71–72, 73, 75; involvement in day care center, 159; involvement in school-age child care programs, 163, 166; making the best of latchkey situations and, 92–93; preferences for child care arrangements, 29; participation in research by, 6, 112, 116; satisfaction with child care arrangements, 26–27; selection of school-age child care programs and, 86; suggestions for, 77–93; support and feedback from, 48; telephone calls to and from, 63; three o'clock syndrome among, 28, 83, 118, 161, 162–163; underreporting of self-care by, 6. *See also* Maternal employment

Parent–child relationship: success of self-care and, 8

Parent groups, 87

Parenting style: susceptibility to peer pressure and, 118, 124

Parent–teacher associations (PTAs): support provided by, 107–108

Peer(s): importance in social-emotional development, 46–47

Peer pressure susceptibility: degree of supervision and, 26, 113–114, 124; parenting style and, 118, 124

Personality characteristics: as dependent variable in child studies, 115

Phillips Extended Day Magnet, 163–164

Philosophy: of school-age child care programs, 171, 178, 181

PhoneFriend, 167–168

Physical attractiveness: adult responses to children and, 39

Physical development: principles of, 39–40; of school-age children, 38–41

Physical knowledge, 42

Piaget, Jean, 41–43; latchkey research and, 125–126

Planning for self-care, 58–59

Play: functions of, 51

Playground programs, 107, 161–162

Playing and Learning in Adaptable Environments (Project PLAE), 165–166

Policy: of school-age child care programs, 171, 179–180. *See also* Public policy

Popular press, 194–195; studies of latchkey children reported in, 19–22

Preoperational thought, 41

Preparation for self-care, 60–61

Problem definition: for research, 112

Problem solving, 43

Psychosocial development. *See* Social-emotional development

PTAs. *See* Parent-teacher associations
Public education: for school-age child care programs, 173
Publicity: for community education, 87
Public policy: on children, 141–142; class advocacy and, 146–147

Questioning of self-care, 67–69
Questionnaires: return rate for, 116

Reasoning: logical, 43
Reinforcement: from adults, 48; among peers, 46
Relativism: shift to, 42
Research, 17–33; on alternatives to self-care, 28–33; on children, 113–119, 134–135; conceptual versus empirical, 121–122; data collection for, 122; defining latchkey and, 123–124; definition of studies and, 125; on environmental context, 25–26; on families, 119–121, 136–137; family context and, 124–125; longitudinal, 122; on maternal employment, 18–19; need for, 112, 121; parental underreporting and, 6; on parents, 26–28; in popular press, 19–22; sampling and methodology and, 6, 112–123; on school-age child care, 29–33; scientific, 22–26; on suburban and rural children, 24–25; suggestions for, 111–130; theoretical guides and, 125–130; on urban children, 22–24
Research instruments, 117–118, 120
Resentment of self-care, 67–69
Resources: sharing of, 158–159, 176–177
Responsibility: ability of children to assume, 128; early, results of, 8–13
Reston, Virginia, Children's Center, 159–160; Senior Satellite Program of, 160
Reversibility, 43
Rewards: exchange of, 128
Risks: associated with self-care, 11–13; in popular press, 20, 21; teacher determination of, 96–98
Rules: for home safety, 83–85, 104–105; published in popular press, 19; for self-care, 60–61. *See also* Instruction and guidance
Rural environment, 24–25

SACC. *See* School-age child care
Safety: assessment of, 78–82; crime rate and, 5, 25, 62, 78; home and, 79–81, 83–85, 104–105; instruction in, 102; neighborhood and, 78–79; safety buffer and, 81–82
Safety buffer assessment, 81, 82

Safety strategies, 82–86; checking in and, 83; emergencies and, 85–86; getting home and, 83; house key and, 82; house rules and, 83–85
Sampling: for child studies, 115–117; for family studies, 119–120; national, need for, 122–123
Satisfaction: of parents with self-care, 26–27
Schedule, after-school, 83–84
School: after-school learning centers and, 161–162, 164; extended-day programs and, 163–164, 177; school-age child care provided by, 107. *See also* Curricula; Teacher(s)
School administrators: as latchkey facilitators, 105–107
School-age child care (SACC): administrative structure and, 172–173, 176, 182; in Charlotte, North Carolina, 148–150, 153–155, 169–173; checklist for identifying and monitoring programs for, 88–89; development of, 170, 176–177; evaluation and, 173; expected advantages of, 30–33; financial support for, 159–160, 171, 182; implementation and public education and, 173; implications of development for, 51–52; initiated by PTAs, 108; lack of programs for, 29; matching level of supervision with development in, 52–53; need for, 13; needs assessment and, 108, 169–171; networking and, 171–172; parental preference for, 29; program development for, 157–174; provided by high school students, 107; provided by schools, 107; research on, 29–33; resource sharing and, 158–159; resources on, 183–185; selecting program for, 86; staff training and, 173; structures, philosophies, and guidelines in, 171; types of, 159–169
School schedules: modification of, 106
Self-advocacy, 146
Self-care, 3; adjustment to, 57–76; alternatives to, 28–33
Self-concept: development of, 46–47; school-age child care and, 31
Self-esteem: development of, 43, 46–47
Self-reliance: degree of supervision and, 22; development of, 58–59
Self-report instruments: in child studies, 117–118
Sensationalism: in popular press, 19–20
Sensorimotor knowing, 41
Sensory mechanisms: maturation of, 40

Seriation, 43

Service agencies: community strategies and, 89–90; location of, 78, 85. *See also* Community organizations

Sex: as independent variable in child studies, 114–115

Sex differences, 22; in physical development, 40

Sex role attitudes: age of children and, 19

Sexual activity: presented by popular press, 21

Sibling care, 5, 6, 63, 124

Sick care, 166–167

Sick Child Home Health Care Program, 166–167

Skill development: physical, of school-age children, 39

Social-emotional development, 45–48; Erikson's theory of, 45–46; implications for activities, 47–48; latchkey research and, 126–127; self-esteem and, 46–47

Social exchange theory: latchkey research and, 127

Socioeconomic status: incidence of self-care and, 4

Sports, organized, 48–49

Staff training: for school-age child care programs, 173

Standardized tests: in child studies, 117

Stigma: research and, 112

Stress: childhood, 90–91; early responsibility and, 11–13; on family, 118; self-care as family's method of coping with, 11

Structure-functionalism: latchkey research and, 127

Suburban environment, 24–25

Summer programs, 165–166; parental preference for, 29

Supervision level: adjustment to self-care and, 26; distal, 53; as independent variable in child studies, 113–114; proximate, 52–53; self-reliance and, 22; susceptibility to peer pressure and, 26, 113–114, 124

Survival skills training programs, 9–10, 161, 168–169; controversy over, 10–11; emergency procedures and, 85

Symbols, 43

Teacher(s): childhood stress and, 90; classroom strategies and, 98–105; determining risk factors and, 96–98; influence on children, 48; observation of emotions by, 102–103; parent–teacher associations and, 107–108; role in teaching survival skills, 10; for school-age child care programs, 164; suggestions for, 95–109; support and feedback from, 48

Telephone calls: to parents, 63, 83

Telephone numbers: listing, 85, 103

Telephone skills: instruction in, 103

Television violence, 50

TenderCare for Kids, 167

Themes: in middle childhood, 49

Thought. *See* Cognitive development

Three o'clock syndrome, 28, 83; employers' attitudes toward, 118, 161; employer-sponsored school-age child care programs and, 162–163

Time: length spent alone, adjustment to self-care and, 62

Time management: instruction in, 101

Toleration of self-care, 70–72

Traffic: parental assessment of, 78

Training: of staff, 173; in survival skills, 9–10, 85, 161, 168–169

Transportation: as barrier to child care, 171

Unitronics: involvement in school-age child care program, 167

U.S. Department of Health, Education and Welfare, 147

Urban environment, 22–24

Videotapes: usefulness in research, 122

Violence, on television, 50

Virginia Cooperative Extension Service, survival skills program of, 85, 161, 168

White House Conference on Children, 141

Women in workforce. *See* Maternal employment

YMCA: survival skills training provided by, 161

Youth service agencies: school-age child care provided by, 161–162

About the Authors

Bryan E. Robinson is associate professor of child and family development at the University of North Carolina at Charlotte. He is coauthor of two other books, *Child Development and Relationships* and *The Developing Father,* and has published more than fifty articles in professional and popular magazines. He has written scripts for national television programs on child development and has appeared on national radio and television discussing children's issues. Dr. Robinson has been active in research and program development for latchkey children in Charlotte, North Carolina. He was project director for the Council for Children's study of latchkey families in the Charlotte-Mecklenburg area, helped design and implement a school-age child care program there, and developed videotapes and an activity manual for training school-age child care staff.

Bobbie H. Rowland is professor of child and family development at the University of North Carolina at Charlotte. She is a leader in statewide efforts to provide affordable, quality child care options for children and their parents. Dr. Rowland has conducted research on latchkey children and designed school-age child care training modules and activities for staff. She has developed creative media kits, songs, and stories for young children, and she has written curricula for preschool and elementary-age children for the United Methodist Church. A leader in child advocacy, Dr. Rowland has appeared on national television and in films on issues affecting children. Internationally, Dr. Rowland has worked with family and children programs in the South Pacific, China, the Middle East, Europe, North Africa, Scandinavia, and Greece.

Mick Coleman is extension specialist in the Extension Division of Virginia State University. He received his doctorate from the University of Georgia in child and family development. Dr. Coleman's dissertation dealt with service delivery for latchkey children and their families. He worked extensively with latchkey families in Charlotte, North Carolina, and the Richmond, Virginia, area and helped design school-age child care training modules and activities for staff. Dr. Coleman is currently helping to lead the development of a Virginia child care resource/referral system and a tristate program for working parents and their latchkey children. His other areas of interest include stress management, sports involvement, family functioning, and men's friendships.